URBAN LANDSCAPE DESIGN

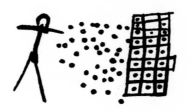

URBAN LANDSCAPE DESIGN

GARRETT ECKBO

McGRAW-HILL BOOK COMPANY

New York   San Francisco   Toronto   London   Sydney

URBAN LANDSCAPE DESIGN

PREFACE

In this book, as in design, I have searched for a balance between order and freedom. I know I am not a poet, and I hope I am not a pedant. A book, like a garden or a city, must have recognizable form within which we can become oriented. But within this form there must be continuity and accent, variety within unity, surprise to match expectation. These should not all be obvious from the first perusal of the table of contents, any more than from the plan of garden or city. Therefore the book proceeds with reasonable but incomplete order, with occasional inconsistencies, repetitions, or irrelevancies, like the stream of consciousness of a reasonable person who knows that life is not entirely rational.

Within the past ten years I have been fortunate enough to have professional assignments in many parts of the continental United States, and also in Mexico, Hawaii, and England. I have spent four months traveling in England, France, Italy, and Scandinavia. I have served as visiting critic at some twenty universities in the United States and Canada; as guest lecturer at several regional and national meetings of the American Institute of Architects, the American Institute of Planners, and the American Society of Landscape Architects; and as panelist or program chairman at two sessions of the International Design Conference at Aspen, Colorado. These travels have given me the opportunity to assimilate the breadth, depth, and scope of our country. It is a great people and a magnificent land. They deserve a better landscape than we are giving them.

The work of designers is not merely a collection of commodities for sale on the open market, although at times that may seem to be its chief property. Their work is also their way of life and their way of communicating, even more accurately than with words, their reactions to the world around them. While words properly used will clarify the designer's work, that work will also reinforce and give true meaning to words. This book draws upon the experience of its author, and of like-minded colleagues, in its specific applications of the thoughts and feelings expressed in the text. The intent is not promotion or public relations, but rather illustrations of the interaction between theory and practice, the mutual impact of generalized hypotheses and specifically variable situations, the development of ideas in this world of hard knocks.

I have endeavored to draw on the work of other landscape architects in various parts of the country, in order to depersonalize the examples and to demonstrate that the landscape revolution of some thirty years ago has now spread well beyond California. This is not, however, a comprehensive anthology of current American landscape practice. I have had neither the time, the space, nor the resources for that. My contacts were personal and sporadic, and I appreciate the excellent and cooperative responses. There should be no thought that the choice of specific people or the amount or kind of work shown by any particular designer is intended as any measure of their stature. The material sent me was what other busy people could produce within the time that my scheduling gave them. Some were unable to produce anything. The selection from this material, on an editorial basis, was mine, determined by examination and analysis of the entire volume of material accumulated from other sources and my own.

Design and photography credits will be found in the back of the book. The text illustrations were largely selected and arranged by Dick Petrie, and the general layout and format of the book are his work, in consultation with Carlos Diniz, Frederick Usher, Jr., John Gilchrist, and John Carruthers. My heartfelt thanks and gratitude to all of these good people for their help and counsel.

Garrett Eckbo

CONTENTS

PREFACE V

DISCUSSION

   I   *Begin at the Beginning* 3

  II *Elements of Space Organization* 7

EXAMPLES

  III *Room and Patio* 37

  IV *Building and Site* 45

  V *Buildings in Groups* 59

  VI *Parks and Playgrounds* 99

  VII *Streets and Squares* 153

 VIII *Neighborhood, Community, and Region* 177

MAINTENANCE

  IX *Maintenance and Design* EDWARD A. WILLIAMS, CO-AUTHOR . . 231

BIBLIOGRAPHY 240

REFERENCES AND ACKNOWLEDGMENTS 240

DESIGN AND ILLUSTRATION CREDITS 241

INDEX 245

DISCUSSION

2

I

BEGIN AT THE BEGINNING

The central concern of this book is the quality of the physical landscape in which we all live. By quality we mean the relationship between an individual, a group of people, or a community and the landscape which surrounds each of them. By landscape we mean the total complex of physical elements within a given area or movement zone.

The physical landscape evolves as a result of interaction between man, as an individual and as part of human society, and "nonhuman" nature, as a set of processes and as a storehouse of materials. The gigantic and accelerating expansion of the technical powers of the human race has produced a parallel expansion in the humanization, urbanization, and sterilization of the landscape. The majority of our population now lives in urban areas which have destroyed the natural primeval or rural environment and replaced it with the least, shoddiest, and most mediocre efforts of the American genius. We have abandoned The Garden to find, not the potential Shangri-La of great architecture and planning, but anarchy, squalor, confusion, blight, and slum. The automatic charm of the handicraft community has become the automatic ugliness of industrial society. Conservationists who want to stop, think, and reexamine nature and man are opposed by the technocrats who think that all problems can be solved by gadgets, gimmicks, formulas, and slogans. Behind them stand the proprietors of the constantly expanding economy, who feel that the only catastrophe is a decline in the rate of production.

Our objective is large and yet modest. We want to consider the entire landscape—but always as experienced by individual human beings. We want to consider general design processes as they are applied today to specific projects—gardens, parks, cities. We want to combine feeling and thinking, enlightened imagination with hard practicality. We want to speak directly to those responsible for the development and maintenance of the landscape—superintendents of buildings and grounds, from home-owners to park executives; those important figures, public and private, who formulate the policies which guide these superintendents; and the general public, who are the ultimate consumers.

Today the final criterion of the quality of our physical environment must be the relations it establishes between three primary elements:

Structure—buildings, streets, roads, highways, parking areas, utilities above and below ground
Open space for pedestrians only
Nature, represented by ground forms, rocks, plants, water

It is well known that the process of urbanization tends to maximize the first, minimize the second, and eliminate the third. These tendencies develop in the absence of adequate foresight, control, and organization. Familiar examples, in England, Scandinavia, and elsewhere, demonstrate that contemporary urbanization can produce balanced humane environments.

All the contributory analyses and processes—sociological, economic, political, planning, engineering, architectural, landscape, traffic, recreation, public security—end up with the production, adjustment, distortion, or elimination of these primary relations. Although each of the contributory processes seems to be of central and singular importance to those directly involved, the ultimate quality of the basic physical relations produced by their joint action will determine the ultimate success of each. Environments controlled by any one alone will be incomplete or distorted, if measured by total human need.

A basic framework of fundamental natural processes surrounds our activities in the landscape—climate, vegetation, wind, flood, ice melting, volcanic action, earth movement; and a basic framework of conservative considerations derives from the impact of man's activity on nature—the need for balance and equilibrium, the pressure of commerce and industry, the increasing intensity in land use, the problems of accelerated soil erosion, water depletion and pollution, flood dangers, and atmospheric pollution. The problems of landscape development include those of waters and shorelines, microclimate control, slope and soil changes, changes in plant and animal communities, waste disposal, extraction of mineral resources, transportation, and the use of the land for work, play, and home living. Conscious design processes as they are

3

conducted today tend to concentrate on land-use problems, primarily in urban areas, touching on the other factors only as they are connected with such use. Design must work within the fundamental and as yet ungoverned forces of nature with clear understanding of their potential effect upon its products. Within the more intimate area of natural processes which can be controlled or directed, design must endeavor to guide human activities toward that constantly adjusting equilibrium of man and nature which is the conservation ideal.[1]

Design is a problem-solving activity, a decision-making process, and at times an art-producing procedure. We might call art those solutions whose effects expand in time and space beyond the immediate scope of the problem. All artists are designers, but all designers are not artists. We think of the landscape as housing various *objets d'art,* but we have not yet come to think of it as potentially a complete work of art in a given area. We tend to equate technology with science, as the wave of the future, and design with art, as a hangover from the past. But technology cannot function without design, and science and art are the two main and inseparable elements of man's constant effort to improve his life in this world. Science expands our knowledge of the world, but art expands our understanding of the meaning of this knowledge in our lives. Science helps us to think more clearly, art helps us to feel more deeply, more accurately, and more constructively. Technology ap-

plies the findings of science, design applies those of art; but technology and design must work together to solve the problems which are presented to them. In this way the discoveries of science and of art may be merged to enrich our lives, *if* both are operating on comparable levels, and *if* the channels of communication are kept open. Otherwise, design may become enslaved by technology, and art may become a weak voice functioning as court jester before the throne of science. Today we tend to glorify science and to treat art as entertainment or as a sales technique.

Design begins with a thorough analysis of problem and resources and ends with a proposed solution which is a synthesis of imagination and practicality. Reality for design must be physical, visual, comprehensible, even though science may tell us that reality is energy in motion. Design in the landscape must cover all decisions about materials, elements, and arrangements within a designated area. Typically this involves the establishment of connections or relations between building, site space, and surrounding landscape. This is a problem that has remained constant through all changes in technology, from the grass, stone, or ice shack to the air-conditioned glass or brick cube. For landscape design the philosophical discussion of the relations between man and nature becomes an exploration of the relations between indoor and outdoor living, in all climates and at all scales from the single house to the multistory apartment. In order to solve prob-

4

lems design must search for form. Relations between technical-functional and sensory-emotional aspects of form will be governed only partially by the requirements of the problem. Much more important will be the background relations between science and art, or between technology and emotion.

Any existing landscape is a result of a constant historical flow of decisions on specific fragments within a framework of general control. Thus we really have two kinds of landscape design, one dealing with the specific development of single sites, the other with the general accumulation of such decisions into a community or regional landscape. Today, with the centralization of control over larger and larger pieces of land in fewer and fewer hands, and with the general concern over landscape improvement being handled through such agencies as urban redevelopment, we have a tendency to fill the gap between these specific and general processes, that is, between planning and design. This tendency brings into question all existing professional design boundaries and competencies. During the past one hundred years public control over the landscape has grown from the pure *laissez faire* of the nineteenth century to the existing structure of zoning ordinances, subdivision codes, restrictive covenants, building codes, and the like. Regardless of the quality of such controls, they establish a precedent which makes it possible to think of moving from Urban Redevelopment, with its negative concern with slums and blighted areas, to Urban Development, with its positive concern for the form and quality of the entire urban area.

Architecture, nature, history, and society are all important in the design of the landscape. Society provides the activating framework of human aspirations, needs, and controls. Nature is the reservoir of materials, inspiration, and repose. History is the background of experience from which we can learn if we avoid imitation, and architecture is the vanguard of human creativity in the landscape, establishing new forces, new directions, new inspirations, and new problems with each new building. Throughout preindustrial history unconscious design produced charming, if unsanitary, environments. Since the Industrial Revolution we have found that we can no longer allow the design of the physical environment to remain in unconscious hands, that we must explore the relevance of conscious design to the constant changes which go on in the landscape around us. All design professions are important in the conscious design of the landscape. Planning, engineering, architecture, and landscape architecture are most directly involved, but graphic design, object design both handicraft and industrial, painting, and sculpture all play important roles. Sculpture in particular seems to have a built-in drive to escape from the pedestal to influence its surroundings. Vigeland in Oslo, Milles in Stockholm, and Noguchi at UNESCO and elsewhere have all demonstrated that, even though their sculpture is much better than their landscape design, there are important things to be learned from the impact of sculpture upon the refinement of its environment.

Collaboration among members of various design professions is demanded by the increasing scale and complexity of landscape problems, and may provide a road to the future development of true master landscape designers. Fear of bureaucratic regimentation may well lead us to question the possibility or desirability of total landscape design at the neighborhood, community, or regional scale. However, this has happened under various autocratic historical regimes, and it is implied now by the complex problems of urban industrial society and by the growing centralization of power and control over the landscape in our society. Whether or not democratic processes can keep abreast or ahead of these proliferating problems is a peculiarly pressing current issue much larger than that of the landscape. As the scale of landscape design expands, there will be an ever more important question as to whether it continues, as in the past, to concentrate on special areas—downtown, economically important areas, cultural areas, better-class neighborhoods— or whether it will begin to move into the long-neglected typical ordinary landscapes, as some renewal projects have done already. Here, as in the special areas, it must ask whether we cannot go beyond technical and functional excellence to search for true beauty in the landscape, beauty which will relax the body, inspire the mind, and expand the spirit. Design for people will attempt to meet their need for a sense of security and creativity, pleasant views and vistas, adequate, comfortable enclosures, graceful continuity and transition, and relation to history. The landscape can be remodeled to help supply such needs through constructive, profitable, and creative social programs: housing, health, recreation, culture, education. Such programs will help us to learn that quantitative measurements of the environment are not enough, that quality, as a relationship between observers and surroundings, can be experienced, described, discussed, designed, but not measured, reproduced, or imitated. The landscape, as the world around us, is one continuous experience in time and space throughout our lives, complete as far as we can see or move at any given time and place. This is the design problem of the future, one which will demand the most sincere, modest, selfless, and yet strenuous attention from all of us.

5

II

ELEMENTS OF SPACE ORGANIZATION

Space organization is a common everyday activity. All of us participate in it at some time. Anyone who moves dirt, places rocks, shapes or directs water, plants plants, builds paths, roads, utilities, or buildings, or arranges furniture, signs, and other impedimenta indoors or out is changing the existing organization of space. This change will affect the nature and quality of the experience people will receive in that specific area.

Space is the invisible ocean of atmosphere at the bottom of which we live. It is given tangible physical form, size, scale, continuity, and volume by the shape of the ground on which we move, and by every other tangible physical element protruding, growing, constructed, or placed on or above it. Everything added to or subtracted from the landscape changes it for better or worse—every chair, table, painting, sculpture, bicycle, auto, building, road, bridge, tree, bush, rock, pond, mound, hollow, poster, billboard, hydrant, or traffic signal. The space-organizing and articulating function of all such elements has central importance, equal to their specific functional or other reasons for existence. This is true because we cannot avoid or evade experiencing their effect upon the space around and between them.

Dimension. The elements of space organization are at first somewhat abstruse—dimension, time, energy. Dimension is our system for measuring the world around us, in commonly accepted units—inches, feet, yards, acres, or their metric equivalents. Dimensions are taken horizontally, vertically, or at specified angles to the primal force of gravity which governs all our physical activities. Dimensions lead naturally into mathematics, which, as Whitehead says, are "the precise ideas which lie at the base of the scientific and philosophical investigation of the universe," beginning with "the relations of number, the relations of quantity, and the relations of space." [2] Such abstract thinking leads us back again to concepts as useful and practical as the contour line. With this, a line every point of which is at the same elevation, we can make two-dimensional drawings of irregular topography which read clearly if one knows the language.

Time

We are accustomed to the thought that every phys-ical object has three dimensions, but time, maintains Einstein, is also a dimension of space, and space is a dimension of time. Neither time nor space can exist without the other and they are, therefore, interdependent. Because movement and change are constant, we live in a four-dimensional universe, with time as the fourth dimension. [3]

Dimensions exist in that continuity of time which measures our lives. We live in the present which extends into both past and future without precise boundaries. The present is an instant which is constantly passing yet always here. ". . . the present is itself a duration, and therefore includes directly perceived time-relations between events contained within it. In other words we put the present on the same footing as the past and the future in respect to the inclusion within it of antecedent and succeeding events. . . ." [4]

Time conditions our experience of dimension. We see so much in a given instant from a given position across a given space; we see so much more as we turn our heads and bodies and move on foot or by more rapid conveyance. Time conditions our experience in terms of continuity and sequence: what we see first conditions what we see thereafter, although what we see thereafter may also condition our memory of what we saw before. Thus what one sees and senses in a given instant, from a given position or circulation route, is a basic concern of spatial design. We must distinguish design from organization because it is concerned with quality as well as quantity.

Energy. Personal physical energy in the individual conditions his experience of time and dimension.

Our own individual characteristics lie at the center of our own worlds, and color all things around us. . . . This personal world consists of things which frequently enter our sphere of activity, and it is limited in general, and in particular, by the extent of our energy.

The more complex an experience is, the greater is the amount of energy and time that we must devote to it. . . . The characteristic time-energy structure of man has two basic qualities: rhythm and quantity. The quantity of our vital energy is rather constant over a given period of time. Fatigue symptoms compel us to a variation of activity. We need a very definite system of regeneration periods which are in close relation to our rhythmically-limited energy. . . . Our energy structure plays a very significant role not

only in our thinking, but also in everything that we associate with order. In addition to the three dimensions of physical space, human space is decisively defined by two additional dimensions: time and energy.[5]

A strong man can cover more space in a given time than can a child or older person. Likewise a healthy and well-fed man can cover more than one who is sick or undernourished. Psychological as well as physical energy will determine how much experience one is willing and able to absorb within a given period of time. Consider, for instance, the bombardment of experience while on a shopping tour, visiting art galleries or museums, or sitting through plays, movies, or musical productions. One must be fresh at the beginning to get the most out of any of these.

Light. Space organization becomes less abstruse when we consider light as one of its elements. Light is the vehicle for vision, our primary sense for orientation in the physical world. Without light we are blind. Light comes from a central source: sun, moon, or light fixture. Indoors it is possible to control light patterns precisely; outdoors this is impossible. The position of the source in relation to the physical elements around us creates a pattern of light and shade. Insofar as these elements are hard fixed forms, like buildings or rocks, they will cast precise and contrasting shadows. But insofar as these elements include moisture and impurities in the atmosphere, changeable elements such as vegetation, and transparent or translucent elements such as glass, plastics, fabrics, and fine-meshed structural materials, the patterns of light and shade will be diffuse, changeable, and subtle. Thus beyond the simple fact of light and shade orienting us in relation to solids and voids, we have the maximum variation in atmospheric seeing conditions between, for instance, the bright, clear Arizona desert and the cloudy, foggy Northwest coast. The daily and seasonal movements of the earth in relation to the sun create a further multiple variation in which the angle of the sun's rays is never exactly the same, except as repeated annually. Shadow patterns move obviously from hour to hour, and less obviously grow longer or shorter from day to day. Seasonal variations are greater as we go toward the poles, less as we go toward the equator. These changing patterns of light and shade change the qualities of spaces and surfaces over which they

play. Spatial design is concerned not merely with arranging solids, broken solids, and voids in clear and pleasant three-dimensional patterns, but with predicting the daily and seasonal patterns that light will make over them. Consider the mysterious dappled light within the forest; the soft, rich light that comes through canvas; the sharp light and shade of adobe towns and mesas in the desert; the mystery of swirling fog in San Francisco or London; the magnificent sparkling clarity of a sunny morning after a rainy night.

Any photographer is acutely conscious of the importance of light in reading the landscape. He will wait hours, sometimes days, for precisely the right pattern of light and shade on a given scene or subject. This will be the pattern which produces a maximum expression of its particular qualities.

Land. Proceeding farther from the abstruse to the concrete, the element most fundamental to space organization is the land which provides its floor and foundation. Land begins as rock—hard or soft, dense or porous, igneous, sedimentary, or metamorphic—the basic structure of our globe. Attacked by the physical and chemical forces of atmosphere, wind, weather, and water, it breaks down into smaller and smaller fragments, moving from rock pile through gravel bed to sand dune and silt bed. As this happens vegetation, animals, and microorganisms take up residence, rooting into it, burrowing through it, filling all the interstices with fantastic microscopic life. This life reacts on the mineral content of the rock to produce organic residues and compounds of constantly increasing quantities and complexities. As the soil develops from the hard rock of the peaks to the soft loam of the valley floor this organic content increases to a balanced ratio with the original mineral. Sometimes, in spots with poor drainage and enough moisture to produce heavy vegetation, the organic material will completely cover the mineral, leaving us a peat bed.

The land has form of great variety and richness. The forces of precipitation, runoff, glaciation, and wind, through eons of geologic time, have shaped the land surface of the earth in remarkable and fascinating patterns. The panorama of land forms is one of our richest landscape experiences: from broad plains that appear level although they actually are not; through gentle slopes, rolls, and swells to those most voluptuous and sensuous plastic land forms, mature rounded hills; and beyond them to the original and still growing mountains in basically triangular patterns, upright, jagged or majestic, rocky. Inseparable from these land forms are the water elements that produce them: streams and rivers, cascading through mountain gorges or meandering across mature valleys and plains; ponds and lakes, still water in horizontal planes of varying colors outlining the contours of the shores; and the variable shoreline formations of great lakes, seas, and oceans. In the arid West the forms and patterns of these water elements exist, quite clearly from an airplane, even though actual water may invade them but seldom.

The vagaries of the subdivision process when applied to the vast orderly topography of the land may bring us any combination of qualities within the legal boundaries of our parcel of real estate. We may have topsoil, exposed subsoil, and/or exposed rock; our soil content may vary from sand to clay, from largely mineral to largely organic; our topography may appear flat, slope at any angle, or be warped in any combination of curved surfaces. Drainage patterns may be simple and predictable or surprisingly complex and difficult to control. Variations will, of course, tend to increase with the size of the property. Smaller parcels of irregular ground are apt to be less understandably related to the general topography than larger parcels. These larger parcels are more apt to contain comprehensible units of topography—a knoll, a ridge, a valley, or a shelf. Subdivision tends to be governed more by economics of lot size, roads, and utilities, than by respect for the natural sculpture of the land, particularly in these days of the bulldozer, carryall, and prime mover.

Roads and Utilities. Next in importance in space organization for people are access roads and utilities. It must be possible to reach the land by car (in all but pedestrian and wilderness areas), and the primary service and sanitation elements must be available. This, along with earthwork, is the basic cost in land development, which establishes the floor for real estate values. Roads may vary from the simple country dirt variety to city streets with curbs, gutters, and sidewalks, and on into the whole complex of highways and freeways. Much excellent re-

1

2

1   2   3

search material exists on utilities, roads, streets, high-ways, and traffic; these problems we have not ignored.

One point tends to be overlooked in our concentration on vehicular problems: they exist to service the primary housing, work, recreation, and cultural elements of the community, not as ends in themselves. The necessity of reaching most land by car does not mean that it must be engulfed in a flood of asphalt. Rather, the closeness and extent of contact must be sensitively adjusted to minimum functional convenience and maximum pedestrian protection and encouragement. The tendency of the traffic engineer to take over all streets and to follow the shortest distance between two points, regardless of what lies between, is devastating to the community landscape. At a regional and community planning scale traffic can be organized and rationalized by tried master planning procedures. At an individual site planning scale our efforts should be toward minimizing invasion by cars as much as possible. Roads should be dead-end, short loops, or peripheral; parking lots, the new asphalt deserts of the twentieth century, must be broken up with planting in a major way to convert them from visual liabilities to assets.

We have reached the point in land planning where car-parking space becomes the primary control of land-use. We have recognized this in widespread requirements for offstreet parking in all types of developments. We have not yet, with rare exceptions, recognized the need for *qualitative* control of parking areas, nor for restricting coverage by buildings *and* parking surfaces to a good deal less than 100 per cent of the site. A parking lot cannot qualify as urban open space, even though it may allow light and air to reach the upper floors of buildings around it. We are, in general, faced with this dilemma: Shall we allow the use of land, measured usually by car-parking requirements, to cover it so completely as to destroy its amenity in the community landscape? Or shall we establish landscape quality as a land-use control, expressed in coverage requirements which guarantee adequate open space for pedestrians and planting? While some may say that the congestion of our cities renders this question irrelevant, expanding renewal programs throughout the country emphasize its importance, and give the opportunity

to meet it. The notion that, as urban density increases, the problems of congestion become more automatic and less soluble is negated by an objective examination of the vast waste of living space in most of our customary and normal land-use patterns; the plenitude of open land around all of our most congested urban centers; and the sensitive and humane patterns for urban living that have been developed by many architects and planners, and that are produced by the dozens annually in most schools of design and planning across the country. It is not that we are unable to solve our problems; it is that we are unwilling to pay the price in organization, control, and disruption of habitual patterns of living and thinking.

Utilities are matters of practical engineering which must be closely integrated with the site-planning process. Problems of sewage disposal, water supply, or drainage can exercise dominant control over development patterns. They must also be subject to imaginative adjustments in the hands of sensitive planners. The fact that most of them go underground gives them second priority after earthwork in development programming. At times their requirements may dominate planning patterns; usually there is a possibility of reciprocal adjustment between the demands of engineering and those of site planning. Overhead power lines are the classical, but not the only, example of the former situation.

Buildings. Buildings are central and dominant elements in most humanized landscapes. They furnish the primary shelter, climate control, privacy, refined environment, and services needed for comfortable civilized living. They are connected with the landscape around them by doors and glass areas, which establish two-way circulation and visual patterns. In built-up urban areas of two- to multistory continuous buildings they are the principal space-organizing elements, forming street canyons, squares, and occasionally more subtle spaces. Landscape elements in these areas tend to be of a minor relief nature, although the occasional urban park demonstrates the potential for balanced contrasting relations between large building masses and large green spaces. Congestion and many attendant ills of urbanism would never occur if these two expanded concurrently instead of inversely.

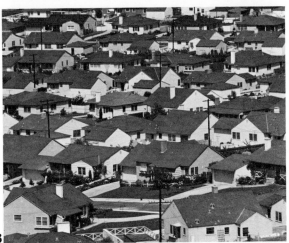

In suburban areas of one- and two-story detached buildings we tend to get an equal balance between houses, trees, streets, and ground forms. This produces, especially in the new mass subdivisions, a monotonous pepper-and-salt landscape without variation in scale or character. The monotonous feeling is aggravated by a tendency for streets to become wider, thus increasing the percentage of asphalt in the total landscape (30 per cent, according to Bartholomew [6]). As lots, trees, and houses get smaller, this monotony is aggravated. Older surburban areas often have by accident what newer ones need—variation in size, character, and space of buildings, trees, and open spaces. But the older area which has this may be on the brink of decline into blight, or it may have so much variation as to be chaotic. There is no substitute for controlled design of landscape relations.

In rural, primeval, or park areas the occasional building can be a jewel of functional or imaginative quality, enhancing the landscape by the integrity of its design. Rural farm buildings are perhaps the best example. The isolated building in the open landscape has always been a fascinating, ideal problem for architect and landscape architect. The National Park Service has begun to recognize this, after many years of self-conscious rusticism.

There is general agreement in architectural circles that, as landscape or community elements, most buildings should be well done but quiet and unobtrusive, using those buildings of special form, color, pattern, or size as accents in carefully planned locations. This is a far cry from the competitive commercial anarchy of most of our cities and towns.

What might be called the two main currents in contemporary architecture are the up-to-date expansion and refinement of traditional post-and-beam construction, using steel, glass, and curtain-wall systems; and the "new sensualism," the search for newer and richer forms and revolutionary structural systems, typified by such names as Fuller, Nervi, Candela, Saarinen, Lautner, and Yamasaki. To these might be added certain other currents—the personal romanticism typified by Frank Lloyd Wright, the "new humanism" of the Scandinavian countries and the San Francisco Bay region, and the hybrid eclecticism of most actual building. All of these together

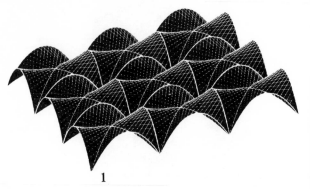

1

2

3

may become elements in good community landscape patterns.

It is refreshing to read that:

Funeral services for the International Style in Architecture were performed without tears by Philip Johnson, A.I.A., one of the prime-movers and founders of that movement some thirty-five years ago. . . .

The world is now so full of so many wonderful things . . . lovely little alleys to explore . . . that it would be a shame to have any straitjacket put on it. It would be marvelous to feel that we could build . . . whatever we wanted to. . . .

This is a terrible thing to say! that we no longer do our buildings on the basis of structure, that we no longer do our buildings on the basis of honesty, of function. . . . All that went out of the window! . . . that we do them the way that we want to. . . .

Freedom of variety is what we should all welcome today. . . .[7]

This is confirmed by Robin Boyd in 1961:

. . . The presently desired state of restless richness in contemporary home design is largely the illogical conclusion of the sober, austere, even puritanical, movement in design which might be called the first phase of modern architecture. . . . This meant two principal fights. The first was to free buildings from the obligation to follow any preconceived forms, allowing them to take any practical shape they wished. . . . The second fight was to set free the technological advances of the nineteenth century. . . .

The most noticeable feature of the earliest modern architecture was a moralistic elimination of ornament, but there was something else equally radical and equally significant: the idea of separating the parts . . . an assemblage of deliberately articulated, deliberately different things each provided with its own separate expression and separate entity within the composition.

. . . today the one consistent idea which seems to be taking shape in the mists of modern architectural thought is not a new idea, but a new, literal, unbending interpretation of another old idea. This is the classical concept of a total unification by design. . . .

. . . starting sometime about 1955 every new building of self-importance sought to be a single thing. It was no longer content just to be composed, integrated, and co-ordinated by a regular "module" (unit of measure) or an even rhythm of similar elements. . . . Suddenly every important building wanted to have a monolithic idea. . . .

. . . gradually in the past five years the monolithic idea has become a passion, or a fashion, and the vari-

ous means now used by architects to create the desired singleness of effect account for most of the apparently unrelated personal styles of the moment.[8]

Such talk emboldens this landscape architect to unburden himself. As he travels through the streets of the city, searching for scenes or elements restful to the eye and the mind, he finds little satisfaction in the average production of modern architecture. Stark stucco or curtain-walled boxes lacking scale, detail, intimacy, warmth, or refinement—one glance absorbs all of the experience existing in most of them. Much more soothing to the roving eye and the tired mind are a multiplicity of more varied elements: old houses, of Victorian or Greene and Greene vintage; church towers, water towers, or what have you, of Romanesque, Gothic, Renaissance, or other eclectic derivation; gas tanks, high-tension towers, steam plants, bridges, dams; mature trees and bits of green or water; even Renaissance office buildings begin to have a strange charm in our harassed, streamlined, super-sexed, phantasmagoric landscape. This is not a plea for a return to eclecticism; it is a plea for a return to humanity. This plea is being recognized in the best work being done in many communities.

Landscape Elements. Landscape elements include all forms of planting and vegetation, all adjustments, refinements or designed developments in ground forms, rock groupings, and water patterns, all construction other than completely enclosed buildings or primarily utilitarian engineering structures—walks, terraces, patios, steps, walls, screens, arbors, shelters, play areas, etc. These are the elements used to develop and refine spaces between, around, or within buildings and vehicular circulation elements, when they occur either intentionally or through accidents of nonintensive land use. The extent and qualitative treatment of landscaped pedestrian open space is a barometer of community concern with the character of its physical surroundings. Bacon's famous line, "Men tend to build stately sooner than to garden finely," might be paraphrased today as "Men tend to build densely sooner than to garden at all."

Trees, rather than buildings, are the best measure of the civilized landscape. A community in which many mature trees survive and more are planted regularly demonstrates a sense of time, history, and continuity on the land which is directly contrary to

12

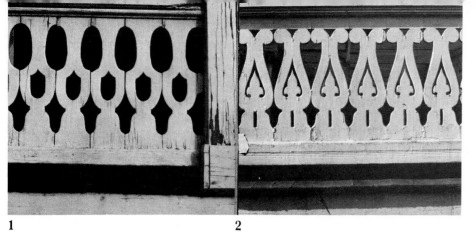

1   2
3

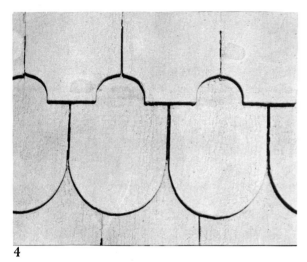

4

6

5

7   8

1

2

3

our normal speculative scramble and the normal real estate drive for higher and better use which regards all green open space as raw land waiting for the magic wand of progress (construction) to touch it. It takes ten years or longer to produce a reasonably mature tree in most parts of the country; few urban land users anticipate a tenure longer than five years. This is not progress, growth, development, or vitality. It is insanity, a squirrel cage in which most of us chase madly round and round only to find the same old ugly city in the end. Those sections in which fine old trees do survive—the better residential districts, institutional grounds, parks—are the showplaces of the city. These are the sections to which the tourists are sent to offset the slums and the blighted areas.

Tree men spend their lives searching for trees which will accommodate themselves to the impossible conditions of urban living—soot, dust, smog, heat, glare, carbon monoxide, barren dry soil covered with paving, no space in which roots or top can flourish. The ideal urban tree is narrow, neat, and inoffensive, somewhat like the ideal urban citizen of these conformist days. Its roots will not push and swell enough to disrupt sidewalks and utilities, its top will not be so broad and dense as to cover signs or windows. It will not drop leaves, twigs, flowers, or fruit enough to make a troublesome mess. The natural cycle of growth and decay which produces the rich humus of the forest floor has no place in our centers of civilization. Now we are even searching for trees that will grow in containers. What a contradiction in terms!

Trees are nature's air conditioners. They moderate the climate, reducing extremes of heat, wind, aridity, and glare. It has been said that an adequate

number of trees in and around Los Angeles would filter out the smog. Likewise trees moderate the visual landscape. Most construction can become acceptable in the landscape, both visually and functionally, if it is so spaced that it can be framed and balanced with adequate groups of trees. Rare is the piece of architecture that is self-sufficient without the counterpoint of natural vegetation. Trees are the friends of man. The environment which is good for trees is good for people, and that which is bad for trees is likewise bad for people. Trees and people should band together against the unwholesome ugliness of most city living. The flight to the suburbs is a sympton of this need. If, instead of forcing trees and people to conform to the demands of today's cities, we were to redesign those cities to conform to the needs of trees and people, the millennium might be near.

Trees range from 20 to 100 feet in height and spread. Their roots occupy volumes of soil comparable to their foliage volume in the air. They will grow best if the ground within the ultimate perimeter of the top is kept in ground cover, grass, or a dry cover which does not seal the surface. Allocation of space adequate for good tree culture should be as much a part of good urban land-use planning as the allocation of adequate space for buildings and parking. The 5- to 15-foot parking strip is inadequate for most trees and does not justify the excessive maintenance which it requires. While it is well known that trees can be found which will tolerate such restricted situations, when we follow this pattern we fail to obtain the greatest benefit from the material. Architecture, trees, and open space are the basic comple-

mentary elements of urban design. City planning which does not make possible good architecture, good tree culture, and adequate open space is failing to reach its potential.

The city which is not beautiful is not functional, and hence is a waste of all the time, energy, labor, and materials which went into its construction. City planning must think more specifically and realistically and less diagrammatically, if we are to avoid repeating the mechanized anarchy in which we live today. It is ironic that the richest country in the world, which boasts of its high standard of living, should live in a landscape so poverty-stricken in visual quality. This bears out Galbraith's contention that all our wealth is concentrated in private goods—public facilities are treated as poor orphans.

These elements of space organization—dimension, time, energy, light, land, roads and utilities, buildings, landscape elements—are primary in all human environments from the small room and/or patio to the community and region. As the scale expands, the emphasis shifts from particular detail to general relations. But the individual human observer is always conscious of precise and intimate close-up experiences no matter what the scale of the surroundings. As the scale expands, the problem of transition and sequence between it and the individual expands likewise. Vast open spaces may be used by authoritarian states to intimidate the masses, or, in more democratic societies, they may provide enriching experiences of spatial expansion and community solidarity. The difference will be determined by the social climate, and by the treatment of the physical surroundings of the open space.

Problems. Design begins as a problem-solving activity. In the landscape these problems stem from the programmatic desires of the owners and developers and from the specific properties of the space-organizing elements. The problems of dimension, time, energy, and light are fundamental to all technical, functional, and esthetic considerations. The problems of the land stem from its natural structure; the movement of water on and under the surface and its suitability as a support for plants and buildings. These are areas of basic engineering which every designer of the landscape must understand in some detail. We must understand that geologic structures, and their rocks and soils, vary from region to region, sometimes from block to block. The techniques of earthwork, water movement, construction, and planting must vary with, and be adjusted to, these changes in geology. Changes in ground forms must be based on careful study of the existing surface and subsurface conditions. The control of water movement—receiving all that enters the land by precipitation, surface, or subsurface movement; moving it rapidly away from structures, or more slowly but continuously through planting; delivering it to public drainage easement or neighbor below in a manner convenient and harmless—is fundamental to the success of any land development. Resolution of the contradictions between good structural foundation requirements—for ground which is hard, stable, inorganic, and dry—and good horticultural requirements—for ground which is loose, friable, organic, and moist though well drained—is fundamental to the happy marriage of structure and vegetation.

The problems of access and utilities are both tech-

15

nical and visual: road alignment, grading and construction, supply and distribution of water, gas and electricity, treatment and disposal of sewage. The technical aspects of these problems are covered in engineering literature. The form and alignment of roads, streets, and highways, particularly on irregular topography, are landscape problems even though usually determined by engineers. Utility elements above ground—power lines, gas and water tanks, sewage treatment plants—are major landscape elements, often landmarks, which are rarely coordinated with the other elements around them.

The problems of building include the development and selection of structural and climate control systems and the solution of functional and esthetic demands. These are discussed in detail in the literature of architecture. Architect Paul Rudolph has said:

We no longer think that when the problems of making a project work have been solved that the exterior form will be found crystallized. . . . there are those who value disorder because it somehow seems "human," and anything else is termed pretentious, regimented, cold, intellectual, dictatorial, etc. Possibly the extremes are illustrated in the USA by the so-called Bay Region style in California on one hand and Mies van der Rohe on the other.

Modern architecture's failure to produce understandable theories regarding the relationship of a building to its environment in the deepest sense is disastrous. The Ecole des Beaux Arts was actually very rich in this aspect. . . . The quickly moving vehicle and unprecedented requirements of sheer bulk have given us new dimensions of scale. Human scale must be coupled. . . .

At mid-century the battle of modern architecture vs. traditional architecture is won, but we find it a dry, limited, timid, monotonous thing, utilizing forms which are merely fashionable, without regard to the fundamental concepts behind the great prototypes. Part of our difficulties come from the concept of functionalism as the prime determinant of architectural forms. There are certainly as many as six determinants. . . .

The first determinant is the environment of the building, which means its relationship to other buildings and the site. . . . Modern architecture has been particularly weak in this respect and indeed even negative, ignoring especially the relationship of the building to the sky. We usually say that our buildings are related to others by contrast, but this works only occasionally. . . .

The second determinant of form is the functional aspects. . . .

The third determinant of form is the particular region, climate, landscape and natural lighting conditions with which one is confronted. Modern architecture is becoming the international style. . . . There are several conditions which tend to limit regional expression. First there is industrialization; second, ease of travel and communication; third, the rising cost of traditional materials and skilled labor; fourth, the influence of the architectural press; fifth, the worship of that which is popular and our desire to conform; sixth, the "do-it-yourself according to manufacturer's instruction" movement; and seventh, the abstract qualities inherent in the new concept of space. . . .

The fourth determinant of form is the particular material which one uses. We are currently going through a structural exhibitionism stage but this will pass. . . .

The fifth determinant of form is concerned with satisfying the peculiar physiological demands of the building. This is accomplished primarily through the manipulation of space and use of symbols. We are particularly unsure in this aspect, partially because the revolution threw out much which still has validity. Thus we must learn anew the meaning of monumentality, how to create a place of worship and inspiration; how to make quiet, enclosed, isolated spaces; how to make spaces full of hustling, bustling activities and pungent with vitality; how to make dignified, vast, sumptuous, even awe-inspiring spaces; how to make mysterious spaces; how to make transition spaces which define, separate, and yet join juxtaposed spaces of contrasting character. We need sequences of space which arouse one's curiosity, give a sense of anticipation, which beckon and impel us to rush forward to find that releasing space which dominates, which acts as a climax and magnet and therefore gives direction.

The sixth and last determinant of form is concerned with the spirit of the times. This is perhaps the most difficult of all and . . . is expressed by its vitality, its tension, its curiosity, its insecurity, its materialism, its desire for comfort, its glorification of the power of man.[9]

The problems of landscape elements include portions of all of those above—rough and finish grading, roads, drives and walks, terminal utility distribution (sprinklers, outdoor lighting) and sewage collection, minor construction—plus the special problems of horticulture in the whole range from turf and annual flower culture to the moving of full-grown trees, the shaping of ground and water forms and patterns,

1

2

3

and the arrangement of rocks for maximum visual refinement. These are discussed in detail in the literature of landscape architecture and horticulture.

In a world in which change is the only constant, land, roads, utilities, buildings, and landscape elements all have special maintenance problems and requirements which must be thoroughly considered during planning and design. The relationship between initial installation cost and early and regular maintenance costs is complex and requires careful study. Proper pregrading surface preparation, compaction of fills, and planting and control of drainage will stabilize new earthwork. Utilities engineered for maximum loads, made of materials resistant to corrosion and abuse, and structures designed to minimize cleaning, refinishing, and repairs indoors and out will soon justify their extra cost. Thorough and deep soil preparation, careful selection of hardy plant species and healthy stock, and installation of well-designed automatic sprinkler systems will reduce maintenance man-hours out-of-doors. However, maintenance is part labor and part love. The landscape which receives a balance of both will have a quality unattainable by any other means.

The Landscape. The landscape is the world around us. It is everything we see or feel wherever we go. It stretches from ocean to ocean; its limits are those of human vision and motion, and such physical obstacles as may exist or be established. It is not only physically indivisible, but this physical landscape is in fact indivisible from the social landscape—people in human relations. These two landscapes, the physical and the social, exist together in a state of constant reciprocal action and reaction.

The landscape is one continuous experience in time and space throughout the life of every human being. It is a composite impression of everything seen, felt, or sensed wherever he or she is during waking hours. It is related in scale to all of the station points and lines of circulation occupied or followed regularly or irregularly throughout life. Its effects upon the citizens are conditioned by all their previous life experiences. These fit them with specially colored glasses through which they see the landscape in special ways. These experiences in turn are conditioned by the educational pressures to which the citizens are subjected throughout life, formally for

3

1

2

17

Sculpture has within it the potential for bridging the gap between building and landscape elements.

eight to twenty years while young, informally daily through the agencies of mass communication.

The landscape is continuous visually as far as we can see from wherever we are. It is continuous physically as far as we can go from wherever we are. These two factors, working together, are the basic design controls for the humanized landscape. We begin with the great natural divisions created by climate, water, topography, vegetation, and soil. Over these we superimpose a network of political boundaries and property lines by a subdivision process. This fragments the landscape legally and socially, but its physical unity remains. Humanized development then proceeds as a multiple series of disconnected, more or less conscious decisions applied to the development of each parcel of land within the subdivision-net separately and independently. These decisions are disconnected in space, so that one does not know (beyond the generalities of zoning) what his neighbor to the right or to the left may do with his land. They are also disconnected in time, so that we do not know why or how the previous owner of our parcel did what he did, or what a subsequent owner may do. These decisions and relations are constantly pressured by all the fast-moving forces of development, growth, and change in modern society: relations between resident and absentee ownership and tenancy on land and in buildings; the forces of speculation and investment, searching for "the highest and best use of the land"; the forces of technological development, which have brought us in recent years to the age of atomic power, automation, jet transport and instant communication anywhere; and the social and political forces generated by all of these. The result, wherever we look about us, is visual anarchy and monotony in our communities, sometimes called the monotony of variety or the American genius for sterility. From across the Atlantic comes refreshing comment by Ian Nairn, architectural observer and critic: ". . . in the United States the divorce of habitat and inhabitants seems almost total. . . . An exceptional new American building may be beautifully treated up to the boundaries of the site . . . but outside the boundary, whether in town or just beyond, is the jungle, a continuous nonsense of non-relation. . . . The argument is not affected by the vast number of American 'urban renewal' projects, which do combine architecture and town planning in a statistical sense. . . . They are seen as isolated geometrical essays . . . and the whole project becomes a big building. Outside it, again, the jungle; inside it, often, an artificially imposed architect's order which makes no attempt to realize the astonishing variety of ways of life still practised in an American urban population."[10]

The individual experiences the landscape both quantitatively and qualitatively as he moves through it, lives and works in it, and with it. Each daily or hourly experience conditions those which follow it. From a very early age memories begin to accumulate. A consistent type of memory may produce a strong bias for or against it, while an accumulation of non-descript or heterogeneous memories may result in open-mindedness or an apathetic approach to the environment. Historical experience, and research such as Lynch's, indicate certain landscape experiences that are consistently memorable—green park-like pastoral scenes, broad panoramas, clear vistas, strong and understandable continuity of relations between elements (paths, edges, nodes), well-distributed and easily identifiable landmarks, districts of consistent character.[11]

Quality. Quality is a relationship between an individual or group and a section of landscape which can be perceived, comprehended, and reacted to. The landscape as a physical fact exists independently of any given observer at any given time. The quality of the landscape is measured by the reactions of human observers. Gestalt psychology teaches us that these are unified reactions to complete units or complexes, that is, to everything perceived at a given time. These reactions are seldom impartial or objective. They are colored by all of the individual's background: childhood, education, training, experience. Sensation and perception lead to intellection embodying experience, emotion, and association. Mankind learned early in history that some of the great pleasures in life come from unifying variety, ordering disorder, harmonizing conflict, balancing imbalance, and generally resolving the contradictions in the world around us. We also learned that unity, order, harmony, and balance complete and pure become stale and lose flavor—each needs a little of its opposite to give it spice and life.

Pleasure in unity and order builds up taste, schools, tradition. Taste begins as individual skepticism, search, and discovery; grows as social recognition and inspiration in schools of followers; matures with community acceptance and integration; flowers occasionally in the high rises of cultural history; sickens and dies as it allows the growth of academic formulae and dogma, measured drawings, authentic reproductions, and rules of design. Tradition is the accumulation and continuity of high rises, seen with the perspective of history.

For some eight thousand years before the Industrial Revolution, mankind tended to group in relatively small social units which developed unified taste and cultural patterns within themselves. The great empires of antiquity may have drawn many such units together under a blanket of fire and sword. But the edges always frayed off into unknown wilderness, and the conquered always tended to absorb the conquerors, or at least to resist absorption. The study of preindustrial cultural patterns has the fascination of variety, individuality, clarity, simplicity. The literature of primitive and folk art is replete with analyses of differences in form and content, finish, detail, technology. And yet the frustrated and searching twentieth-century eye finds certain fundamental unifying continuities in preindustrial art—fitness to purpose, economy of means, richness limited only by resources, intuitive forms, similarities in quality, flavor, form, or pattern across great gaps in time and space, and always the constant small variations among similar elements that are as natural as nature herself.

It remained for the 200 years of industrial culture to make known the entire world, in quantitative generality if not in qualitative detail. Its tendency to equalize or cosmopolitanize culture around the world, through rapid communication and transportation and aggressive commercial enterprise, has exceeded the wildest dreams of khans or emperors. Hollywood, Madison Avenue, mass production, and the Chase Manhattan Bank have been more effective than all the legions of Rome. Aldous Huxley, in *Brave New World Revisited*,[12] finds that the homogeneous and sterile culture which he had predicted some thirty years ago for the twenty-sixth century is now almost upon us.

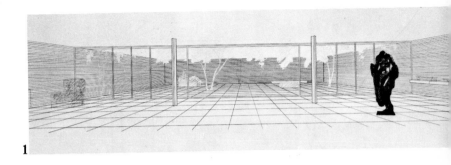

1

Quantitative relations in the landscape exist within themselves, and can be measured from outside themselves, in dollars, acres, or miles. Qualitative relations in the landscape exist only in connection with one or more human observers or participants. Without people to measure it by reaction there can be no quality in the landscape. Thus a qualitative discussion involves two factors—the physical landscape, and the people who experience it and participate in its formation. One who would design the landscape in more than quantitative terms (art is a search for quality) must have understanding and sensitivity for both factors. This is well demonstrated by Kevin Lynch in his search for "the image of the city."[13] He searches, not for an idealized, abstract, or professional image, but rather for that which exists, actually or potentially, in the minds and hearts of those who experience the urban landscape most intimately and continuously. By seeking out, even in a limited research, the forms and elements in existing cities which produce clear and lasting responses, he points the way toward urban design of truly organic quality. Similar concepts are relevant to landscape design in general, at all scales from back yard to region. Indeed, with the monstrous acceleration of urban development throughout the country, urban and landscape design will soon be synonymous.

2

Structure. The basic relations in the humanized landscape at all scales are those between floors, walls, and ceilings. These may be the obvious concrete, wood, and plaster; or the less obvious grass, shrubs, and tree tops; sand, rock, and sky; prairie, distance, and stars; street, buildings, and clouds. The production of these primary relationships is either natural, technological, or both. Human relations to them are arranged by planning and detailed by design. Arrangement is conditioned by design; planning must consider detailing. Vice versa, design-detailing must have in mind the arrangement objectives of planning. This expanded arrangement of floors, walls, and ceilings involves infinite variety in material, detail, form, and pattern, infinite range in scale and subtlety, infinite cargo of imagery and symbolism, even as in the garden, but immensely more complex in scale, context, technology, and social organization.

Floors are all the materials with which we cover the exposed surfaces of mother earth: concrete,

3

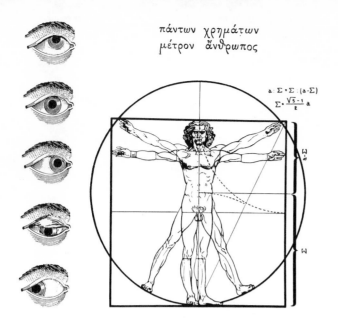

πάντων χρημάτων
μέτρον ἄνθρωπος

$a = \frac{\Sigma \cdot \Sigma \cdot (a - \Sigma)}{\Sigma \cdot \frac{\sqrt{5}-1}{2} a}$

1

2

3

asphalt, grass, brick, stone, pebbles, sand, ivy, brush, forests, water. Walls are all the elements which protrude, grow, or are built, placed, or piled above or below the general surface of this floor: hills and mountains, canyons and valleys, boulders and rock outcrops, trees and shrubs, structures of all sorts from the row of posts through the glass wall to the solid masonry wall, of all sizes from 1 foot to 1 mile. Ceilings are the tops of caves and trees and the roofs of buildings (man's primary improvement on the wild landscape). These spaces are enriched with an endless array of smaller-scale elements of interest, pleasure, inspiration, or utility—small plants, flowers, pebbles, rocks, sculpture, painting, furniture, mechanical equipment, vehicles, signs, lights, utility outlets, animals, people, clothes.

Floors, walls, ceilings—this may still seem too simple a summary of the vocabulary of the landscape. But think of hardwood floors, rag rugs, brick terraces, neat lawns, vacant weedy lots, ankle-deep litter on the forest floor, grassy meadows strewn with wild flowers, glassy lake surfaces, beaches wet and dry, cobble-strewn stream beds. Think of stucco, glass, boards-and-batts, concrete-block walls, split-rail fences, cedar-sapling fences, wide-board fences, narrow-board fences, building walls of steel and glass, brick, stone, ornate terra cotta, polished granite; trimmed hedges, shaggy shrub borders, neat rows of flowering fruits, free drifts of white-trunked birches, impenetrable earth banks and rock cliffs, contoured grassy mounds and hollows. Think further of flat plaster ceilings, sloped-beamed ceilings, cantilevered roof overhangs, geodesic domes from within, hyperbolic paraboloids from beneath, the fabulously variable structure of tree tops—trunks, limb, branch, stem, twig, petiole, leaf arbors, pergolas, pavilions, gazebos, exedras, lath houses, tents, carports, posts, beams, rafters, lath, one-by-ones, two-by-twos, one-by-fours on edge, two-by-fours on edge, egg crates, fiberglass sheets, expanded metal panels, the clear blue sky, the dull gray sky, magnificent castles built of clouds. All these, and many more, are the floors, walls, and ceilings, which shape the spaces that create the sequences of landscape experience.

Perception and Control. These sequences are continuous throughout our lives. The memory of the first spaces we were able to sense is still embedded in our subconscious. Each subsequent space in the sequence of life is judged in terms of those which preceded it. This judgment is colored by the physical quality of the space and the psychological quality of the specific experience we had within it. Friendly, warm, sympathetic, loving experiences may endear bad-quality spaces to us, and conversely harsh, cold, arrogant, or exploitive experiences may turn us against spaces of high physical quality.

How, if we were interested, would we define, measure, and control the quality of landscape experience? We have said that by quality we mean the relationship existing at a given time and place between an individual or group of individuals and the landscape around them. We have said that the landscape experience is continuous from birth to death, wherever we are or are moving, and that it is composed of all tangible elements we can sense around us—sights, sounds, smells, feels, streets, buildings, trees, streams, hydrants, signs, cars, dogs, people. These perceptions are screened through a background of intellectual and emotional experiences, associations, and attitudes which produces a reaction —applause, scorn, faint praise, or apathy. Thus the objective of landscape design is to establish such relations between landscape and people as will lead to applause either loud or quiet.

This visual problem is not a simple straight-line right-angle problem, as the old formal designers thought, nor is it concerned entirely with subjectivity and literary associations, as the romantic informalists think. It involves a pair of mobile eyes, in which the retina as a whole sweeps through a visual angle of some 240 degrees, while the fovea or fixation point subtends an angle of only about $1\frac{7}{10}$ degrees, giving us a small cone of direct vision within a large semi-sphere of variable consciousness.[14] The combination of these two may be abstracted as a cone of perception of about 60 degrees for basic landscape relations. Quite unlike the camera, whenever we look directly at an object or portion of the landscape, we see it in specific detail within a large periphery of general consciousness of the surroundings.

Vision itself, the nature of perception of space, upon which every architectural effect depends, should be the basis for resolving all of the conflicting factors in city building. The eye is always at the converging point of a pyramid of visual lines extending from the object perceived, and various perceived objects are in a visual circle having the eye as its center, so that, with respect to the eye, they form a concave line. This is the natural basis of the principle of perspective that was so effectively used by the Baroque masters. Only by taking full account of the nature of perspective, to make a maximum number of related objects perceptible at a single glance, can we attain the best effects.[15]

These eyes are backed up by nervous and intellectual equipment which instantaneously combines sensation, perception, and intellection involving the entire accumulation of memorized analogies and emotional associations to produce a reaction—"Isn't it beautiful!" or "How ugly!"

The sense organs are borne symmetrically upon the human chassis. Two eyes and ears, one nose and mouth, paired hands and feet, and all the other sensory areas of skin are arranged in bilateral balance on, or on either side of, a central vertical axis symbolized by the backbone. This has been one of the time-honored rationalizations for formal axial design—as though we could see ourselves in Versailles. But this symmetry is never exact. The well-known trick whereby your photo is split, each half duplicated and put together to form two faces, neither like you, and both strangely uninteresting, is one of the best examples. This variance within symmetry extends throughout the body, and is a part of the large and constant rhythm of nature whereby elements which are similar but never identical are repeated with variable regularity. Jagged mountains,

rounded hills, beach pebbles, buttercups, stars, people, amoebas—within each group the individuals are all alike and yet all different.

Human Symmetry. Unless restrained by straitjacket or plaster cast, human symmetry is further varied by flexibility and mobility. The eyes move within the head, rolling complete circles which swing the small cone of perception through almost the entire range of consciousness. The head turns, 180 degrees from left to right, somewhat less up and down, to expand the range of consciousness into more than half a sphere. The body twists, with feet fixed, 180 degrees from left to right, and bends somewhat less down and back, to complete the sphere of consciousness swept by the cone of perception. The hands, on triple-jointed arms, move freely through the air to touch, stroke, seize, or strike. And finally, the feet move on triple-jointed legs, carrying the sensory and perceptive body wherever they can find support and it can balance or hold on. The consciousness, compounded of intellect and emotion, past and present, guides movement while absorbing the experiences which it generates. The almost symmetrical body, in whimsical, capricious, balanced but asymmetrical motion, defies, or plays counterpoint to, the regimentation of axial planning, bringing us back to the classical definition of symmetry. This reference becomes more meaningful when we consider the current development of new symmetrical classical forms in architecture and landscape architecture.

Sitte says:

The notion of identical figures to the right and left of an axis was not the basis of any theory in ancient times. . . . In short, proportion and symmetry were the same to the ancients. The sole difference between the two is that in architecture proportion is simply a relationship agreeable to the eye, like the relationship between the diameter and height of a column, while symmetry is the same relationship expressed in numbers. This meaning remained valid throughout the Middle Ages.

When Gothic masters began to form architectural patterns and became more concerned with the axes of symmetry in the modern sense of the term, the notion of similarity of figures to the left and right of a principal line was established in theory. An ancient name, with its meaning altered, was given to this idea. Writers of the Renaissance were using it in this sense. Since then, the axes of symmetry have become continually more frequent in plans for buildings, as they have in plans for cities.[15a]

It is difficult to determine who has most influence on future cultural development: he who produces the first mature prototype for a given problem, or he who interprets this prototype for posterity.

The human relationship to the landscape, primarily visual, supplemented by the other senses, is thus a peculiar compound of symmetrical structure, particularly in the head, and free movement of the body. Perhaps this is what leads us to search for compounds of stability and movement, regularity and irregularity, incomplete balance, equilibrium not quite achieved, in our environment.

Each individual human is connected directly to

1

2

the landscape by the twin cones of perception projecting from his eyes (reversing symbolically the actual pattern of light reception), like the beam of light from the miner's cap. These cones have an unlimited extension—we can see stars many light-years away. The extension of perception is conditioned by the relationship between distance and size or brilliance of objects perceived. Across the patio we study the tile pattern in the wall fountain; across many miles of open desert we study the structure of distant mountains; across thousands of miles of empty space we study the features of the Man in the Moon. Distance, scale, and detail are closely related. We know from intimate experience the exact sizes of the wall fountain tiles. If the desert mountains have recognizable trees or buildings on them we can guess their size and distance; otherwise, this is impossible. The moon is merely a globe in the sky; we may know its size intellectually, but we have no emotional connection with it. That connection awaits the return of the first men on the moon.

We scan the landscape as we read a book, by rotating or swinging our eyes across it. In this way we determine the dimensions of space and our relationship to them. We move mentally forward, up, down, or sideways into space, following our eyes, whether or not our bodies move. This pattern of visual connection and movement leads us to establish certain typical relationships.

The vista is a space whose primary dimension is length, along which we feel compelled to look and move. This may be established by enclosure at the sides—a hall, a street, an allée of trees, a canyon in the west. It may be established by an element so distinct from or important to its environment that all eyes and feet are drawn toward it—the Chrysler, Empire State, or Rockefeller towers in the New York skyline, single dogwood or redbud in the spring forest, the white birdbath in the green garden. It may be these two together, a rewarding combination in city streets, the classical terminal feature at the end of the allée. This is the simplest and most direct pattern for creating visual impact, perceptible organization, and a system of landmarks through garden, forest, or city.

The vista is determined not only by the predominance of length over height and width, and the com-

3

pelling quality of the terminal element, but by the control of circulation patterns leading to and from it. These may be carefully controlled, as in formal garden or park; or completely accidental, as in ordinary forest, meadow, or city; or any variation between. This last is the largest and richest area for design exploration.

Although length predominates in the creation of vistas, they are three-dimensional structures at any given moment, four-dimensional in total passing-through experience. Relations may vary—long/narrow/low—long/narrow/high—long/wide/low—long/wide/high. As width assumes more importance in relation to length, height, and terminal feature, the sense of vista—the long shot, compelling depth, single direction—tends to become dissipated in more complex multidirectional qualities which might be typified by room, square, plaza, court, and meadow in woods or mountains.

These are spaces which we live in and enjoy as enclosures, rather than looking down and walking through. They might, in diagrammatic overall proportions regardless of actual shape, vary from circles or squares to rectangles, polygons, or ovals twice as long as wide. Their enclosure, internal arrangement, and connective possibilities have all of the multiple potentialities covered by Sitte's description of the old squares of European cities; Olmsted's projection of the pastoral meadow as a park prototype; and the variable concepts of modern painters, sculptors, architects, and landscape architects. The academic tendency to convert these room-spaces into vistas by placing terminal features at one end of the main axis, or in the exact center, has been one of the principal means for missing or evading their experience potentials. The one exception is, of course, the theater or concert hall designed to focus on a central stage. Room-spaces, singly and in sequence, are the basic units of the humanized landscape (see Saarinen),[16] variable in approach and circulation patterns, dimensions, color, texture, and detail of enclosing elements. In these the directional quality of the cones of perception becomes diffused in multiple directions, the emphasis on enclosure rather than features, or the placement of features to emphasize enclosure. The other sensory impressions, and the general consciousness of environment which surrounds perception, become more equal in importance.

As enclosure reduces and horizontality expands, room-spaces become uncontrolled open spaces, source of agoraphobia to city folk and of romance to westerners. Empty parking lot, great plain, flat desert, suburban tractscape, wherever horizontality without direction dominates, man loses scale and meaning and must develop shelter and transitional elements—room-spaces—for comfort and security. Inside or near such enclosures, great spaces can become magnificent experiences.

Special-quality room-spaces, or even wide open spaces, develop with many vistas focusing on one center, as in theater, symphony or convention hall, sports arena, or auditorium. The primitive prototype for this occurs with the impromptu speaker on any green, the soapbox orator in Hyde Park or elsewhere, who immediately transforms a bland stretch of green, open in all directions, into a net of dynamic sightlines focusing on himself.

The reversal of this focusing space is what might be called panoramic, in which interest does not concentrate but pans across a width equal to or greater than its depth. This may vary all the way from the private garden which is shallower than its width as approached from the main portion of the house, through various larger public spaces of similar proportion (including the minor axis or side approach to the long space), to great panoramic views from high places—Rio de Janeiro, San Francisco Bay, Los Angeles from the Santa Monica Mountains. On a smaller scale, panoramic spaces are problems in structuring to create a sense of depth and concentrated interest. At larger scale, with views beyond the property, the problem is one of creating a sense of security and transition in scale, often by breaking and framing the view so that all of it cannot be seen from any one point, or so that it changes from point to point, in spite of the dollars-per-panorama-foot of the real estate sales pitch.

We might say, then, that there are three basic types of landscape spaces—vista, room, panorama. This is, of course, a gross oversimplification of the multiple variations in size, scale, material elements, proportions, and arrangement inherent in all three,

1

2

and in the transitions in dimension and direction between them. But it is useful. For instance, the typical urban landscape is a gridiron of endless circulation vistas dominating and locking in blocks of congested and confused room-spaces for living needs. Panoramas and cross-block vistas may come with accidents of topography or planning, or by intention in park and civic design, as in the hills of San Francisco, or the Chicago lake front. Expansion, coordination, and integration of room-spaces at superblock and larger scale; reduction, rationalization and rearrangement of uncontrolled vehicular vistas, and articulated integration of accidental panoramas might be called the order of the day for the American cityscape.

In the suburban landscape the street vistas may be more open, farther apart, more variable in curves, loops, or dead ends; the room-spaces more open, flatter, simpler, less congested, but more continuously similar in scale and character. Panoramas and other vistas come by accident or by design to take advantage of irregular topography. Rural landscapes are patterns of room-spaces—yards, crop fields, orchards —or of greater open spaces—pastures, corn and wheat fields, ranges—with vistas and panoramas developing from accidental combinations of topography and planting. The orchard is both a gridiron of multiple vistas and an abstract forest. In wild landscapes, all three types of spaces are mixed in complex and unpredictable forms and patterns, resulting from relations between topography, water, grassland, brushland, meadow, savannah, and forest. A loose generalization might say that the comfortable humanized landscape is a rich and variable pattern of room-spaces, taking advantage of, rather than dominated by, vistas and panoramas. Loss of control over rigid vistas and accidental panoramas, or proliferation of the former, is comparable to loss of control over the machine—dehumanization sets in. The balanced dimensions, variable arrangement, and multiple noncompulsive directions of the room-space make it the central or primary environment for human life. Vistas and panoramas service it, enrich it, multiply the experiences radiating from it. But the room remains central as the enclosure from which people survey, assess, control, use, and enjoy their world.

Detailed Space Organization. The private garden (private to house, office, shop, cultural or civic building) and the small public square are the most primary and basic exercises in outdoor space organization. They differ fundamentally in that the garden is usually a dead-end space with building between it and public street. In the typical residential block. (most typical of private garden relations), the private lots are like a filing cabinet or storage wall, a row of vermiform appendices open to the street, though guardedly. Life goes on in the houses, lapping over into the gardens with more or less freedom, varying with locale and development. Though the gardens may be room-spaces in proportion and treatment, their dominance by the house, usually at one side only, adds a vista or panoramic quality dependent upon whether the maximum dimension of the garden is perpendicular or parallel to the house wall. The fact that, regardless of quantity of glass, life tends to center just within the garden wall of the house emphasizes one visual direction—perpendicular to the house into the garden—over the others, even when design is multidirectional. The public square, on the other hand, is usually approached and looked into from all sides, even when the approaches are devious to maximize enclosure (see Sitte) and is thus a more truly multidirectional problem.

In the garden, design gives form to the feeding of living patterns from the house out, into, and around the garden. Thus we have the typical progression from living room to terrace, lawn, border, and background planting. This is a progression in various terms—utility, from more to less intense; visual, from living center into spatial depth; symbolic, from architecture to nature. Well-known modern design efforts to render this progression more subtle or complex, to extend the terrace beyond or around the lawn, to develop multidirectional patterns giving more movement to the garden picture and more incentive to move physically through it, have enriched but not changed the primary dominance of house-to-garden over garden-to-house, even in California. We experience the garden from the house more often than we experience the house from the garden. Likewise, praiseworthy and exciting modern architectural efforts to decentralize house sections irregularly over the site, in order to multiply and diversify house-

24

1

2

garden relations, have not materially reduced the basic American tendency, dictated by economics and practicality, to think of the house as a box placed across the site, confronting the street on one side and the garden or view on the other.

Space organization must begin with the elements which exist, and with the circulation patterns which give access to and from the space to be organized. It is concerned with continuity of experience, with accents and landmarks which give that experience emphasis, richness, meaning, and depth. We approach the house through a front yard or entry garden which is a transition space from the noise, exposure, and movement of the street. We enter the house, passing from an entry hall—an airlock between public and private spaces—into the private living and working quarters, and those even more private for sleeping and bathing. From these we see, and may go into, the garden, a space of sun and shade, firm paving and resilient lawn, secluded within walls and foliage which make it a world to itself. This, at least, is the objective. It may seem a forlorn hope to the owner of the new tract house, looking across a 5- or 6-foot fence into the upper half of the neighbor's windows under 8-foot eaves and 12-foot ridge lines. Like most dreams this can be accomplished, with time, energy, money, and planning.

The quality of garden space in relation to the house is determined first of all by the nature of the enclosure—earth, fence, wall, or planting. It is determined still more by detailed relations between the types and dimensions of enclosure at sides and rear. Strong lines and colors at sides and soft forms and shades at rear will create a greater sense of depth. Continuity of the same treatment around three sides will create maximum enclosure with minimum sense of depth or extension. Structures which obscure the exact location of the rear boundary—vertical freestanding trellises or baffle walls, arbors, shelters, or trees creating shady depths, free shrub patterns—will create a sense of mystery and seclusion, even on the tract lot surrounded by close neighbors.

Color, texture, and detail all affect the quality of space enclosure. Bright, warm, strong, hard, or shiny colors will come forward toward the observer; quiet, cool, mild, weak, or dull colors will recede. Coarse textures will come forward, fine textures will recede. Detailing will establish relations between colors and textures in both plants and structures which can be rich and harmonious, rather than confused and disquieting. Height, width, depth, and form all contribute to color-texture relations.

The pattern, color, and texture of ground surface or floor materials will also have a major impact upon the quality of landscape spaces. Overemphasis upon ground pattern, resulting from concentration on design in plan, has been a disease of landscape design. Weak enclosure patterns may be completely overbalanced by insistent ground patterns. Good enclosure patterns around a garden with primarily one floor material may create the most satisfactory space. Surfacing patterns may be strong, linear, and directional, as most typically, concrete next to grass. Such patterns seize and direct the eye and must be most carefully controlled and related to enclosure and circulation patterns. The reverse curve which looks so well in the photo may be taken from a point rarely seen by the ordinary observer. Surfacing patterns may be nonlinear, as with the use of freely placed large flagstones for paving, feeding irregularly into lawn or ground cover areas. Lawn, by its mowing and edging requirements, creates linear patterns at its boundaries which may be almost as strong as those of concrete. They are, of course, dependent on maintenance. The dichondra lawn of the south requires no edging and merges easily with shrubs or ground cover.

Shelter patterns, of structures or trees, create volumes of shade or diffused light into which we look or move, and strong shifting patterns of light and shade which are the life of the landscape scene. This is maximum space organization outdoors, approaching the complete indoor control of architecture. Trees and buildings complement each other, not only in scale, but in degree and richness of definition of space.

All this discussion has to do with gardens which must create their own internal views because of the nature of their surroundings. Gardens with views beyond their boundaries, resulting from hillside, countryside, or parkside locations, have problems which are similar but more complex. Public and private landscapes begin to be more intimately related, often because distance lends enchantment. Surfacing pat-

25

1

3

2

terns should function to connect house with view without conflicting with it. Enclosure elements become security and framing elements, designed to minimize danger at the boundaries of level or property and to provide adequate transition in scale and security of outlook. (Completely enclosed intimate spaces may well be desirable also, for contrast with, or escape from, the view. All variations between the open panorama and the casual peep hole have validity.) These may well merge with shelter elements—arcade and gazebo are time-honored for comfortable overlook purposes. Trees are the primary and most flexible connecting, framing, and transitional elements between man and landscape.

While the reality of the garden problems with which landscape architects are faced daily is infinitely more variable and complex than these oversimplified examples, they are nevertheless typical of vast areas of mass-produced or semi-mass-produced housing at all levels from luxury to minimum tract. Our purpose in discussing them here is only to use them as the most commonly experienced and understood prototype for outdoor space organization. Most of the area of most cities and urban areas is devoted to residential use. The basic relations between floor, walls, and ceiling, color and texture, form and scale, and mass and structure continue through public squares (which we impoverished Americans must experience abroad or through Sitte, Zucker, and Kidder-Smith) [17, 18] and beyond into streetscape, shopscape, bankscape, rowscape, apartmentscape, factoryscape, institutescape, schoolscape, playscape, parkscape, muddlescape, stripscape, scatterscape, highwayscape, and that greatest product of American culture, adverscape. It has been said with some justice that the garden designer or house architect is at a loss when first confronted with public space problems, because of the expansion in scale from individual to group, the increased complexity of circulation and intensity of use, and the increased wear and tear on materials. However, these are hurdles which any competent designer can clear, given the opportunity and the incentive.

Public open space is usually accessible from all or several sides, is thus centripetal rather than having the cul-de-sac character of the private rear garden. Once we escape from the academic Renaissance and informal precedents, it is much less easily prototyped than garden spaces. The patterns of approach and entry circulation and of enclosure by buildings, traffic, topography, or vegetation are infinitely more variable in both scale and detail than are those of gardens. Use requirements and pressures are apt to be much more complex and less predictable than in gardens. The garden designer has a client known through direct contact; the public space designer produces for a constantly changing, heterogeneous, unpredictable, unknown, or partially known client represented by entrepreneur or public official. The sense of equity and interest developed in this public client will determine his morale and responsibility or the reverse, expressed in vandalism, hooliganism, delinquency, and crime. These factors condition the designer's attention to materials, details, refinements, and cultural improvements.

Types and Variables. While these relations tend to be typical, as described, in the majority of cases, there remains a large minority with relations which are enormously variable in form and function. Variables result from natural conditions of topography and weather, hangovers of old forms, experimentation by individual owners and designers, and the confusion of precedents and influences introduced by modern communication. Types resulted historically from a continuity of solutions of similar problems, within similar social and regional conditions. Types today result from decisions which may be arbitrary, functional, or both, reproduced in an increasingly vast scale through mass production and communication. Occasional inspirations or whimsies, thrown into this vast machinery at the right time and place, may produce new types which render the old obsolete. The selection and reproduction of new types is conditioned by the basic contradiction between two powerful forces: the conservatism of finance, which does not want the value of its established investments disturbed by innovation, and the radicalism of merchandising, which bases itself on designed obsolescence and annual restyling. Neither of these forces alone is good for the landscape; together they provide opportunity for constructive maneuvering.

The other common elements of the humanized landscape are also subject to similar processes of typing through communication and reproduction, and of variation through individual inspiration or whimsy and adjustment to local conditions. Schools, colleges, parks, hospitals, shopping centers, city halls, streets, and signs all tend to begin with prototypes which result from a fresh look at a problem. The fresh look may be stimulated by new programming, new conditions, new technology, or individual inspiration. Prototypes so produced last until upset by fresh inspirations. The relation between typing and variation goes on at different levels with varying frequency. Details, colors, and materials can change readily to suit styling whimsies. Plans and forms in buildings and open spaces change less readily. Community relations in land-use and circulation patterns are slowest to change. These rates of change seem to be much more easily accelerated by technological change than by ideological change. The gridiron is the most consistent and typical feature of the American landscape. The large scale and curving alignment of new freeway systems, arbitrary and destructive of community patterns though they may be, nevertheless represent a healthy and more organic impact upon the gridiron.

The issue is complicated by what seems to be a sadly typical American pattern, that of building a superb building in a new style at the first attempt, and then not bothering to experiment any further, or even to profit from the merits of the lone swallow. . . .

Something similar has overtaken all the new structural forms that ingenious engineers are bestowing

upon architects. The novelties are used seriously once or twice, taken up en masse for a year or so, then thrown away for the next fashion, all with their true qualities unexploited, yet with the form so debased by repetition that nobody can ever use it again with freshness. . . .

. . . the situation is not a very healthy one, and with architectural photography at its present stage of expertise it is almost impossible to distinguish good from bad without actually going to see. . . .[19]

Continuity and Accent. The relation between continuity and accent or emphasis provides a thread of design principle that runs through all landscape problems from back yard to city and region. In the garden, park, or public open space we may have horizontal continuity in surfacing of grass or concrete, with accents of flower beds, water, or shrub and ground cover areas. In enclosure we may have quantitative relations between vegetation and frame or masonry construction in which any one may accent the others by virtue of position and area or the continuity of any one may be accented by a change in its own detailing. In shelter, a tree may accent a court among buildings; a structure may accent a grove of trees; a peak-roofed gazebo may accent a long horizontal arbor; deciduous or evergreen trees may accent each other; and changes in size, form, texture, or color may establish emphasis within continuity. Enriching elements—sculpture, rocks, furniture, lights, signs—are accents and points of focal concentration.

Such relations expand from single to multiple spaces among groups of buildings on large sites. Continuity and emphasis are developed by the size, form, and arrangement of buildings, tree groupings, and the spaces between. The movement and rhythm of circulation, relations between origin and destination and the experiences between, are the essence of campus-type space organization. The long walk through grass and trees; the constricted dark tunnel between buildings; the open sunny courtyard with sparkling fountain; the broad stepped portico—these are the sequences of experience that lend richness and meaning to the traverse from room to class. Cranbrook, in Michigan, is one of the best examples of this potential richness. Similar sequences could give equal importance to the basic traverses between home, work, and recreation that frame our daily lives.

Continuity of experience characterizes specific areas, centers of activity or concentration, and circulation elements such as quadrangles, freeways, turnpikes. Accent or emphasis points up important portions of these spaces: direction changes in circulation, transitions between different spaces or centers of action, important objectives, circulation centers, points of decision. Accents become landmarks in the continuity of the local or general landscape.

At the community scale, the relation between continuity and accent—the movement of circulation and the emphasis of landmarks—proves itself a reliable basis for quality space organization. The lower-Manhattan skyline, symbolizing the aspirations of every downtown center in the United States, is the most

27

1

2

concentrated and exaggerated collection of architectural accents and structural emphases in the world, a landmark between old world and new, a beehive of activity in which old buildings are going down and new taller ones going up at an accelerated pace. From airplane or nearby shore this is one of the seven wonders of the modern world. From within, it is a carnival of urban life, an architectural kaleidoscope, in which vertical scale dominates the horizontal as completely as in the narrow streets of Old World cities. Here is the nerve-racking competition of American life in its sharpest expression. Every building tries to outdo every other in height, form, brightness, glassiness, elegance, detail, or gadgetry. Here we have a continuity of accent saved only by the quietude of Central Park—exciting for visitors, exhausting for residents—a landscape which seems to have everything, yet in which something new (all glass!) appears every year; lacking today only Frank Lloyd Wright's mile-high building. Should that be built in Chicago instead, New York would suddenly have a major competitor, would no longer be preeminent on the American skyline. (Of course some say it can never be built at all, but we still believe anything can happen in America.)

There is implicit in the physical structure of lower Manhattan, and to a lesser degree of every downtown center, a qualitative change in scale by which the strangling small-scale network of auto traffic will be eliminated. The application of the superblock principle will make possible the development of the pedestrian malls and oases, projected by so many architects and planners as solutions for downtown deterioration. The unhampered continuity of pedestrian traffic thus achieved, plus the weeding out of marginal and blighted buildings, would create a wholly new relationship among the structures and spaces remaining. Corbusier's vision of *la ville radieuse* may yet prove to have been one of history's greatest prototypes.

The suburban landscape, by contrast with the downtown skyline of accents, is all continuity. Streets, houses, trees, and yards have similar scale and relationships without interruption for mile after mile. Breaks come first through shopping centers which, if of the supermarket type, do provide that change in scale, space, and atmosphere which the suburbs

need. Schools, churches, and parks provide similar accents, landmarks, and changes of pace which are a welcome relief in suburbia. Too often, however, these fail to achieve their potential through that mistaken and timid emphasis on "domestic scale" (it should look like a house even if it isn't) which is commonly considered good neighborhood design. It is only a step from this to the quaintness of the Cinderella house, the ⅞ scale of Disneyland, and the general conception of the suburb as a cross between a sanitarium and a summer resort. Other breaks may come from topography, water, bits of wild or rural landscape, or escaped industry. Rarely do any of these result from conscious design for visual quality. Usually they are the product of accidental combinations of pressures—the availability of land and financing, the objectives of developers, the strength of demand for community facilities made by public agencies and citizens. Community facilities tend to run a poor third in the struggle for vanishing land. Thus the forces which produce a monotonous continuity in the suburbscape dominate the scene, making minimum concessions to the community facility pattern. Shopping centers are rarely equal, in terms of visual, spatial, or social experience, to schools, parks, and churches as suburban landmarks.

The vast middle urban areas, between built-up downtown center and sprawling suburban fringes, are complex and unpredictable jumbles of blight and quality construction, all types of residential, commercial, and industrial land uses, tangled traffic patterns, miles of buildings without quality, scale, or visual meaning, lightened by occasional islands of vegetation or of careful land use in institutions or well-to-do neighborhoods. This middle ground, a jumble of continuity and accent without rhyme, reason, or reciprocal relations, is the great area for redevelopment and renewal activity with or without Federal aid. Here we find the most complex and special problems, subject to most ingenuity and design inspiration and least prototyping, vulnerable to big-time preconceived design patterns which will substitute a deadly continuity of overscaling and oversimplicity for the existing jumble with its many unexpected accents and emphases on human warmth, inventiveness, humor, and private creativity.

The rural or primeval regional context which sur-

1   2   3

rounds these urban and suburban areas has its own problems and potentialities for continuity and accent. Natural patterns of topography, drainage, and vegetation usually have their own consistent rhythms, repetitions, breaks, and contrasts. The patterns of agriculture have an inherent orderliness derived from their dependence on natural processes. The control of the disorderly leapfrogging of suburban development in order to preserve for it the potential benefits of these existing landscape amenities might be called the principal problem of regional design.

Landmarks. A landmark is an accent, terminal feature, or focal or turning point in the landscape. It is identified by its contrast in size, form, color, texture, detail, function, or content of symbolism or sentiment with its surroundings. Landmarks are found in nature—water bodies, rocks, hills, mountains, trees that are placed or shaped so they stand out from their surroundings. Landmarks also exist in rural and urban areas—special buildings, street intersections, open spaces, sculptural, water or landscape features, or functional, cultural, or historical centers that likewise stand out from their surroundings either visually or in the consciousness of observers and users.

People orient themselves in the physical world much more simply and naturally by relation to landmarks than by such intellectual abstractions as verbal directions, signs, or maps. Our first visit to a new locale or center is guided by conscious objective reliance on these abstractions. Each subsequent visit lapses a little more into unconscious subjective reliance on assimilated memories of physical elements and relations in the landscape. Habitués and long-term residents of communities and regions move through them as freely, effortlessly, and unconsciously as animals through forest, fish through water, or birds through air.

The glib rationalization of the gridiron, with streets numbered in one direction and lettered in the other, as simplest for human orientation, does not stand up under this kind of analysis. This is only a paltry abstract substitute for the human need for a landscape rich in coherent and sensible relations between general continuity and accenting landmarks. This rich and balanced physical landscape, in which people will live and move as naturally and

as simply as wildlife in its habitat, seems to be beyond the imaginations of those to whom the gridiron is the peak development of 8,000 years of world planning experience.

Although landmarks are thought of as features of community, regional, or national landscapes, they are also typical of smaller controlled private gardens or public open spaces. The birdbath, seat, change in paving pattern, sculpture, fountain, shelter, screen, specimen plant, bed of color, or special-use element —play apparatus, swim pool, game court—functions as an orienting, focusing, or guiding landmark in the small or limited landscape as surely as larger elements in the general landscape. Even in that large continuity, certain small signs, lights, seats, or mechanical elements may be so placed or detailed as to take on landmark significance. Thus the scale of landmarks is related to the scale of continuity around them, and to changes and transitions in that scale.

Change. Each change in the structure or use of the existing physical landscape disorients those who are accustomed to it. A more or less extended period of conscious intellectual reorientation, comparable to that involved in passing through or moving to new localities, will then be required until reciprocal relations between people and landscape are once more stable, easy, and natural. It will be seen from this that those who undertake projects of physical construction and development in the landscape take on a responsibility beyond the specific limits of their programs. This responsibility is rarely recognized on a community scale, except in the occasional development of public projects officially viewed as landmarks—civic, cultural, and sports centers, monuments, major traffic and transportation elements, landscape conservation, or park projects. The general responsibility of all physical developers to the community structure of continuity and accent seems to be beyond their normal consciousness.

We need community design plans which project a reasonable and imaginative structure of continuity and accent, flow and interruption, direction and change, area and boundary, landmark and context. All too often we get instead the familiar hodgepodge—civic landmarks lost in a sea compounded of commercial enterprises each endeavoring to become the dominant landmark in the area (as in

29

1

3

4

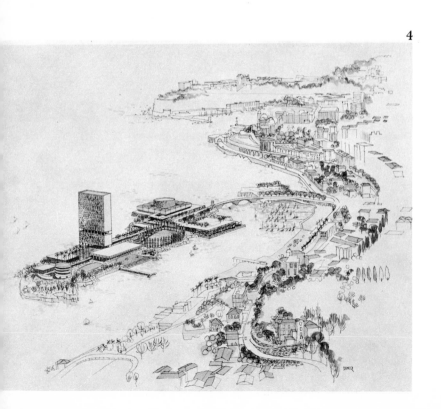

Philadelphia); corporate enterprises with similar objectives and greater resources; industrial areas of purely empirical functionalism with little regard to appearance—though apt to become competing landmarks through sheer size, noise, smell, or interest; and residential areas of a general flat sameness which increases as "progress" (a euphemism for mass-produced regimentation) gradually eliminates individualism and variability. These traditionally American qualities are found more and more only in the pious platitudes of editorial and sermon, and as a hangover from the past in slum and blighted areas waiting for efficient and sanitary renewal or redevelopment. Private and public financial and development interests emphasize continuity classified in economic levels and eliminate accents of a meaningful nature as being disruptive, inefficient, impractical, or irrelevant. Thus the dominance of our community and regional landscapes by commercial, speculative, and investment incentives produces a structure which has little relationship to the visual physical reality and needs of those who inhabit and use it. The commercial landscape is all accents of generally discordant and even raucous character, save the occasional discreet monument of corporate enterprise. The residential landscape is all continuity, a flat sanitarium for living, an escape from the hurly-burly of the workaday (commercial) world, so quiet as to approach monotony for its full-time residents, housewives, senior citizens, and children. Contrast enforced between these areas makes it difficult for either to achieve visual balance. Both the continuity of accent in the commercial landscape and the absence of accent in the suburban create a monotonous confusion in which the basic enlivening and enriching function of accenting landmarks is lost to the landscape.

This community may well be truly beautiful to the financial and real estate interests who see it as a healthy structure of sound, stable, and developing investments. The gaps between the picture seen by this potent and influential minority, that seen by the sensitive but less potent architectural-landscape-design minority, and that seen or ignored by the harassed and apathetic general public are among the cultural landmarks of our times.

The elements of space organization, which add up

to one experience for the citizen, are sorted into special separate vocabularies for the various space-planning professions. Architects deal with the elements of building—floors, walls, roofs; masonry, wood, metal, glass; furniture; mechanical equipment; enriching art elements—in all the multiple richness which their combinations can produce. Landscape architects deal with analogous elements outdoors—paving, grass, ground cover; ground forms, hedges, and shrub plantings; fences and walls; trees and shelters; flowers; water; rock; sculpture; furniture; equipment. Engineers deal with major elements of continuity and accent—earthwork and drainage; streets and highways; bridges and dams; utility systems and specialized buildings; mass transit, railroads, airports, harbors, canals. City planners, intentionally or not, deal with overall urban form elements—site forms, urban textures, green areas, circulation facilities, paved open spaces, significant architectural masses, perceived by means of panoramas, skylines, vistas, urban open spaces, and experience in motion (Williams, 1954); [20] geometric patterns, linear features, landmarks, lookout places, areas of distinctive character (New York AIA-AIP, 1958); [21] paths, edges, districts, nodes, and landmarks (Lynch, 1960). [22]

A more somber picture of community development is sketched by Harrison Brown and James Real in *Community of Fear*, a study of the nuclear arms race:

If the arms race continues, as it probably will, its future pattern seems clear in broad outline. As a result of the emergence of the current tremendous capabilities for killing and destroying, programs will be started aimed at the evacuation of cities, the construction of fallout shelters in regions outside the major metropolitan areas, and the construction of limited underground shelters. . . .

The new development will cause people to burrow more deeply into the ground. Factories will be built in caves, as will apartment houses and stores. Eventually most human life will be underground, confronted by arsenals capable of destroying all life over the land areas of the earth. . . . Once the shelter program is underway, it will constitute a significant retreat from the idea of the obsolescence of war.

Once the people are convinced that they can survive the present state of the art of killing, a broad and significant new habit pattern will have been introduced and accepted, one grotesquely different from any we have known for thousands of years—that of adjusting ourselves to the idea of living in holes. From that time onward it will be simple to adjust ourselves to living in deeper holes.

Tens of thousands of years ago our Mousterian and Aurignacian ancestors lived in caves. The vast knowledge which we have accumulated during the intervening millennia will have brought us full cycle. The epic of man's journey upward into the light will have ended. [23]

We are reminded of H. G. Wells' greatest work of science-fiction, *The First Men in the Moon,* in which a race of intelligent cave-dwelling gnomes are discovered. We cling, however, to a stubborn and perhaps irrational optimism that the human race, which somehow always has the intuition and sympathy needed to solve major problems of survival, will somehow manage to slow down or stop the arms race, remain above ground, and move toward greater light and broader life.

Subdivision. Subdivision of the land into individually owned parcels is normal to our physical development procedures, once basic land-use and circulation patterns have been projected. This results from historical processes such as the opening of the West through the Homestead Act and the sectioning process, and is a direct expression of our social and economic principles. The conflicts existing today between the traditional pattern of small individual land holdings (both urban and rural) and the growing area of large corporate or public agency holdings is a direct expression of the social conflict between traditional free competitive enterprise and the established dominance of some two-thirds of the national economy by about two hundred large corporations. Historically private ownership of the land has been a symbol of freedom and the opportunity for privacy and self-development. In all of the backward, underdeveloped, or peasant countries of the world, land reform (distribution of large holdings among many small owners) is a battle cry of progress. Oversize and absentee ownership are the abuses which tend to undermine the virtues of land ownership. As industrialized societies become more urbanized, private ownership becomes less relevant to personal development, as participation in community patterns becomes more relevant. With urbanization, private ownership may become more relevant to personal

31

1

2

aggrandizement. Thus the process by which large feudal holdings break up into the small ownerships of young industrial societies tends to reverse itself as those societies mature.

We are concerned here, not with the social content or direction of the subdivision process, but with its impact upon design processes and their qualitative results in the physical landscape. Analyzing in these terms, we need not involve ourselves in determining whether or not subdivision in itself is or is not desirable, but rather in determining how the technique is used, and particularly at what point in the chronological timetable of physical development.

Normally, subdivision follows master-planning of land use and circulation (if any) and precedes the detailed design of all physical elements—roads, utilities, buildings, landscaping. Roads and utilities are usually closely coordinated with, or may be an integral part of, subdivision design, out of certain minimum functional engineering necessities. Buildings are much less often tied closely to the subdivision process. When this does occur, as in tract housing, the connection is usually of the most arbitrary and mechanical kind, derived from setbacks and similar zoning ordinance provisions. Recognition of a functional pattern of varying building types—houses, schools, churches, shops, playgrounds, parks—usually occurs only on request by established community planning agencies. Subdivisions do, of course, follow existing zoning requirements—single family residential, multiple housing, commercial, and industrial. Landscape development is almost never considered in the subdivision process, except in the most decorative and superficial patterns. The one exception to this is the general acceptance of mandatory street tree requirements. The occasional developer who makes the effort to preserve worthwhile segments of existing topography, water, or vegetation stands out in isolated contrast to his "practical" and bulldozer-happy colleagues. Practical is that which produces most return for least effort; impractical, that which requires extra effort.

Creative design functions most productively within a framework of discipline which includes only those requirements which are organically or unavoidably part of the problem. Other preconceived or arbitrary

requirements serve only to reduce the potential contribution of the design process to solutions which will expand the frontiers of living. Thus the organic requirements of problems of neighborhood and community development center around the production of integrated structures in which housing; workspaces; educational, cultural, and recreational facilities; distributive, service, and administrative elements; and circulation patterns achieve the most harmonious balance of technical, functional, and sensory solutions. Subdivision and zoning requirements, insofar as they set up arbitrary preconceptions as to neighborhood and community form before most of its details have been considered, eliminate a major segment of the contribution which creative design could make to community development. To the argument that these arbitrary controls are necessary in order to prevent worse forms coming from the hands of developers who know or care nothing about qualitative standards we must ask, why does society allow the development of the priceless environment which houses its life to remain in hands which know little and care less about quality? The greatest opportunities exist when land is virgin; once physical development has begun the improvement process is infinitely more difficult and costly.

Whatever connection it may have with the planning which may precede it, or the physical development which follows it (sooner or later), the primary function of subdivision is viewed as the production of a system of parcels of land which can be bought, sold, and developed independently of one another. Controls limiting this independence have developed as concessions to community concern with the results of uncoordinated individual actions. This structure of existing land-use and development controls represents awareness that the entire body of disconnected decisions by individual landowners accumulates constantly into the community landscape which we see.

The subdivision landscape is an abstract landscape embodying, at least in theory, the protection of certain basic individual rights to life, liberty, and the pursuit of happiness on the land. We are now, and have for some time been, engaged in working out the problems which develop in urbanized living when these individual rights begin to compete and to can-

32

1

2

cel each other out. The actual physical landscape which we experience and use is a structure of physical elements—buildings, streets, open spaces, trees, and many others. The detailed design of these elements, and the relationships established between them on the land, determine the actual quality of the landscape for us. This process, by which designed relationships must conform to subdivision patterns, is another example of the cart pulling the horse.

Rational and sympathetic design processes place first things first. They insist on thorough understanding of all physical and human components of a problem first, then on precise and sensitive development of proposed solutions from inside out, beginning with the most important functions and relationships. In the humanized (urbanized) landscape, those most important are: first, the detailed space organization within buildings; second, the detailed relationships between these interior spaces and the outdoor spaces immediately around the building; third, the detailed relationships between such building-site units and neighboring buildings and open spaces; fourth, relationships between such groups in continuity and the streets and public ways which connect them; fifth, general relations between buildings, open spaces, and streets at the neighborhood, community, and regional scale. These relationships affect each other continuously; it is difficult to consider any one in a complete design sense without considering all the others.

The subdivision process, when it precedes these design processes, must of necessity make arbitrary and mechanical assumptions about the design patterns which will follow. On this basis it establishes a system of site boundaries, speedily frozen into legal documents and streets, utility and drainage patterns, which becomes a straitjacket for all subsequent design processes. If—and this is obviously very iffy—two, three, or more of the above design relationships could be worked out *before* subdivision takes place, the problems would find better solutions and the land would be subdivided in more truly reasonable patterns. All this has been recognized in the programs and procedures of urban redevelopment, which embody the collection of many small parcels of land into fewer larger parcels, suitable in scale to organic and functional replanning.

Inasmuch as building design is a more or less organic process which tends to produce the size and form of the structure which best solves the problem (unless the site is actually too small for such a solution), the burden of patching up the faulty relations between such organic structures and arbitrary land subdivision patterns is passed on to landscape design. This process, last and least honored and budgeted in the construction industry, must make up for all mistakes which have preceded it, give quality and value to all spaces left over between building, auto parking, and site boundaries, and at the community scale do the same for all spaces left over between the disconnected processes of private and public development. The amount of waste space, or inadequately used space, which is a by-product of these disconnections between land subdivision and physical development would be truly staggering if measured and totaled for community areas. Side, rear, and front yards, and miscellaneous areas improperly proportioned or related to their buildings, and therefore inadequately developed and used, exist wherever the pressure of urbanization has not reached the level which covers all land with buildings and paving. This level, of course, is not better; it is the final disaster of urbanism.

This waste of land and of potential living space and amenities is expressed directly and specifically in the gap between the owner's concept and the optimum budget for adequate site and landscape development. In common practice, especially on raw newly developed land, this gap can be surmounted only by herculean private efforts or the most devious and persistent bargain hunting. The average owner, private or public, is not prepared, or has avoided considering, the total budget requirement for optimum development of all his land. If one accepts average professional standards as optimum for site development, he will find most land beyond minimum building and auto-paving areas, in most communities, is underdeveloped, often not developed at all. This land must be considered either wasted or lying fallow for higher and better use. The visual price, in shoddy, messy, poverty-stricken landscape pictures, surrounds us wherever we go. Few sections of our communities rise above this level.

33

FIG. 1. PEOPLE WHO ARE TROUBLED BY THEIR NEIGHBORS

Fig. 1. "The above illustration represents a common scene. The neighbors suspect each other, and they destroy the beauty of their grounds in the attempt to shut each other out. Suspicion and selfishness rule. Regardless of rights of others, animals are allowed to trample to pieces the sidewalks, to destroy shade trees and to despoil the neighbor's yard. Inharmony, disorder, and ill-feeling among the people are characteristics of the neighborhood."

Fig. 2. "This illustration represents a neighborhood where the people evidently do unto others as they wish others to do unto them. They trust each other. The barriers between them are removed. No animal is allowed to do injury. Enjoying peace and beauty they evidently desire that the neighbor shall share the same. This cooperation, kindness and regard for all give the beauty, the harmony, the peace, and the evident contentment which are here presented."

FIG. 2.   THE NEIGHBORHOOD WHERE PEOPLE LIVE IN HARMONY

EXAMPLES

III

ROOM AND PATIO

Patios are enclosed spaces, flexible in use, content, and form. They are for general social activity without compulsion (save perhaps that of conformity); they are nonspecific, mixed, quiet to boisterous, single-relaxing to crowded-partying. They provide facilities for social intercourse in groups of all sizes—spaces for outdoor living, eating, dancing, talking, listening, watching, serving, shopping, sleeping, bathing—hospitals, country clubs, public administration buildings, homes, public housing, exhibits and fairs, community centers, churches, hotels, commercial buildings. Patio spaces include terraces, plazas, malls, squares, anything more organized than parks and less organized than playgrounds, and any space where people mix comfortably in random patterns to any degree of intensity. Their primary function is social intercourse, human contact, meeting of friends, relatives, neighbors, fellow-citizens, those with common interests, beliefs, or principles, landsmen, alumni. Typical patterns are: stand-up socializing, sit-down socializing, eating and drinking, dancing and playing games. Swimming can be a social activity, as was the Roman bath. Patios can be spaces for relaxing when they are not being used more intensively, and if large enough, they may serve for both relaxing and intensive use. They have a considerable range in scale, from private patios up through social spaces serving neighborhoods, communities, and regions. They have been indispensable social elements around the world throughout history. They are highly developed social spaces of flexible use and content.

At the scale of small room and patio, the precise dimensions; precise detailing of floors, walls, and ceilings; selection of furnishings and *objets d'art;* and patterns of plant structures, foliage, flowers, and fruit are all primary in determining quality and character. Such single enclosed spaces are used by people for work, recreation, relaxation, or the details of daily life. They require careful study of the exact nature, intensity, and duration of required functions and activities. From this can be determined the probable relationship of individuals and groups to the details of the space; how much design is concerned with its specific functioning in activity and movement; how much with passive relaxation and intimate detail.

1. Living rooms in houses and apartments, social rooms in all sorts of community centers, hotels, social and country clubs, all with their patio or terrace extensions, are spaces for both active and passive social life for individuals, families, friends, and larger groups. The enclosure of these indoor-outdoor units will comprise the inner walls of the rooms and the outer boundaries of patio or terrace. More and more typically, the wall between, used primarily for climate control, is made of movable glass for maximum visual and physical movement. While active and passive may be in variable proportions at different times, these spaces need generally serviceable and handsome flooring, furnishing, and equipment to meet the demands made upon them. The quality of design will result largely from the detail of the functional elements, of the enclosure, and of the way they are arranged together in the total space.

2. On the other hand, living spaces in difficult climates, bedrooms, bathrooms, hospital rooms, waiting rooms for professional services and administrative and service centers, churches and other assembly spaces, may be connected visually by glass walls to landscape spaces which have no other function than to be seen into. These are real three-dimensional pictures, visual extensions of indoor space, the difficult-climate answer to the mild-climate patio. Here detailed and sensitive arrangements of plants, rocks, water, sculpture, and structure can run the gamut of design, imagination, and expressive insight. Such attention will be justified by the intensive inspection these spaces will receive from contemplative eyes within the air-conditioned or heated buildings.

3. Workspaces in home, office, and shop—here we run the gamut, from primary efficiency and economy, where outdoor spaces handle extensions of indoor activities, to the expansion in scale, richness of detail, and recreational or relaxing elements which may come with affluence. From utilitarian service yard we expand to the kitchen patio for eating and socializing, or to the kitchen garden to rest the housewife's or maid's eyes. Offices may have patios for outdoor conference or coffee break, garden pictures to rest the eyes, or more elaborate social-recreational developments. As we pass from white collar to blue collar in shop or factory we are less apt to find more than the most efficient and economical physical structures, though industrial recreation is an established field.

To consider providing the textile worker or machinist with a pleasant view out the window would perhaps be a gross violation of the principles of industrial efficiency. The ideal factory today appears to be a hermetically sealed box with controlled artificial light and climate, in which nothing distracts from concentration on production. What automation and its attendant shift of emphasis to more highly skilled workers may do to this concept is conjectural.

4. Passing-through or entry spaces for all types of buildings—the front yard at any scale from country cottage to city hall or factory. Here public relations enter; the passerby will look in or perhaps slow down to look more closely. Everyone who uses the building will pass through this space, looking casually or carefully, depending on his haste and its quality. Seating and paving may be provided for those with time to linger. These spaces will not require the detailed design of 2 above, as inspection is not apt to be so intensive or continuous. But they do require fine space concepts in relation to building and street, adequate to leave an impression in the mind of pedestrian or motorist passing by or through.

We pass now to the second stage of space organization, the relations between single free-standing buildings and their sites. In this, the room-and-patio becomes a detail of the whole, articulated into a larger concept. It may nevertheless retain its own integrity.

PATIO FOR TURNER & STEVENS, FUNERAL DIRECTORS
Pasadena, Calif.

This space is formed by a U-shaped brick building. It opens south through a covered walk directly onto the street. It provides circulation to and from the family room and was formerly merely a walk among plants, very hot because of its southern exposure.

The redevelopment produced a court adequate in scale and arrangement for the group movement and gathering, quiet conversation, and contemplation, which attend times of sorrow. A Douglas fir arbor overhead filters out a good part of the sun's heat and glare. Brick paving provides freedom of circulation and gathering; substantial redwood benches provide seating; redwood screens provide group privacy. A small fountain in a metal bowl provides splash and coolness. Specially designed lights make evening use possible. The entire complex of elements is arranged to facilitate use by groups of various sizes and to make possible subgroupings within larger groups.

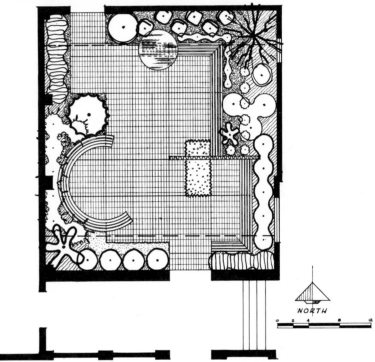

NORTH

39

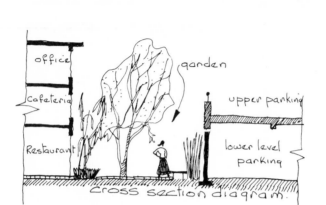

office

garden

cafeteria

upper parking

Restaurant

lower level parking

Cross section diagram.

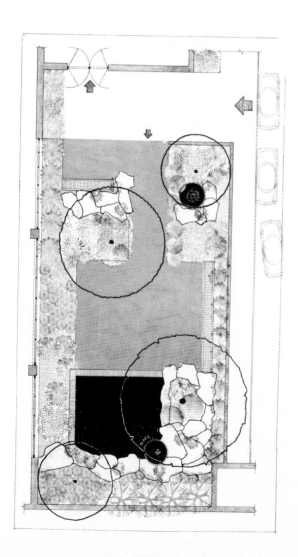

A RESTAURANT GARDEN
Raleigh, N.C.

The garden is approximately 54 by 30 ft and is located in the center of a suburban shopping center. It is approximately 20 ft below street level. A restaurant opens onto one long side of the garden. On the opposite side is a brick screen wall hiding an unsightly view of the lower level of a two-level parking deck.

FUNCTION: *It provides a pleasant garden setting in which diners may enjoy the view of plants, rocks, and moving water in the heart of a busy city shopping area. The garden also provides a pleasant space in which friends may meet before dining, and may delay their departure afterwards.*

PLANTING: *Construction and planting were completed in May, 1961. As the majority of plants were in full leaf, they were planted and kept under an atomized mist system operating approximately 4 sec. in each 60 sec.*

CONSTRUCTION ITEMS: *"Feather rock," a lightweight rock, was used because of the impossibility of handling heavy local rock and overloading the parking deck during its moving. Various water effects occur on a cycle with a small waterfall operating continuously. Paving throughout the restaurant and the garden is brick laid on sand. The garden is illuminated at night. The project has proved successful for owners and restaurant users and as a contribution to the area.*

1

2

28th CHURCH OF CHRIST, SCIENTIST
Westwood Village, Los Angeles, Calif.

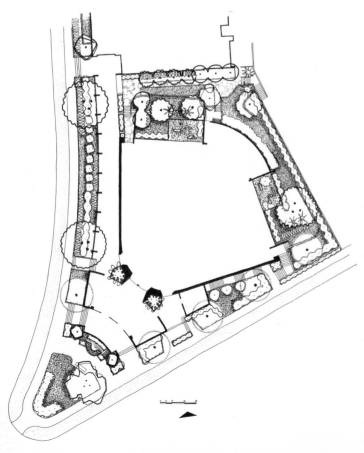

On a limited triangular site, adjacent to an existing building which became its social and administrative center, this large church reveals a handsome and impressive form. The architect, Maynard Lyndon, designed a fine tall curved colonnade connecting the new and old buildings and an elegant pierced wall backing a fountain at the point of the triangle. The most important architectural concept from the landscape point of view was the 10- by 40-ft fixed glass panels set in the walls on either side of the main meeting room. These look into sunken gardens about 25 ft wide, retained by brick walls. These gardens, developed in structural patterns of plant and rock forms, become visual extensions of the indoor space, three-dimensional dioramas, richly detailed compositions for intimate contemplation, demonstrations of the experience-expanding function of the glass wall in any climate, without physical circulation through it.

The soil in this area is a heavy adobe, offering maximum resistance to the movement of water and air through it. The sunken gardens, 10 ft below all surrounding levels, offered a serious drainage problem, exaggerating the difficulty of obtaining good plant growth in heavy soil. Vertical holes 12 in. in diameter were drilled on a 10 ft grid throughout the sunken areas. At depths of 10 to 25 ft a layer of sand was reached. The holes were then filled with crushed rock to a point 2 ft below the surface, covered with building paper, and filled with soil. Drainage and plants are still doing well. The most difficult planting problem is under the wide solid overhangs on the north side.

3

4

5

6

7

8

IV

BUILDING AND SITE

The single building on a site larger than its ground floor area has been the typical concentration of modern architectural and landscape thinking. Much good work has been done, and many good examples publicized, particularly in the residential field. The problem may be summarized as follows: the site is a piece of real estate, variable in size, form, and topography, produced by land subdivision. The building, dominated by the economics of construction and the demands of functional design, will tend to establish its own size and form, even if conditioned by some preconception of form from without. Thus the landscape design problem is to achieve the best possible development of a space or series of spaces determined by the relationship between the building and the site boundaries. Within these, the specific demands of the program must be satisfied. Problems of orientation and climate control—sun, wind, heat, glare, reflection—must be resolved. Visual demands created by the form and height of the building and the size and position of glass areas must be satisfied. The exterior landscape, beyond the site boundaries, must be analyzed and included or excluded by judicious screening or framing elements. Finally, yard spaces which do not relate to building or specific function must be developed in meaningful forms. All of this will be more difficult if the building has been conceived as a self-sufficient unit, and less difficult if the organization of building and site spaces is conceived as one coherent pattern at one time.

The relation between building size, lot area, and auto-parking requirements will also be critical. More and more the auto becomes the enemy of the landscape, as its asphalt requirements destroy or make impossible green space around buildings. Our land-use patterns are so pinched and penurious that we seem unable to control this expanding force by recognizing the positive value of landscape and pedestrian space in land-use and coverage controls. Another factor might be the control of car sizes in the public interest. This would, of course, be considered a gross. violation of the individual freedom of choice between large and small cars. We are reminded of the famous freedom of choice of rich and poor alike to sleep beneath bridges.

On sites larger than the joint requirements of building and parking—a shrinking and idyllic condition—we have a range in scale from the bare minimum and almost useless strip of foundation planting around the building, through walled patio spaces of minimum or adequate size, to that expansion in comfort and luxury which allows lawns, trees, and the ultimate richness of woods and meadows. The growing tendency for housing and productive enterprises to migrate into the open country may provide them with the temporary illusion of manor house affluence, overlooking other people's farms or woods. But, unless this outlook is over some guaranteed land-use such as a water district or regional park, the forces of exurbanization will soon catch up with them. The peculiar hodgepodge checkerboard leap-frog pattern of modern urbanization renders no open country safe without adequate planning controls by local government. Even these tend to give before the pressure of big-time power structures.

Within basically similar land subdivision patterns, we may have a range in building-site concepts as wide as that from the New England colonial house, standing four-square with its neighbors on a sea of grass with only occasional trees or shrubs to suggest boundaries between them, to the Latin patio house which encloses the entire lot for private living space, creating structural continuities in which individualized architecture is hard to find. These extreme contrasting forms have obvious roots in severe and mild climates, but perhaps are related even more to social attitudes: the puritan combination of tight economy with "I have nothing to hide from my neighbors"; the Latin expansive and rich concept of daily living, combined with demand for absolute family privacy. In our heterogeneous culture the relations between privacy and neighborliness are more variable. The former tends to be self-centered and antisocial while the latter tends to produce self-conscious do-goodism and social maneuvering. Balanced relations between the two are made difficult by social conflicts between individualism and togetherness, competition and cooperation; and by our heavily institutionalized structures of subdivided land-use, with minimum consideration for relations between the parts. The pressures of technology and of community needs are forcing their way through these structures; larger and larger parcels of land are being assembled for unified design and development.

45

STANFORD MEDICAL CENTER
Stanford University, Palo Alto, Calif.

1 *Hanging gardens and integration of existing live oaks at the end of one hospital pavilion.*
2 *Topiary planting in interior court.*
3 *Planting and fountains in front of the Center.*

1

3

46

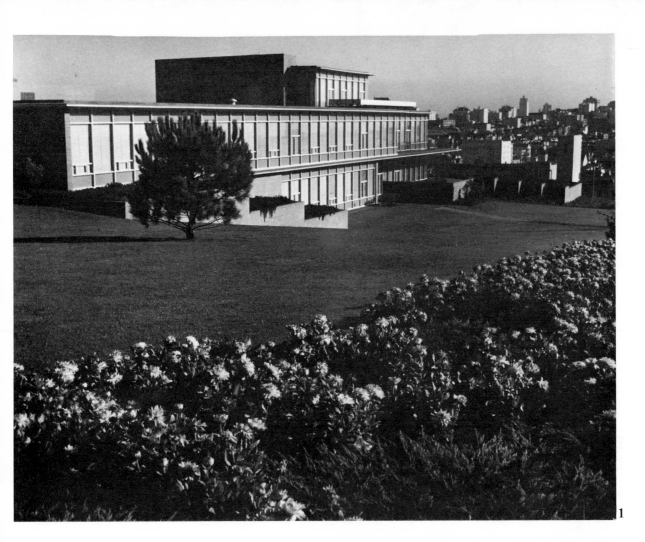

1

FIREMAN'S FUND INSURANCE COMPANY
San Francisco, Calif.

Of the 10.2 acres in the Fireman's Fund Insurance Company site, approximately 1¾ acres are devoted to the building and 2¾ acres to parking, leaving the major portion of the site for gardens.

Considerable care was taken in the arrangement of the building, parking areas, and levels to save all the existing trees. Some of the trees were left on mounds of earth where the ground was depressed, and others were contained in wells where the ground was raised. In all cases, special pruning, feeding, aeration, and watering were done during construction to help the trees make the necessary adjustments.

The most impressive of the trees saved are the beautiful specimens of Monterey cypress in the parking areas on the California Street side of the building. Here, too, three very large blue gums are retained. In some ways, the most distinctive specimens saved are the large red-flowering eucalyptus near the corner of California street and Presidio, and the magnificent native toyon or Christmas berry in the parking area above Presidio. In addition to these, six live oaks and a very large redwood and Monterey pine are saved.

Taking the cue from the existing trees and from the special climate features of the site, the live oak and red-flowering eucalyptus were chosen to predominate. Secondary themes are carried by the Monterey cypress, olives, redwoods, and Bishop pines.

In addition to the general landscaping of the areas between the building and the streets on all sides, there are two special gardens of note. The first is the entrance court, and the second is the terrace adjacent to the cafeteria.

47

2

3

The entrance court off Presidio Avenue is U-shaped, its major paving of brick and asphalt, with adequate parking space for those visiting the executive offices. Dominating this court is the 80-ft reflection pool in the center, planted with water lilies. Two planting areas straddling the pool contain a specimen live oak and ground covers of creeping myrtle and pink-flowering sunrose. All along the arbor-covered walks around this court, between arbors and building, are shade-loving plants in great variety, including rhododendrons, azaleas, ferns, fuchsias, and bluebells. Along one side, a long row of alternating blue and white *Agapanthus* provide a splash of color against a low brick wall.

The terrace off the cafeteria and lounges is particularly useful and colorful. Since it is situated on the east side of the building, it is protected from the prevailing west wind and is elevated so that there is a good view of a large part of San Francisco. Benches have been provided, so that employees can relax in the sun during lunch or coffee breaks. Specimen oaks and magnolias have been planted in this area, and springtime is particularly colorful when the flowering cherry, wild lilac, camellias, Mediterranean broom, wild strawberry, and St.-John's-wort are in bloom. One bed is filled with star jasmine, which provides a delicious fragrance in the summertime.

Careful attention has been paid to the arrangement of the shrubs to provide interesting combinations of foliage, color, and texture, so that at all times of the year there will be something of special interest for the passerby to see.

4

5

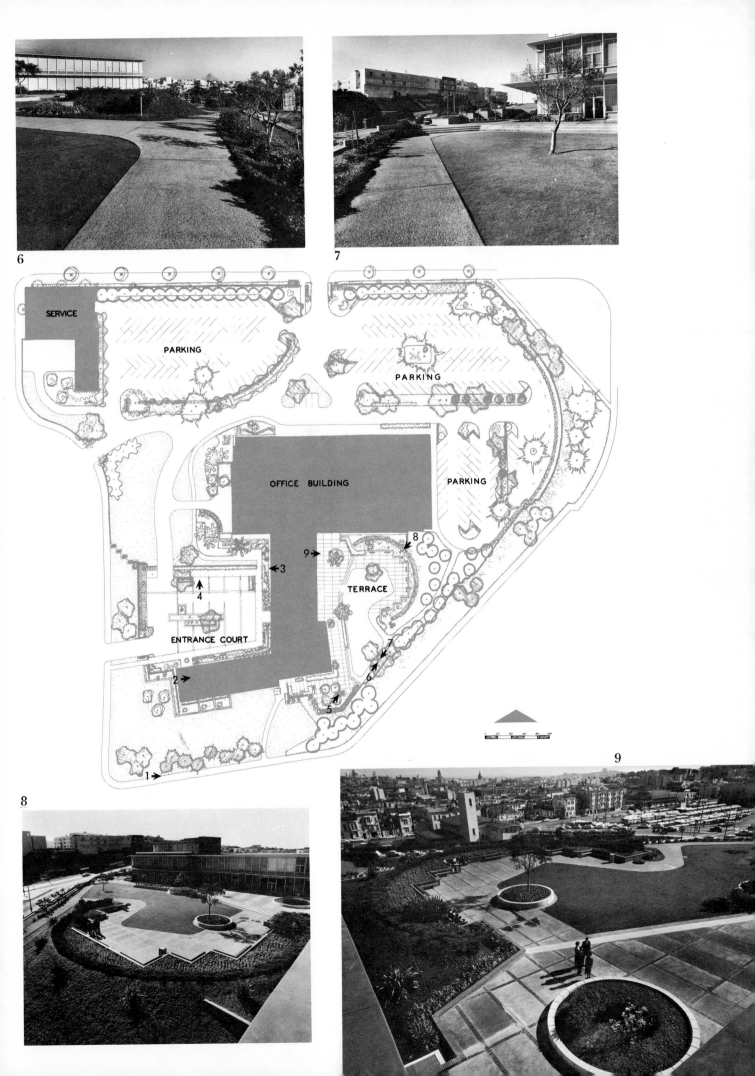

6

7

SERVICE

PARKING

PARKING

PARKING

OFFICE BUILDING

9

3

4

8

TERRACE

7

6

ENTRANCE COURT

2

5

1

8

9

1

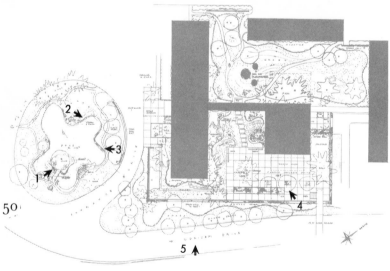

50

WASHINGTON WATER POWER COMPANY
Spokane, Wash.

This project is a consolidation of many far-flung offices from various parts of the state of Washington into a unified command center. The Washington Water Power Company is a private utility company which owns and installs dams for electric power. This facility is their central operating plant and includes a six-story office block, a service center, large warehouses, and a cafeteria-auditorium for employees.

The new facility is built on the outskirts of Spokane along the Spokane River. The design was coordinated with the architects from the beginning. Water, the source of power for the company, serves as the theme of the gardens. These waters are carried around in runnels, jets, and fountains, through various parts of the gardens and finally end up in a pond which serves as a reservoir for sprinkling and an overflow for the heat pump system.

The company decided that the gardens would serve not only as a facility for employees, but also as a park for the city—this public relations gesture seems to have had an effect far beyond expectations.

2

3

4

5

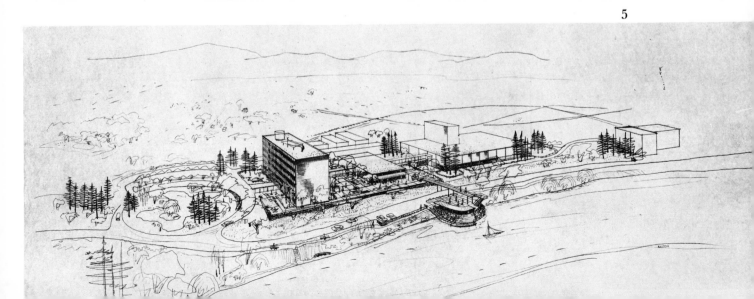

1

2

3

INDUSTRIAL INDEMNITY COMPANY
Fresno, Calif.

The job represents the current trend toward the decentralization of one master urban center into self-contained units dedicated to the service of the local community, the car, and the coffee-break.

And in many respects, it was an ideal job.

The site selected was adequate for present and future needs; there were excellent trees to provide shade for the hot summers and the soil was good.

Further, the owners' representatives knew that landscaping was greater in scope than merely planting a pair of cypress at the front door. Collaboration with them and the architects was constructive and congenial and was begun early enough in the planning phase.

The architects had proposed to set the building high enough on the site to protect it during a possible flash flood in the rainy season. However, the filling to meet the grade of the building would then jeopardize the trees. A redwood deck, adequate in scale to complement the building and provide easy access to the garden, was suggested as an alternative solution.

The site was dominated by the pecan tree which influenced the placement of the building. Its sculptured quality in winter is enjoyed from the cafeteria, which also enjoys its shade in summer. The oasis it creates invites the employees into the garden during the hot weather.

The open and closed baffle fences were used to suggest privacy for the garden area while providing circulation of air and a suggestion of things to come to a prospective employee approaching the front entrance. On the orchard side the fences clearly define the area under development.

Low-maintenance plant materials were used throughout except for the small grass areas which seemed imperative for visual relief in a hot climate.

The employee parking area in the rear is adequate and easily accessible. It is planted with fast-growing Modesto ash to ensure quick shade.

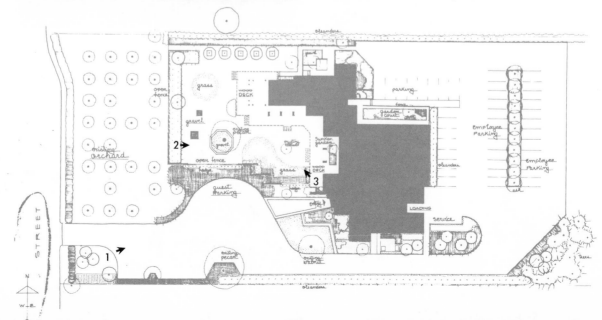

FACULTY CLUB
University of Washington, Seattle, Wash.

The new faculty club at the University of Washington replaced an old Elsworth Story building which had been used for years as a faculty club. This old building, with all its nostalgic charm, no longer satisfied needs and was in a state of disrepair. The very handsome new clean structure has attempted to capture some of the quality of that old building. The existing trees, maintained at the entry, were of very significant value in the total development of the exterior spaces. The entry ramp, working in contrast to these tall vertical trees, is very graceful and lifts one gently off the lower floor area. The building is generally used by the faculty on campus and presents an atmosphere of relaxation, including a poolroom, lounges, and related exterior space, in addition to eating facilities. The interior court at the main floor level separates functions within the building, but being completely glassed-in, provides a pleasant visual relief from the surrounding corridors. One moves from the entry and lounge area to the dining room over an enclosed bridge which allows a view into the lower garden; this enhances the vertical space while one is looking through the dining room into the long and extended horizontal space. The very careful siting of this building has allowed a complete unobstructed view across the waters of Lake Washington and the surrounding residential areas.

53

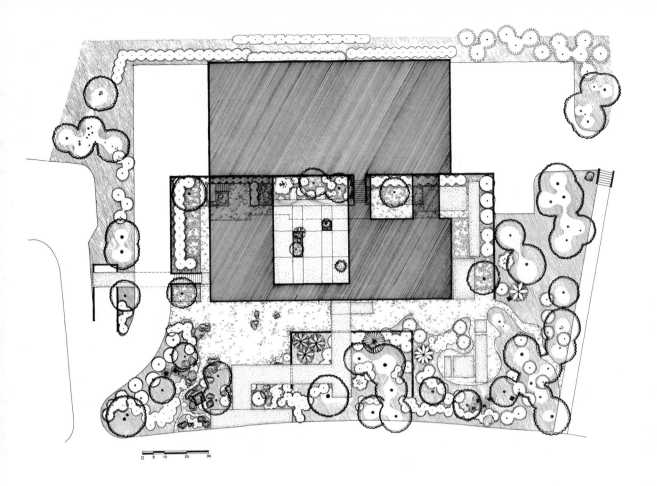

1

2

3

TEMPLE, BRANDEIS CAMP INSTITUTE
Santa Susana, Calif.

A hillside site of 25 acres within a 1,200-acre ranch-camp-institute, an hour's drive from Los Angeles, gives a magnificent outlook onto the surrounding hills and valleys. The building, to house worship, culture, and social life—the House of the Book—is secluded in a Garden of the Bible. The latter has been well planted with biblical trees on many annual tree-planting festivals. In 1959, as a service for Lag B'Omer, *the festival program, written by Norman Corwin and Dore Schary, repeated the refrain: "To a day when the shade of the oak spreads wider than the shadow of war."*

One will walk to the temple through the garden, from parking areas secluded on its periphery. Access paths will lead through five garden terraces, each developed as an expression of one of the basic landscape elements—rock, water, earth, vegetation, structure. The visitor, already an hour removed from the pressures of urban living, will thus pursue a leisurely and contemplative walk to the House of the Book, pausing en route to commune intimately with the detailed composite elements of the garden and the fine panoramas and vistas beyond it. The house, surrounded by fine broad overlook terraces and quiet intimate gardens, will sit at the heart of this network of landscape experiences like a wise and benevolent spider at the center of a rich and luxuriant web.

1   *Entering the garden.*
2, 3, 4   *Views out from the garden.*
5   *The water garden.*
6   *The foliage garden.*
7   *The earth garden.*
8   *The House of the Book.*

56

FOLIAGE GARDEN

5

6

7

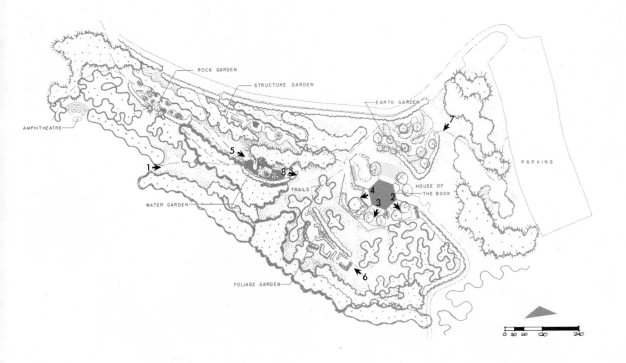

ROCK GARDEN

STRUCTURE GARDEN

EARTH GARDEN

AMPHITHEATRE

PARKING

5

1

8

HOUSE OF
THE BOOK

4

3

2

TRAILS

WATER GARDEN

FOLIAGE GARDEN

6

7

0 30 60   120   240

57

8

V
BUILDINGS IN GROUPS

The next stage in space organization is the development of groups of buildings on single parcels of land. Here we immediately take a major step from the centrifugal influence of the single building to a more balanced and subtle play of forces between buildings. While each building still radiates functional and visual requirements, these may meet and be absorbed in the spaces between, which should be designed to function with the buildings on all sides of them. The development of such group construction on single sites—multiple residential, religious and cultural centers, schools, colleges, universities, civic centers, shopping centers, office groups, research and industrial parks, hospitals, urban renewal developments—makes possible sound technical, functional, and esthetic relations at that expanded scale. Spaces between buildings can be designed to conform with their size, form, and exterior requirements. Beyond the economics of mass housing and the functional needs of institutions and commercial and industrial groups, which have created the typical group building projects with which we are familiar, lies their potential for fine balanced relations between buildings, trees, ground and water forms, circulation patterns, and the smaller details and furnishings of site development. This is perhaps best exemplified in some of our older universities and cultural and civic centers.

Group building is a normal result of functional programming and site selection, but it is remarkable how often its potentialities for rich relations between buildings and open space are lost through mechanical, habitual thought patterns. Important institutions on large sites are laid out on gridiron patterns, similar to subdivisions, as if the gridiron was the most functional pattern, when in reality it is a straitjacket from which a large site gives an opportunity to escape. Thus the design potentials inherent in group building by contrast with single building are sometimes gained through open-minded imagination, and sometimes lost through hardheaded habit.

Outdoor space forming possibilities of grouped buildings were discussed with great sensitivity and insight by Camillo Sitte in 1889.[24] His words, and those of his American sponsors, Charles Stewart, Eliel Saarinen, Ralph Walker, and Arthur C. Holden, are as relevant today as in 1945 when first presented to American readers. His discussion of "the relationship between buildings, monuments and public squares; open centers of public places; the enclosed character of the public square; the form and expanse of public squares; the irregularity of ancient public squares; groups of public squares; and, the artless and prosaic character of modern city planning" is a masterful analysis of historical prototypes in relation to modern practices. While concentrating on the high art of urban centers, these words are relevant to all serious design of building groups. His discussion of the natural art of building architecturally enclosed open spaces on the site, adapted with sensitivity to specific conditions, as contrasted with slick modern drawing board design within the sterilizing block framework of modern cities, is devastating to the latter. Widely accepted by architects and urban designers here and abroad, showing their influence in a number of excellent developments and projects, and in many urban renewal studies here and in England, these principles have had little, if any, effect upon the city fathers, the politicians, the bankers, realtors, builders and developers, city planners, and engineers who dominate the building and rebuilding of our towns and cities.

Group building patterns may, of course, be developed at any scale from one to several hundred acres. As the scale expands we grow from simple architectural-open space relations to more complex patterns and multiple groupings, including vehicular as well as pedestrian circulation patterns. Thus an elementary school has a simple building and open space pattern; a college may have a superblock of buildings enclosing a pedestrian quadrangle, and surrounded by parking spaces, connecting roads, and service elements; a major university is a small community, including several or many building groupings, each requiring parking and vehicular access, administrative, health, cultural, social, and service centers.

Whatever the size of its site, the institution or other group of buildings has boundaries which demark its characteristic development patterns and bring it into contact with the neighborhood and surrounding landscape. Wherever such boundaries occur, there are breaks in the continuity and character of the landscape; changes in the qualitative level which are at times shocking and disastrous (as the slums which once existed around Washington's Central Composition); maladjustments and dissonances which need harmonizing by careful design procedures.

59

CHERRY HILL SHOPPING CENTER
Haddonfield, N.J.

In this shopping center all shops open onto completely enclosed public spaces. A constant temperature of 70° and humidity of 35 per cent in winter and 50 per cent in summer is maintained. Merchandising—kiosks, displays, and exhibitions—generally takes place in the central mall.

The landscape architect had to design a completely new atmosphere, using the customary outside materials inside. Atomized mist systems, electronically controlled, provide additional local humidity around plants for certain types of ecologies. Photoperiodism is regulated by artificial light.

Design within a completely controlled artificial environment is becoming increasingly important in the large shell buildings of contemporary architecture.

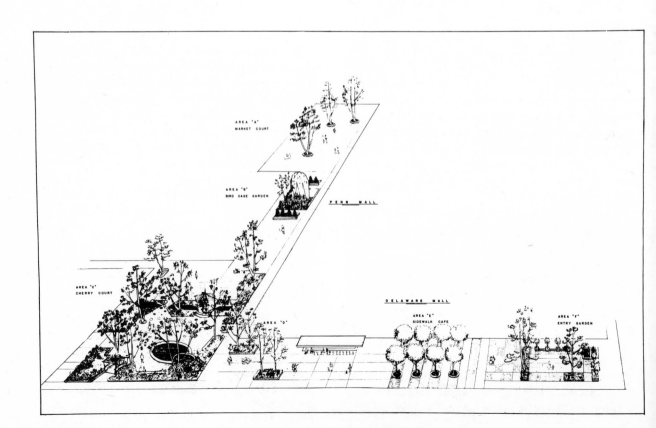

OLD ORCHARD
Skokie, Ill.

This very large shopping center, developed by American Commonwealth Builders, has as its principal tenant Marshall Field. It is west of Evanston and north of Chicago, about 45 minutes by car, and taps a North Shore population of about 1½ million people. There is space for 6,500 cars. The plan is interesting in its layout aspects in the sense that all the principles of shopping center design have been violated. The malls are very wide and irregular in outline. There was some effort made not to block all the signs, but there is no compulsion to see everything at once. Large islands of planting have been placed throughout the parking areas. In fact, the shopping center has a quality of being in a park, interspersed with plazas, almost in the European sense.

In spite of all these violations of presumed business practicalities, the owners feel that it is the most successful shopping center in the United States and does a huge volume of business. The theory is, and it seems to work, that if people enjoy being in an area, they'll shop there as well.

1

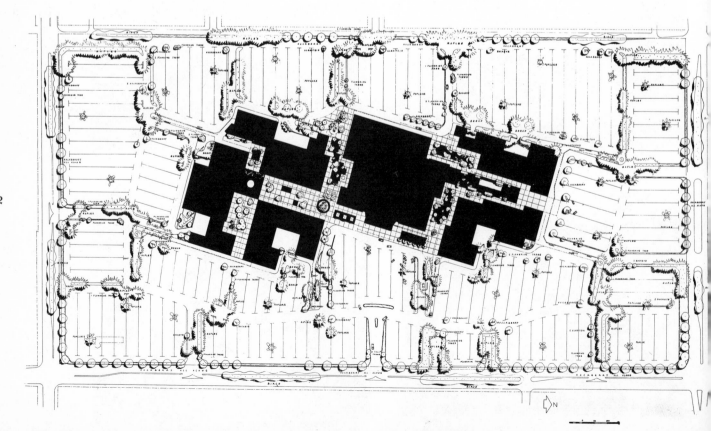

2

3

4

5

6

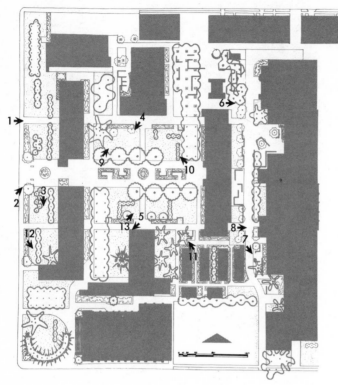

POLYTECHNIC HIGH SCHOOL
Long Beach, Calif.

This school received a minimum of landscape development. Student use of the grounds wore out the grass and exhausted the maintenance program every year. The redevelopment program was aimed at developing the site spaces between and around the buildings to serve more than the bare functions of circulation, light, and air. The site spaces were viewed as outdoor living spaces for students and faculty during all nonclass times and as visual environments for buildings and people. Tree patterns were developed to complete and enrich the architectural organization of the site space and to provide light-filtering protection for the long east and west façades of the buildings. An extended and fairly elaborate system of seat walls, in patterns designed to promote group socializing, was developed throughout the campus—in the center of the main quadrangle and lunch area, along the mall between the gym and classroom buildings, and around the entrances to these buildings. The asphalt lunch area was planted with a grid of plane trees for shade.

1

2

3

4

5

6

7

8

9

10

11

12

1

AMBASSADOR COLLEGE
Pasadena, Calif.

Orange Grove Avenue in Pasadena was once the center of wealth, ostentation, and high living. Now its fine large old homes, too expensive for contemporary incomes to maintain, are deteriorating and being replaced by "luxury" apartments of nondescript design. Ambassador College, a small institution of 400 students, is performing a cultural service by buying up these old homes and converting them to academic use. Six fine old homes of varying architectural character—Renaissance, Mediterranean, Tudor—have now been refurbished and placed under careful maintenance. Along with the rear blocks of cottages once inhabited by domestic help, a total superblock of about 25 acres is gradually being assembled. The cottages will be replaced by new college buildings—auditorium, dining hall, administration center, gymnasium.

This unique college development poses site planning and landscape design problems of special interest. Large old gardens of individual character must be merged, connected, integrated, and redeveloped to campus scale and character. Fine specimen trees must be preserved; smaller plants salvaged and re-

used. Circulation patterns connecting principal buildings and functions must be developed. Detailed intimate spaces, serving more intensive uses than the buildings were originally designed for, must be developed.

Most highly developed of the original houses was the Merritt house, now called Ambassador Hall, converted to classrooms. Of Renaissance vintage, this property was surrounded by an enclosure of wrought-iron fencing and cast concrete urns and piers of magnificent scale and detail. To the west, the house fronted across an open lawn to a large formal sunken garden. This is being redeveloped with a long reflecting pool, beds of green and color, tall slender lemon gums giving a sense of height and space above the sunken level, and coniferous accents. Ultimately there will be a new and special sculptural fountain at the west end.

To the east the house looks down a terraced grassy slope, framed in tall deodars, and centering on a cypress allée leading down to the classical Renaissance pool. This pool had to be bridged to solve circulation problems. A hardwood bridge on curved

2

1 *Merritt house from the east about 1905.*
2, 3 *Ambassador Hall from the east today.*

laminated beams, of slightly Oriental character, was designed and built. Two pieces of bronze sculpture, of abstract-organic form, have been installed at the centers of the semicircular ends. Although this mixing of forms may seem heretical, the designer is convinced that it produces an expanded richness, while clinging to conventionally compatible forms would have resulted in sterility. This feeling may be analogous to the mixing of modern and period furniture in some modern houses.

This former Merritt property forms the north end of the present campus. Along its southern boundary some portions of the enclosing structure had to be rearranged or removed in order to open it up to the balance of the campus. It was found possible to open up a basement swimming pool to a new sunken sunning patio by piercing the basement wall with double sliding doors (see page 76).

South of the eastern sloping half of the former Merritt property (now Ambassador Hall grounds) a long and elegant expanse of contoured and terraced lawn, studded with fine specimen trees, extends the length of a city block through the heart of the

3

4

4 *Sculpture and stream inlet in Renaissance pool.*
5 *View from Ambassador Hall down main lawn and stream.*
6 *View into east garden of Ambassador Hall from south before walk construction.*
7 *View toward Terrace Villa from main path and stream crossing. Urn from Ambassador Hall grounds.*
8 *View toward Ambassador Hall from main path and stream crossing.*
9 *View toward main crossing from Terrace Drive entrance. Pool patio fence enclosure beyond.*

5

6

7

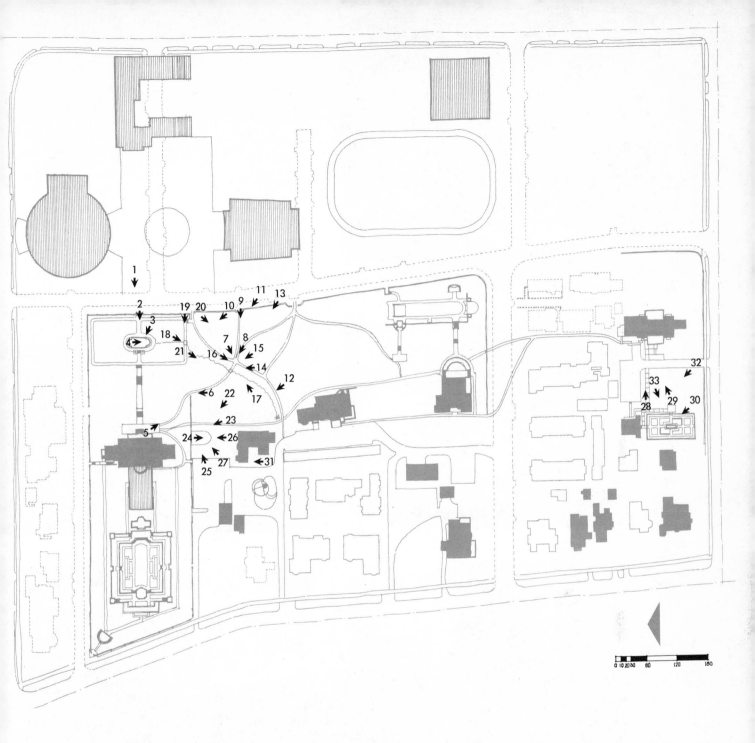

8

9

10

10 *View from Terrace Drive northwest toward Ambassador Hall grounds.*

11 *View from Terrace Drive entrance toward main crossing.*

12 *Stream detail.*

13 *View from Terrace Drive toward main crossing and Ambassador Hall.*

14 *Main crossing.*

15 *Waterfall in stream near main crossing.*

16 *Waterfall under bridge.*

17 *View across stream at main crossing toward Terrace Drive.*

18 *Bridge across lower end of stream.*

11

12

13

14

15

16

17

18

19

present campus. Formed by the designed merging of five large old gardens, it forms a foreground for the redeveloped old houses, leading down to Terrace Drive, ultimately the main mall of the completed campus. Across this lawn diagonal paths have been carefully curved in a criss-cross pattern which carries the main campus foot traffic. Parallel to one path a stream with a cascade has been created which runs for several hundred feet. Channeled in granite boulders brought in from the nearby mountains, it originates as a spring in the highest group of rocks and follows a variable course ending in the aforementioned classical Renaissance pool. This stream is a central feature in the daily experience of most students and faculty, bringing coolness and sparkle to the hot, dry glare of southern California.

At the southern end of the campus, Del Mar Hall, a fine old Tudor mansion, has been remodeled as a men's dormitory. To the east a sloping lawn has been terraced to provide space for free play. To the west a long pergola has been constructed to connect the main house with a former stable-garage converted to a recreation room, and an old formal sunken garden remodeled by the introduction of two paved areas with wood seats on two sides of each. Carefully developed new planting patterns keep the garden colorful.

Many other detailed new and remodeled spaces and special problems have been worked out. This campus is in a constant state of active development. All work is performed by college personnel and students. Mr. Herbert Armstrong, president, and Mr. Jack Elliot, dean of men, have participated actively in development decisions.

Existing trees are primarily deodar, camphor, Canary Island pine, olive, Ficus elastica, Pittosporum undulatum, Podocarpus elongatus.

19 View across lower end of stream toward pool patio enclosure.
20 View toward Mayfair up main path and stream from Terrace Drive entrance.
21 View upstream toward Mayfair.

20

22

25

26

23

27

22 *Pool patio enclosure from southeast.*
23 *Pool patio enclosure.*
24 *Pool patio south toward Terrace Villa.*
25 *Pool patio enclosure from west. Existing metal grill and concrete frame turned 90° from position left of picture.*
26 *Pool patio partially excavated. Pool behind lower windows.*
27 *Pool patio completed. Deck drain grill standing against wall between openings.*
28 *Del Mar pergola.*
29 *View toward Del Mar house from formal garden showing connecting pergola.*
30 *Seat and paving added to formal garden.*
31 *Terrace Villa patio.*
32 *View toward Del Mar pergola and playroom. Neighboring apartments beyond.*
33 *Entrance into remodeled formal garden at Del Mar. Pergola, seat, and pebbly concrete paving added. Old overgrown laurel specimens trimmed up into tree form.*

28

29

30

31

32

33

THE UNIVERSITY OF NEW MEXICO
Albuquerque, N. Mex.

This is a state university of about 9,500 students on a campus of some 500 acres close to downtown Albuquerque. About 200 acres constitutes the campus proper, the balance being taken up by a golf course, medical center, stadium and its attendant parking space. Although the university is nearly 100 years old, most of its structural development has taken place during the last 35 years. All of those buildings were designed by architect John Gaw Meem of Santa Fe. He developed a remarkably sensitive regional vocabulary based on local Indian and Spanish precedents. The new College of Education complex, designed by architects Flatow, Moore, Bryan & Fairburn, updates this vocabulary with equal sensitivity.

During all of this development little was done with the outdoor spaces of the campus. Most of them were in grass, and the older portions were quite well planted with trees dating from the 1930's and earlier. But the campus was laced with streets and parking spaces, and there was not a qualified gardener in the Physical Plant Department when this study began.

Feeling the pressure of the postwar expansion of the West, the university retained architect John Carl Warnecke of San Francisco to prepare a master plan. This projected an ultimate campus for 20,000 students, including future building pattern, exclusion of cars within an outer ring road, and hypothetical landscape relations between green spaces, water elements, and desert planting. All of this was quite diagrammatic. The current study, presented herewith, represents a much more detailed and specific

development and adjustment of such ideas. Working closely with the administration through Dr. Sherman Smith, the designers made a careful analysis of the master plan (for the central 200 acres), the exact physical condition of buildings and grounds, the management and maintenance organization, the current administrative thinking on future development, the nature of development under way, local climate, topography, material resources and skills with reference to site development. Regular and irregular population was surveyed building by building as a basis for a precise pedestrian traffic pattern study. Exploration was begun of the possibilities for use of native plant material from the mountains above, the mesa nearby, and the desert below (Albuquerque is 5,000 ft above sea level) in relation to standard available nursery stock. The peculiar problems of dust and sand movement in a windy desert with little natural cover were discussed.

All of these studies culminated in the drawings shown here, which constitute a master plan for central campus development. They have been expanded and implemented with many more precise working plans and details for immediate development, as well as with diagrammatic projections for areas whose future is not yet specific. The general objective of these plans has been a pedestrian campus unified by a fine sequence of open spaces enlivened by variable patterns of light and shade, and diversified by many intimate arrangements of a sculptural and furnishing nature. The main public approach via Cornell Mall between Johnson Gymnasium, Fine Arts Building,

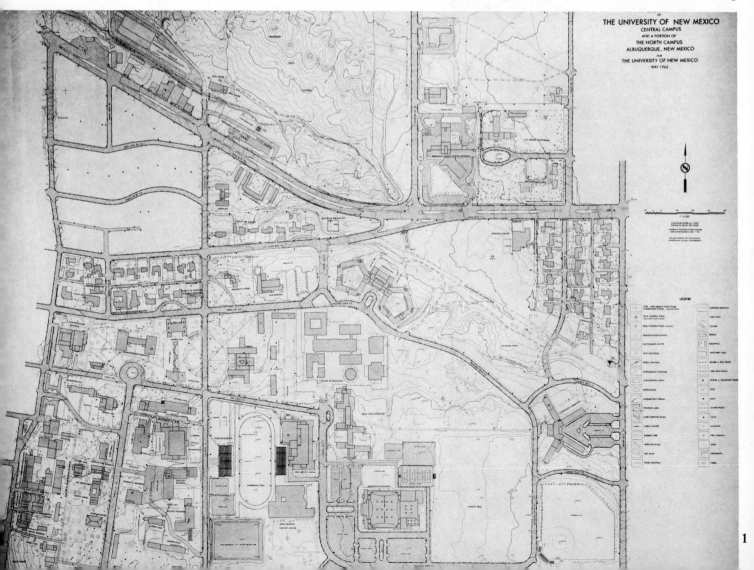

1

Student Union and future Student Affairs Building is planned as a free-moving paved plaza, broken by a grass carpet and trees in seat-height boxes, and culminating in the sculptured fountain at the College of Education entrance. Turning this corner, one will look from a broad raised terrace under a pavilion of trees down the parklike Humanities Mall, bordered with irregular masses of ponderosa pines and spring-flowering trees, to the fine little chapel at the far end. This mall will be laced with freely curving paths within oval and circular frames, designed to combine overall form with functional circulation. Crossing it at right angles, parallel to Cornell Mall, a long canal will bisect the campus, centering on a large lagoon in front of the library. This canal will be bridged by several main crosswalks, which will make it part of the daily experience of most students and faculty. It is proposed further to bridge it with several buildings at second-story level, to break up the bisecting force.

Throughout these main spaces, and others yet to be developed, there will be intimate and comfortable seating areas. These areas are part of a program for furnishing the campus as a space for living, studying, socializing, and interaction between the various academic disciplines. A pattern of recreational facilities, such as picnic, barbecue, and game spaces, will be developed. Further proposed is a series of permanent wall-and-platform installations to house outdoor displays and demonstrations by various departments. By such means it is hoped to develop the campus open spaces into integral parts of university life, rather than negative by-products of building.

1 *Central campus*
2 *East view of library*
3 *Central campus master plan*

2

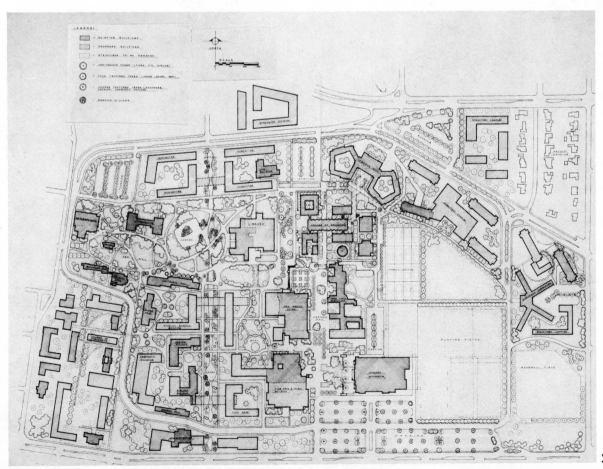

3

79

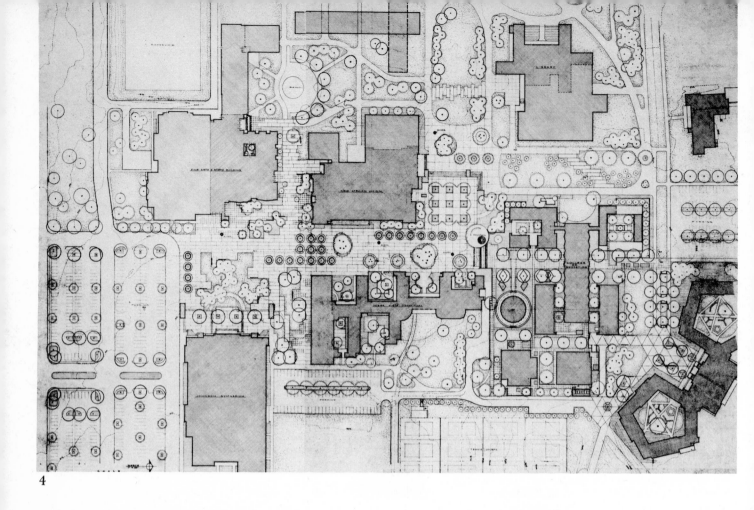

4

5

4 *Cornell Mall*
5 *Cornell Mall*
6 *South end of Cornell Mall*
7 *Ash Mall*
8 *West view of Ash Mall*
9 *Sitting area, north of chapel*
10 *East end of Ash Mall*

6

7

8

9

10

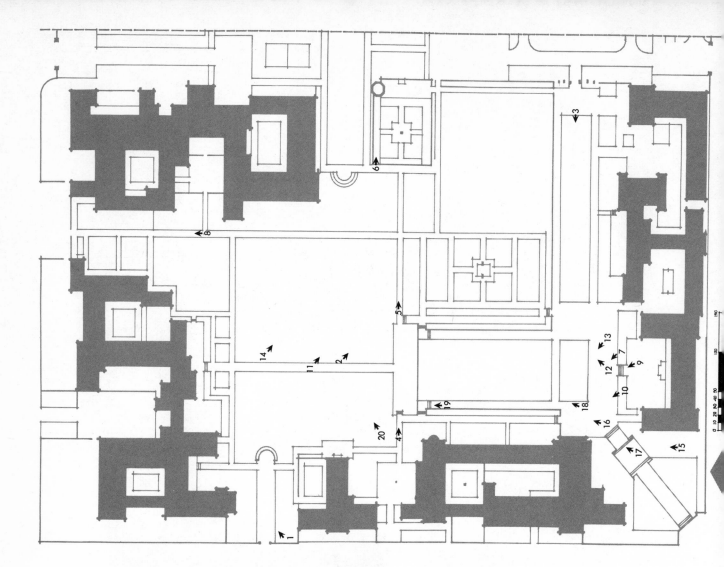

SCRIPPS COLLEGE
Claremont, Calif.

Scripps College is a residence in the midst of a residential gridiron. It is designed for such reasonable conformity to its site as will enable it to sit comfortably within its rectangular boundaries. Buildings—administration, library, classroom, residence hall—join hands by way of walls, walks, and courts to form a self-enclosed paradise, which does not strain against or fight its confinement, but capitalizes on it.

The leitmotif of the plan was a search for the

ultimate in simplicity, for the inevitable answer, for the least common denominator in design.

The short diagonal walk, the main entrance, leads directly to an open space which is the intersection of the two major axes of the scheme. Across this intersection, the auditorium, on the east-west axis, faces the Elm Tree Walk and the president's house (and incidentally Old Grayback, Mount San Gorgonio). The art building looks north toward the bowling green and Toll Hall (and incidentally the adjacent peaks of the Sierra Madres). These axes together make the structural backbone of the plan. They give it strength and stability to contrast with the free form of trees and other plant materials, and with the vagaries and varieties of associated detail in which the human equation is dominant. This holds true for the entire grounds, since a controlling objective was the creation of an academic residence for some 200 women students. Garden courts are frequent throughout. Everywhere there are shade trees, the all-important element of the Californian outdoors which is designed to be lived in.

Permanence and economy of continuing cost have led to a liberal use of walls rather than hedges, and of trees rather than shrubs and perennial flowers. Originally the great interior yard was to be plain earth with mostly trees. However, nostalgia for the ancestral grassland soon prevailed against this economy. The quadrangle of the residence halls and the elm-tree allée are both now in lawn.

Service entrances and parking areas have been restricted to the perimeter. There is no place for the automobile in the academic and residential grounds of the college.

2

3

4

5

6

7

8

9

10

12

11

13

14

15

16

17

18

19

20

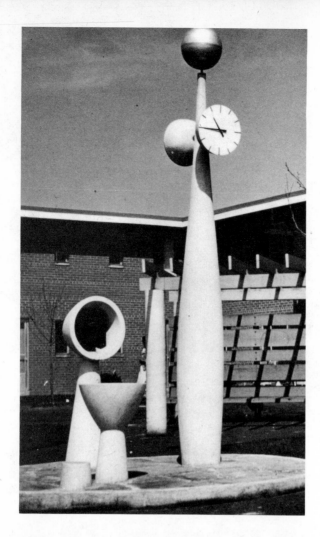

LONGWOOD REDEVELOPMENT
Cleveland, Ohio

Urban renewal is coming of age. All across the country, blighted sections of our cities are being cleared and plans for their reconstruction are taking shape. These projects are of all sizes and shapes. As an antidote to some of the vast and pompous malls decried by the editors of Fortune *(in "The Exploding Metropolis"),* Longwood *in Cleveland, Ohio, is small, neat, well planned, rich in facilities, and socially constructive.*

The Cleveland Redevelopment Agency earmarked 29.5 acres of downtown slums at 40th and Woodland. The total project, calling for 700 housing units, was divided among three sponsors. Land of 12.4 acres with approximately 300 units was awarded to the Longwood Redevelopment Corporation, representing sponsors James H. Scheuer of New York and Raphael Silver and Richard A. Keller of Cleveland.

The site is flat, next door to the Cedar-Central Housing Project, one of the first in the country. It is surrounded by the slums and blighted areas from which it was cleared. The development comprises 28 two-story, four-family buildings, in which two front doors share a path to each broad side, and two kitchen doors share a path and service area at each end. Although this creates a multiplicity of paths, the development provides quite good housing—quatrefoil in pattern, one family to each quadrant of each building, living downstairs and sleeping upstairs. In addition there are 15 three-story twelve-family apartment buildings with main and subordinate entrances centering on the long walls. There are also a community building with social, store, office, and basement utility space; a round colored-brick maintenance building with climbing bars projecting from the walls; S-shaped colored brick telephone stands; one large central play park, four small play parks, and four smaller playground areas; a central social plaza complete with curved exedra and sculptured clock–telephone–drinking-fountain stand by Leo Lionni; and a series of small bricked social areas with seats, checker tables, and cantilevered shelters.

Planting concentrated on trees for shade and color, with some mugho pines, Taxus, Euonymus, *and* Ampelopsis *around the buildings, and a few hedges screening play and social areas. This wealth of facilities exceeds FHA standards by a good deal, thanks to the courage and vision of the sponsors.*

EAST 37ᵀᴴ STREET 60'

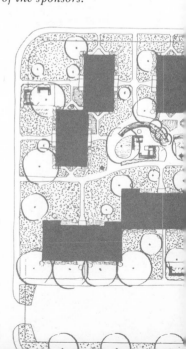

A special effort was made so that the detailed design of the play and social areas would equal the warmth and variety of the site planning and architectural design. The central play park became a playscape: a bowl of contoured grassy mounds and hollows, bordered with sheltering specimen trees, and incorporating a little grove of steel poplars, a family of concrete turtles, a fantastic village, a contoured sand pit, a saddle slide, a jumping platform, and the terraced tile wading pool developed around William McVey's abstract sculpture. The community-building terrace overlooks this playscape as the manor-house terrace once overlooked the meadow and pasture. Of the other play areas, one concentrates on a mock cityscape with a wall maze of varying textures, a gable roof of amber plastic, tile tunnels, and another fantastic village. Another play area incorporates a pattern of intimate beehive sand boxes around a wading pool, a hexapod sculpture, a silo gym, and tunnel bridges. Each play area provides shaded seating for parents. Most of the equipment used comes from two New York firms— Creative Play Things and Playground Associates.

Trees planted included Quercus palustris, Quercus borealis, Acer rubrum, Acer saccharum, Acer platanoides, Acer platanoides schwedleri, Platanus acerifolia, Ginkgo biloba, Gleditsia triacanthos inermis, Tilia cordata, and Cercidiphyllum japonicum. Smaller flowering trees included Crataegus in two varieties and 6 species of Malus. Shrubs included Prunus spinosa purpurea, Ligustrum regelianum and vulgare, Euonymus alatus, Viburnum tomentosum, Chaenomeles lagenaria, Weigela Eva Rathke, and Ribes alpinum.

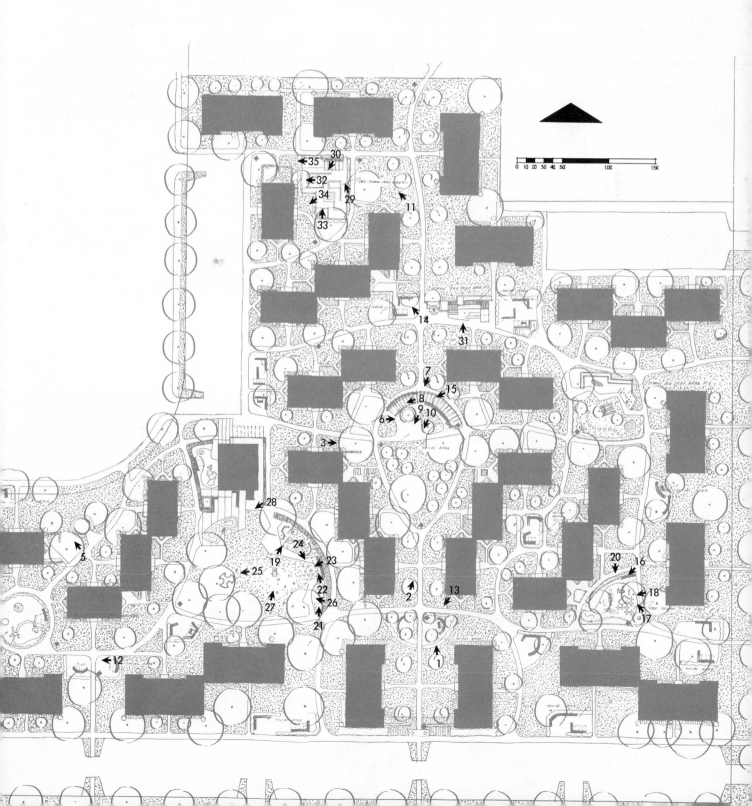

1 *Social space toward central exedra.*

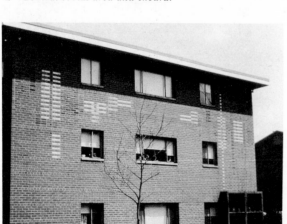

2 *Central social area and exedra.*

3 *East across central social area.*

4 *Colored-brick patterns in apartment buildings.*

5 *Maintenance building in colored brick.*

6　*Exedra and time-space unit—clock–telephone–drinking fount.*

7　*Detail of 6.*

8　*Seat in exedra.*

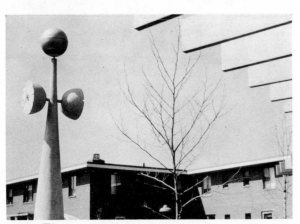

9　*Time-space unit.*

10　*Time-space unit.*

11, 12, 13   *Social spaces.*

14   *Social space and service yard.*

15   *Exedra.*

16

17

18

19 *Fantastic village in central play park.*

16, 17, 18, 20 *Preschool age play area with hexapod, tunnel, bridges, beehive sand boxes, wavy wall and arch climbers, parents' shelter. Curb encloses wading pool.*

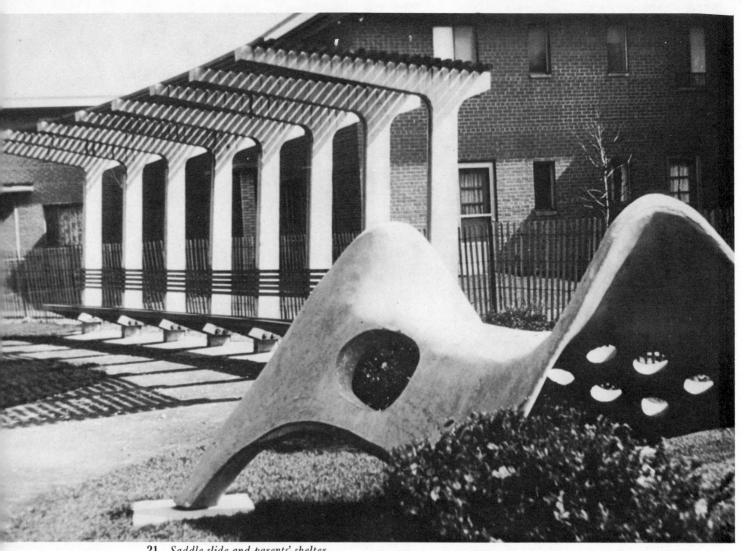

21 *Saddle slide and parents' shelter.*

22 *Turtle family and fantastic village toward community building.*

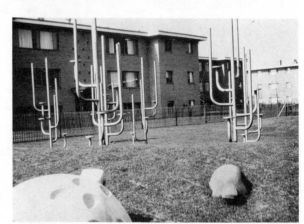

23 *Turtles and poplar trees (steel).*

24 *Turtle family and saddle slide in central play park.*

25 *Sculptured sand box and contoured turf.*

26 *Central play park—saddle slide, jumping platform, sculpture, community building and terrace, Christmas tree.*

27 *Poplar trees, jumping platform, mounds, fantastic village.*

28 *Play pool and sculpture by William McVey. Snow fence is temporary, to protect new sod.*

29 *Parents' shelter, city play area.*

30 *House frame and maze, city play area.*

THE UNIVERSITY OF DENVER
Harper Humanities Garden
Denver, Colo.

This project involves the replanning of some 12 acres at the center of the campus, and the precise design of a garden area of two to three acres within this. The general space is enclosed by the library, Carnegie Hall, Science Building, Student Union, dormitories, a new science-engineering group, and some parking lots and temporary buildings on the neighboring Iliff Theological School grounds. Centered in this open space is Evans Chapel, a small stone building which was Denver's first church, built in the downtown area about 100 years ago by Colorado's first governor. When this church was threatened recently with demolition for parking lot development, it was saved through the inspiration and energy of Chancellor Chester Alter and the generosity of private donors, and moved stone by stone to the university campus. From this effort developed the idea and support for a Garden of the Humanities in the same area.

Analysis of architectural and landscape space relations, and of potential pedestrian circulation patterns, led to projection of the garden as occupying the space between library and chapel and thus forming a connecting link between these two most important architectural elements. This also made possible the inclusion of two fine groups of Colorado spruce and one large Siberian elm within the garden. A fall of over 20 ft. from library to chapel promised interesting topographic adjustments. While fairly complete planted enclosure of the garden was probably necessary, a strong future main line of circulation between the Science Building and the Student Union, directly past the chapel, would bring students into the heart of the garden.

Development of form concepts to express the humanities was not so easy. Research revealed little agreement as to their precise content. While the conventional division gives them all but the physical and social sciences—philosophy, history, languages, literature, art—some writers did not agree. Ralph Barton Perry included in the humanities all those studies conducive to freedom, that is, enlightened choice. Careful thought and study led the designer to propose that the garden, enclosed for control, will conduct the visitor through three levels of experience. First he would enter through Elements of History—columns, capitals, well-heads, etc. From these he would pass through a series of spaces containing Elements of Creativity. These probably will be a series of sculptural projects, more or less modern or abstract in nature. From these the visitor will emerge in a Philosophical Center, an open space in which grassy ground forms, large round boulders, water, and trees are arranged to produce a contemplative and inspiring atmosphere. This concept was approved, and the plan endeavors to give it specific form.

While the architectural and tree relations might have suggested a symmetrical terraced pattern, the designer felt that the garden should take more free-flowing forms expressing the total environment of the Rocky Mountains and the West. Water became the backbone of the scheme, originating in a formal fountain and cascades on the architectural library terrace, proceeding through a curving stream and a 4-ft waterfall into a series of terraced lagoons ending in a quiet reflecting basin in front of the chapel. This basin is bridged by the main crosswalk. The main hard paved circulation follows the water, leaving the special Elements of History and Creativity in soft surfaced spaces. At two points conical earth mounds, reflecting the mountain structure visible on the western horizon, are proposed. Around the chapel a series of intimate social spaces, reflecting its ceremonial use, are indicated. Surrounding the entire garden will be a planting of spruce and hawthorn, carefully aligned within but filtering out into the surrounding open space outside. The spruce will serve not only for enclosure, but to screen out the boxy dormitories as one looks west to the mountains from the library terrace.

96

SECTION B-B

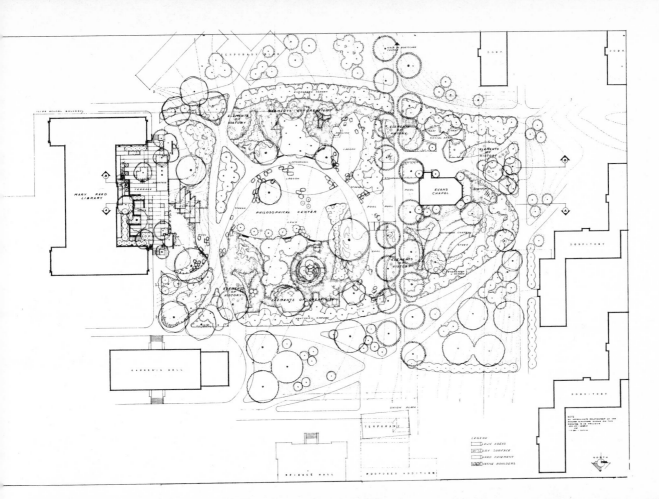

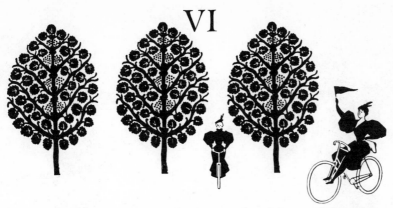

VI

PARKS AND PLAYGROUNDS

Parallel to the scale of design of building groups of various sizes, with their attendant open space and site-planning problems, is the entire field of park, playground, and recreation area design. In the former the buildings dominate the open space; in the latter the open space dominates the buildings. The possibilities for healthy intermediate combinations are largely frustrated by the double standard which governs the relations between construction and park land. In the eyes of many of our leaders, park land is merely raw land waiting for development by construction. But land once built upon, rarely, if ever, reverts to park status; this would be considered a catastrophe by the forces of "progress." The possibilities of master planning and urban design, by which construction and green space could play a gay and variable counterpoint throughout our communities, are just beginning to make some small impact upon our development thinking, though forecast one hundred years ago by Olmsted.

Parks are spaces of limited use and flexible form, developed with a minimum of construction and a maximum of natural unprocessed materials, for general relaxing-viewing, contemplating, meditating, sleeping, dreaming, making love, quiet socializing, free play. They are spaces of limited intensity and nonspecific use. Some are spaces to be seen only from outside themselves, in passing—"keep off the grass." These include front yards of all sorts, reservoir, drainage, and watershed areas, quarries and waste land, agricultural lands, and nature preserves. Some are spaces to be occupied quietly, supplying visual composition and circulation plus provisions for sitting, eating, relaxing, contemplating, meditating— parks, hospital grounds, cemeteries. Park spaces are highly developed meeting grounds for man and nature, in which each makes adjustments to the other.

Playgrounds are spaces of specific use and form, in which to participate in active play and organized activities, or watch specific performances, all with freedom of choice as to the extent and kind of participation. They are developed with largely structural materials for specific programmed facilities of all types—children's playgrounds, playfields, golf courses, race tracks, theaters. They are highly developed social spaces of relatively fixed or regular use and content.

Park and play areas run the full gamut in size, from the neighborhood tot lot and play area on a vacant lot or two, and the neighborhood park of 5 to 10 acres, through district and community parks of 10 to 50 acres or more, regional and county parks, wilderness areas, and forest preserves of hundreds or thousands of acres, to state and national parks of many thousands of acres. In all of these there is a general problem of relationship between active and passive elements. The latter are represented by the traditional park movement initiated in Central Park in New York City one hundred years ago. It has stood for the importance of natural green space, developed within urban areas to counteract their excessive and unhealthy congestion or preserved outside them to provide a weekend and vacation refuge for their exhausted citizens. Active elements, beginning with playground and playfield programming at a physical culture level, have expanded to incorporate all sorts of cultural, social, handicraft, nature study, and informal educational and recreational programs and activities. Recent years have seen a strong tendency to merge formerly independent park and recreation departments. This concept, correct in the abstract as producing a balance of active and passive recreation facilities and programs, has, of course, had varying results depending upon the relative strength of the personalities and organizations involved, the available acreage and facilities, and their distribution. The socially oriented recreation director may have little feeling for physical planning or landscape quality; the physically oriented park superintendent may have a paternalistic or negative attitude toward the people who use his facilities. If enthusiastic recreation programming takes over too completely, beautiful parks representing many years of development may be ruined by badly planned overuse. On the other hand, stubborn resistance by park authorities to active recreation may deny the citizens of a community the opportunity of creative and imaginative recreational leadership. Much depends upon the relative flexibility, open-mindedness, sensitivity, and cooperative spirit of these leaders. Rigid minds and empire builders are obstacles to progress. Sometimes a wise general manager may serve as moderator and coordinator, like George Hjelte in the city of Los Angeles.

1   2

Equally important in the integration of park and recreation facilities is the physical structure existing when it is initiated. Adequate acreage is primary: at least 1 acre of permanently dedicated recreation space per 100 to 300 persons. This should be distributed as follows: neighborhood park (elementary school complement) 10 acres or more with ⅛–⅜ mile service radius; community or district park (high school complement) 25 acres or more with a service radius of 1–1½ miles; city and regional parks larger and in strategic locations. (*The Guide for Planning Recreation Parks in California* is an excellent example of an imaginative and practical basis for determining local recreation space standards.[25]) With this pattern it is quite possible to design balanced relations of active and passive facilities adequate for all age groups and temperaments. More ingenuity and sensitivity may be needed to make adjustments to existing facilities and practices than to design a new system from scratch. But the difficulties will be much greater, and may be insurmountable, if one attempts to produce balanced facilities in badly distributed or inadequate acreage. Thus the great slogan for city councils, city managers, and park and recreation bodies everywhere is, "Get the land now, while it's available!" Once built upon it is gone forever.

In "The Crisis in Open Land," the American Institute of Park Executives says:

Today the standard of one acre of park space to 100 people is outmoded. To meet today's crisis, metropolitan communities must base their acquisition of open land not on today's population, but on the estimated population of their areas 40 or 50 years hence.

Judged even on out-dated standards, it is doubtful whether 10 per cent of our metropolitan areas have acquired enough open land. Almost none has a program massive or aggressive enough to meet the requirements of the next 10 or 20 years.

Most have added little to their park lands since the early 1930's, when many cities acquired needed parks by foreclosing on tax delinquent properties. . . . Not only are they failing to acquire new lands fast enough. Many can not even hold what they already have. . . .

How can we determine our present need for open space? Is there danger that we may go too far and acquire too much land? If such a situation were possible, a surplus of open land would be a better asset than a surplus of depreciated properties or slum areas!

Where time is of the essence, detailed planning may not always be possible. The best policy with which to meet such situations has been formulated by William H. Whyte, Jr; "When in doubt, get the land now and rationalize the purchase later!" [26]

While the primary demands of recreation programming are for open space adequate for needed facilities, it must not be implied that recreation is limited to the formal open spaces of the city. Recreation is creative use of leisure time, release from compulsion, and the opportunity to grow, develop inner capacities, release tensions and frustrations. Recreation facilities are indoor as well as outdoor, and all resources of the community, private as well as public, obscure or indirect as well as obvious, will be explored and integrated by a resourceful and competent director. Typical of such broad planning is the tendency to integrate school and park facilities on the same site, and the tendency to encourage local private-resource people with special skills or knowledge to participate in public recreation programs. Advanced thinkers like Wayne Williams seem to say that life should be a constantly re-creational process, with the total physical environment as its basic resource and home. However, it is clear that surroundings of rich and varied quality will provide more resources for recreation than the physical monotony and shallowness of most American communities.

Old-style park design of primarily passive space for the enjoyment of all citizens of all ages based itself on the pastoral meadow prototype developed by Olmsted. Rich variations, in terms of topographical, water, rock, and vegetation formations of natural inspiration, developed around this central concept. Introduction of classical or romantic architectural elements was judiciously controlled as to location and proportion. Great park landscapes have been produced by this approach in many cities—New York, Chicago, Cleveland, San Francisco, others. Greatness is not necessarily a function of acreage. Some quite small parks have the free flow and wonder of natural scenery.

Increasingly, congestion and density of land-use, plus pyramiding of the speculative spiral in urban land values, have developed a penurious and myopic

approach to American city planning. Bursts of civic imagination leading to great gestures in richness and scale have become irrelevant to our cautious, practical, minimal approach to public improvements of any but the most utilitarian nature. Exceptions such as 4,600 acre Mission Bay Park in San Diego, currently under development, are few and far between. Gestures of benevolence, prestige, and power, such as Mellon Square in Pittsburgh, the proposed Franklin Delano Roosevelt Memorial in Washington, and the proposed new Los Angeles Civic Center Mall, do still occur. Great parks—great in design, concept, and/or size—will be done again, for the American creative spirit has a way of bursting bonds.

The balanced recreation park is a different and more complex, though perhaps less subtle and poetic, problem than the primarily passive green park. Specific programs will be written by specific directors and communities, but in general the park must serve all age groups and balance active with passive, physical with mental, and intellectual with emotional facilities. Preschool and school-age children, adolescents, adults, and senior citizens all have special needs, interests, and urges. Balancing these special considerations is the need to encourage the family to play together in the same area. Rational categorizing of facilities by age and sex tends to support the general tendency in our culture toward the atomization of the population into mutually irresponsible units. It is socially healthy and necessary to reverse this pressure by emphasizing the reciprocal interdependence and responsibility of all groups in our population. Recreation is of many kinds—active play, social activities, music and rhythmic activities, arts and crafts, imaginative play and dramatics, nature study, mental and conversational activity, service activities, and relaxation are only a few. The high-standard design of recreation parks which will provide varied facilities for individually creative use of leisure time within a framework of rich green space and handsome, elegant structural elements is in its infancy. The primary limitations are inadequate budgets for development and maintenance, and the same psychological handicap which makes it difficult to enrich other public facilities. While condoning, or even applauding, any extravagance in private en-

1

vironments, we fear greatly "wasting" the taxpayers' money in public.

Play area design is an especially detailed and demanding segment of recreational design. Children need adventure, safe scares, limited hazards, complex climbers, junk yards, castles and caves, water, and unpredictability. Play should be experimental, not set; risky, not secure; a frontier of normal life—a release from frustrations.

Play should not duplicate school or home facilities or activities. There must be close collaboration between program and facilities. Those in charge of programming should make contact with resource people in the community who can supply such things as contact with animals and other sources of adventure and experience. If collaboration with school programs can be developed, experience with such elements as live animals and actual construction with building materials can be greatly expanded and made more flexible.

Play areas are centers for physical and social orientation. Learning to orient physically is probably most important for the preschool group as it involves learning to judge space relations up and down, sideways, forward and back, and scale and general physical maneuvering. Social orientation is also, of course, important from the beginning, in learning to live and play together; it grows in importance. As children's ages increase, their interests expand and they learn more and more about the real world around them. Not everything should be done for children. They should participate in planning, take responsibility for maintenance, putting things away, etc.

Older children can help to take care of the younger ones and thus eliminate mutual hostilities and fears of molestation. Facilities can be arranged so that they can build together and play together. There is some question about how separate the preschool and school-age areas should be. Although the preschoolers need more physical control to prevent their wandering off and to reduce supervision problems, growth is a continuous process and there should not be too mechanical a separation between these groups. If their play areas can be connected with an intermediate space in which transitions and mutual visiting can be developed, the results may be beneficial.

Just as there is a relation between the planning of facilities and the planning of supervision, so there is a relation between the design and selection of specific equipment or play elements and the design of the entire space set aside as a play area to include them. It is not enough to collect a number of separate pieces of equipment, no matter how good they may be in themselves. The character and scale of the organization of the spaces, surfacing, and enclosure around them, and the way they are connected and related, are equally important in producing a

2

small private world which the children can feel is their own. The scale of this world must be related more closely to the size of children than of adults. Research has shown that children like a green world, and the most enduring recollections carried over by adults are landscape elements such as trees, grass, and water remembered from their childhood. Most playgrounds, even the most modern, are hard, barren, and dreary in character.

The equipment and play elements incorporated in the designed play area may be bought ready-made, secured as junk from miscellaneous sources, or custom-designed for construction on the site, but they must be integrated in design on paper and in practice by a unified construction process on the site. This design process must not forget the importance of movable toys, blocks, and building materials for all ages.

Play is not just a safe way of getting rid of the children for a certain time; it is not just a way of developing children physically, nor just a way of developing better coordination, nor just a way of teaching children to entertain themselves. . . . Play is nature's way of preparing the child—or any young animal—for the struggles of maturity. In its unspoiled state it is a universal educational system which allows a child to discover his natural rights and natural limitations. (PROF. JOSEPH BROWN, *Princeton, New Jersey*) [27]

In designing equipment which would help "to prepare children for the struggles of maturity," Prof. Brown set three interrelated requirements:

1. Play equipment must be continuously challenging and creative for the child—not merely for the designer. (Accidents on playgrounds result from boredom, he believes, after the child has been lulled into a false sense of security.)

2. To provide continuous challenge, equipment must be unpredictable. "Unpredictability, within reasonable limits, is the factor which gives physical activity the creative quality which is the very soul of play." It necessitates decisions and makes each experience a different and new achievement—"a tacit reminder that success is a process, not an end."

3. Play equipment should be so designed as to permit various age groups to use the same apparatus

without getting in each other's way and with a minimum of supervision. "In too many cases, supervisors have become to the child what the lawyer and the policeman have become—too often—to his father; a substitute for judgment and conscience."

What we wanted was a playground with a maximum of do's and a minimum of don'ts. We wanted a project that was not large, not expensive, and not exclusive—one that others could copy and improve upon. We wanted to skip the fanfare, the side shows, the souvenirs and the popcorn wagons. Standing in line and spending money are not among children's natural activities. But here are things that children do: run, slide, jump, wade, balance, dig, swing, pretend, crawl, hang, dodge, hide, sit, climb, roll. . . . Children love to pretend. Take that apparatus we put together which adults can describe only as "The Thing." It does not look like anything any adult would use, but to one child it is a space ship; to another, a huge fish; to two girls, a castle; and to all of them, it is rampant with opportunities to slide, hide, crawl, jump, climb—and pretend. (HANK KETCHAM, *Creator of* Dennis the Menace) [28]

The primary factors in play-area design may be listed as:

1. *Surfaces:* Concrete, blacktop, sand, water, grass, tanbark, dirt

2. *Sun and Shade*

3. *Activity:* Sliding (slides, slopes); swinging (swings, rings, trapeze); balancing (beam, bench, rail, mounds, log stacks); hanging (horizontal ladder, bar, trapeze, rings); walking; running; crawling (tunnel); rolling (grassy slope); lying (sand, grass); sitting; climbing (tree, jungle gym, rope, slope, change of level); jumping (board, platform) over (obstacles, bridges), under (tunnels), around (walls, mazes, dodgems); exploring (mazes, dodgems); getting lost (mazes, dodgems); getting found (mazes, dodgems); digging (dirt, sand); building (wet sand, blocks, etc.); riding (tricycles); pushing (wagon, wheelbarrow, merry-go-round); pulling (wagon); wading (pool, spray); splashing; learning to live in the world—nature (plants, ground forms, materials, animals), houses (play houses, building), streets (ride around), vehicles (cars, boats, planes), animals (sculpture), community (all these together); creating (building, putting together, rearranging, planning)

Once the boundaries of the old mechanical approaches to play area design are lifted, endless possibilities open up and all sorts of specific ideas develop. For purposes of organization and control, these seem to fall into six typical groups:

1. Play structures, regular or special, including apparatus, space structures, play sculpture, trees for climbing

2. General play space is mostly landscaped; small-scaled, contoured grass areas for younger children; open play fields for the older children

3. The "vacant lot," messy, junk, or adventure space; for the younger ones a paved court and sand for playing with blocks and wheel toys; for the older ones a large enclosure with a soft surface and a lot of miscellaneous building materials and junk elements on which they can exercise their imaginations and ingenuities by putting them together in various ways over and over again. This may include transportation elements—cars, boats, planes—which are brought in; live animals—barnyard or other; special facilities for nature, science, and gardening activities

4. Play community including a riding track or freeway for tricycles

5. Water and sand play

6. Sheltered area for quiet play, parents, play houses, and storage for movable equipment, etc.

Of these six types of play elements, all are relevant to preschool areas. The first, third, fifth, and sixth are most relevant to school-age areas, since the others may be provided by the general park space.

Finally, as with buildings in groups, parks and playgrounds always have boundaries where they meet the neighbors and surrounding landscape. However, with these areas, the problems of reciprocal action at the boundaries are much more acute and subtle. Parks and playgrounds should be integral elements in the life of their neighborhoods and communities, with constant two-way relations. Often they provide the principal outdoor living space for their service areas. If they are designed as interlocking parts of the social and physical patterns around them, they will succeed. If they are designed as preconceived abstractions, without reference to context, they may fail.

103

1

2

CHILD STUDY CENTER
Los Angeles, Calif.

A small play yard for a specially selected group of young children, completely fenced and sheltered overhead by open frame extension of building roof, contains elaborate climbing structure to accommodate the entire range from timid to daring, including a fireman's pole. A compartmental sand box is designed to promote social grouping; an elevated balcony permits dramatic play, sheltered space beneath, and equipment storage. Steps with 4 in. risers and 8 in. treads are scaled to children—teachers find them difficult.

PLAYGROUND STUDIES

These models present a variety of imaginative ideas for play facilities and arrangements. They incorporate climbing experiences, material experiences, and space experiences with various qualities of environment from precise to wild.

1

2

1 *Tricycle freeway.* (*Krusi Park, Alameda, Calif.*)
2 *Sand box with concrete mountain, merry-go-round, tricycle, garages.* (*Krusi Park, Alameda, Calif.*)
3 *Preschool play area.* (*Mitchell Park, Palo Alto, Calif.*)
4 *Climbing wall.* (*Krusi Park, Alameda, Calif.*)
5 *Gopher tunnels.* (*Mitchell Park, Palo Alto, Calif.*)
6 *Gas station.* (*Krusi Park, Alameda, Calif.*)
7 *Climbing structure.* (*Krusi Park, Alameda, Calif.*)
8 *Play area.* (*Married students' housing, University of Utah.*)
9 *Balancing rail and mound.* (*Hayward, Calif.*)
10 *Climbing tower and slide.* (*Mitchell Park, Palo Alto, Calif.*)

PLAYGROUND DETAILS

A variety of well-built and creative play facilities developed for communities in northern California and Utah.

3

4

5

6

7

8

9

10

PLAYGROUND
Duarte, Calif.

A large playground designed to serve all age groups together. The cylindrical form was a concrete reservoir incorporated to save the cost of wrecking. A long pergola was built straddling it; the exterior and interior were painted in gay color patterns. The interior was designed for quiet play and occasional shows or exhibits. Other facilities include a tricycle freeway with overpass-underpass, rest rooms, vegetable gardens, an apparatus area with a concrete mountain in built-up slabs, play sculpture, and open green space.

CHOPIN MEMORIAL PARK
Zelazowa Wola, Poland

This charming house and garden was the birthplace of Frederic Chopin, and have been dedicated to him as a memorial.

1 *The house from the north.*
2 *The living arbor before planting.*
3 *The house from the east.*
4 *Open-air music theatre.*

1

2

3

4

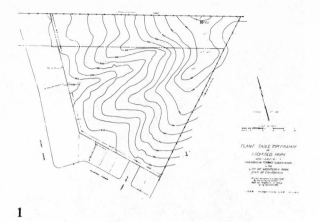

1

LA LOMA PARK
Monterey Park, Calif.

A 10-acre site, partly within a power easement, was left for park use, being too rough to subdivide. The drawings illustrate the stages in developing the design for a sound and useful neighborhood park.

   1   *The topographic plan shows slopes from 2:1 to 5:1 over most of the site.*
   2   *The grading plan shows the cut and fill necessary to develop the areas shown on the land-use plan.*
   3   *The tree plan indicates the structuring that carefully selected tree forms can bring to the land-use plan.*
   4   *The land-use plan shows the development of level terraces for active sports; picnic areas and a tropical glen on the sloping areas; play areas; social center; auto-parking.*

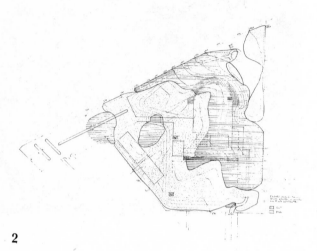

2

3

4

5 *The central-area plan suggests the refinement of form and function resulting from more detailed study of spaces for play, socializing, and quietude.*

6 *The bird's-eye view demonstrates the three-dimensional structure which will develop when topography, trees, structures, form, and function are all studied together.*

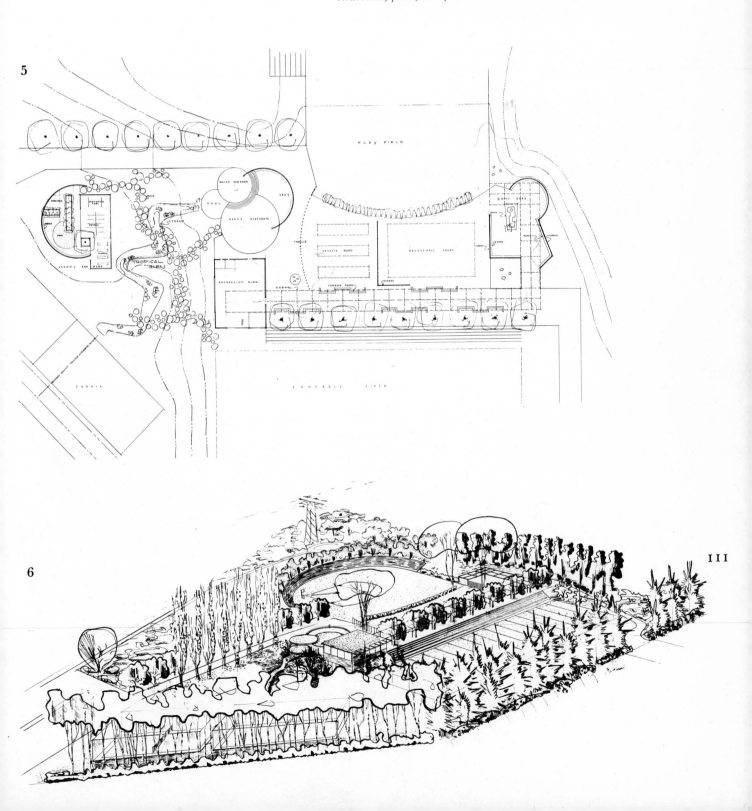

5

6

III

1

2

MUNICIPAL PARK
Buena Park, Calif.

An 18-acre flat site with a 200-ft wide power-line easement across the north quarter. The program included all the normal elements of a community park except ball fields, which were located elsewhere. This made possible the housing of the active elements in a more impressive parklike or pastoral environment, including a lagoon, contoured topography forming a large bowl, and carefully studied tree patterns exploring various relations among size, form, texture, color, and arrangement.

1 Entering the park east of the community building.
2 Main terrace toward play areas.
3 South from north end of lagoon.
4 Bridge and water feature at south end of lagoon.
5 Main terrace and control tower.
6 Buena Park tree-analysis plan, indicating size of trees. Dark areas represent large trees; medium areas represent medium-sized trees; light areas represent small trees.
7 Buena Park tree-analysis plan, indicating texture of trees. Dark areas represent rough-textured trees; medium areas represent medium-textured trees; light areas represent fine-textured trees.

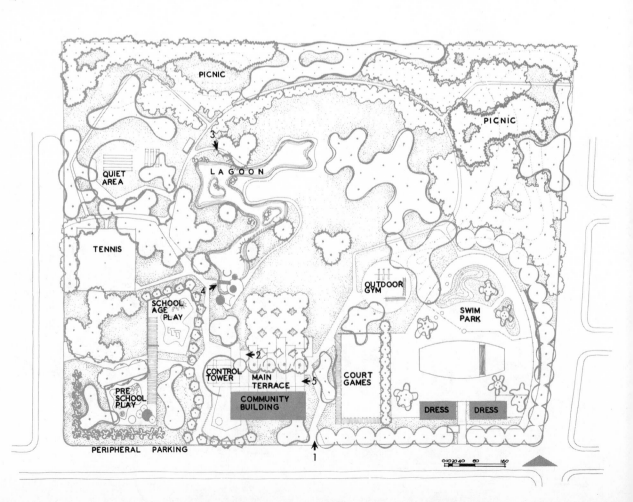

3

4

5

6

7

EAGLE ROCK PARK
Los Angeles, Calif.

The site was 18 acres of rough topography—two large gullies framing a knoll on which stands the well-known community building designed by Richard Neutra. In order to capture the space needed for community facilities, the gullies were filled and leveled, an operation requiring over 100,000 cu yd of earth. The larger area to the west was given one main level for a large playfield housing three ball diamonds and a smaller terrace containing a multi-family picnic shelter, children's play area, future campfire ring, and outdoor theatre. The eastern area was terraced in three levels: the upper containing picnic facilities, quiet games, and an outdoor gym for teenagers and young adults; the center

containing picnic facilities and children's play space; the lower, a depressed bowl, containing a so-called wilderness area of sand and boulders rimmed with pine trees, for western games.

On the upper street level, extensive parking areas were developed. Patios were designed to extend the livability of the community building. The existing playground was expanded to include additional apparatus, a contoured area of mounds and hollows housing a "fantastic village," and a play mountain with terraced wading pools. This was surrounded by a promenade overlooking the other park areas and the city beyond, repeated halfway down the sides of the knoll with another overlook pathway.

115

2

3

4

Tree patterns were designed to complement the finished topography and to give pleasant form and enclosure to the various terraces and levels. The tree-analysis plan, shown below, indicates the size of the trees. The dark areas represent large trees; medium areas represent medium-sized trees; light areas represent small trees.

5

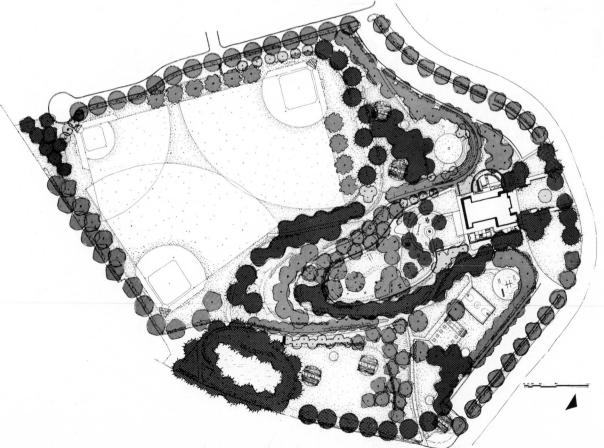

JOSE DEL VALLE PARK
Lakewood, Calif.

On a site of 15 acres, this park includes a large play-field, surrounded on three sides by extensive contoured filled mounds and ridges averaging 4 ft in height, and incorporating a series of circular, sheltered picnic units; a youth center building, and a proposed recreation building; carefully designed pre-school and school-age play areas, at present installed with more standard temporary equipment; a multi-purpose game court slab with handball wall; a proposed quiet area for senior citizens; a control building, maintenance area, and parking area. Tree patterns, structural development, and ground forms are all designed to interact to produce a whole park landscape greater than a mere accumulation of facilities.

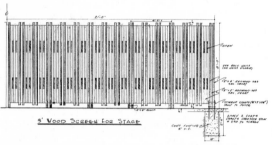

5' WOOD SCREEN FOR STAGE

STREET

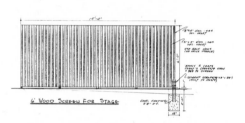

6' WOOD SCREEN FOR STAGE

ELEMENTARY SCHOOL

SCALE

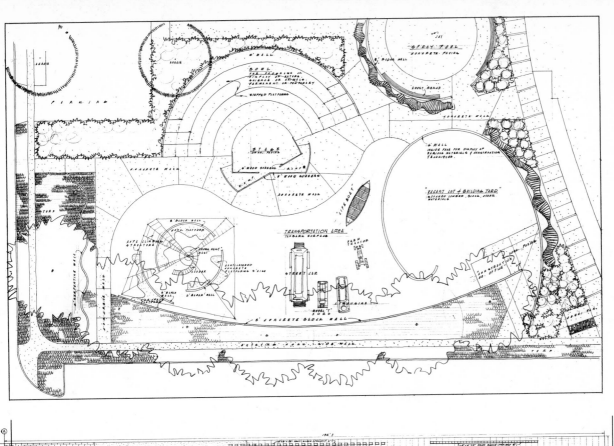

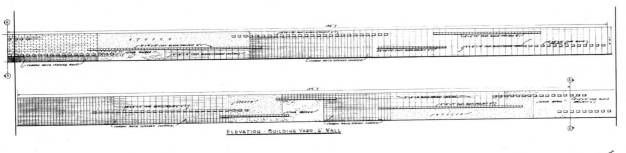

ELEVATION - BUILDING YARD, 6' WALL

119

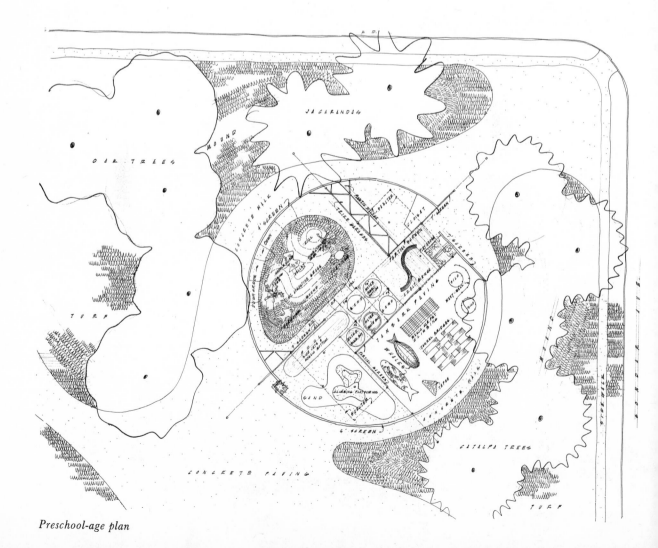

Preschool-age plan

SIMON BOLIVAR PARK
Lakewood, Calif.

On a 10-acre site, this park includes a swim-park facility designed to serve the west side of town as another serves the east side. The pool incorporates standard functional swimming and diving requirements with some playful irregularities in form. It is designed to be surrounded by a water environment; a lagoon provides wading, model boating, and casting and returns to the city the lake for which it was named, now hidden in the center of its golf course. Detailed facilities as above are provided, minus youth center and with playfield reduced to one ball diamond and a free-play area. Detailed design of play facilities is varied for individuality, although basic structural units are repeated for economy. Complete integrated design concepts are developed for this park as for all.

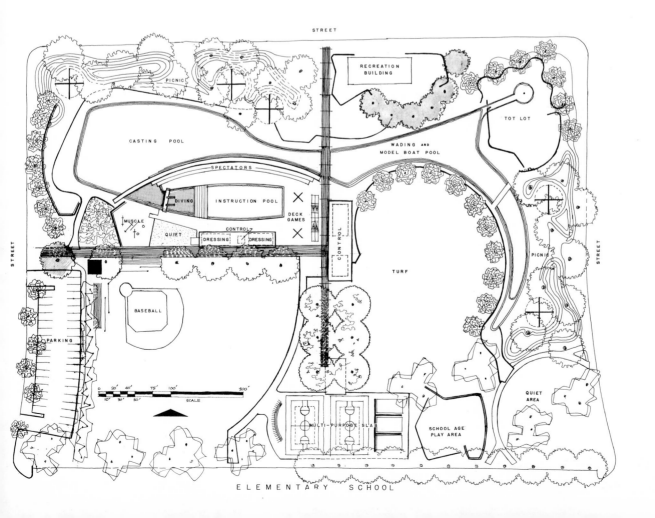

121

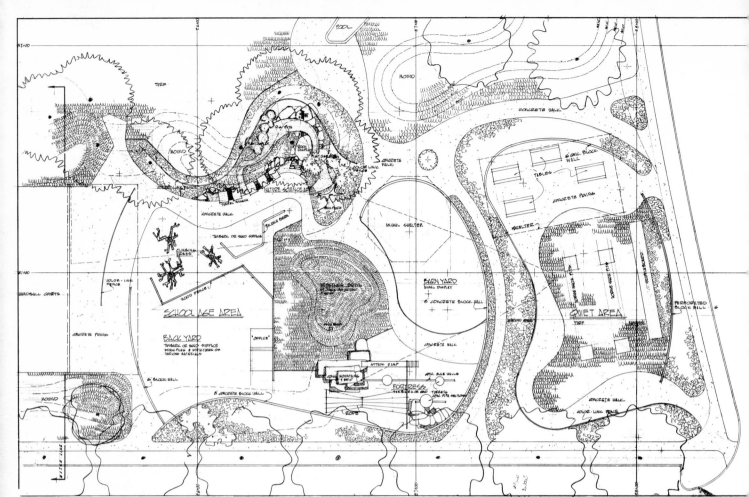

School-age plan

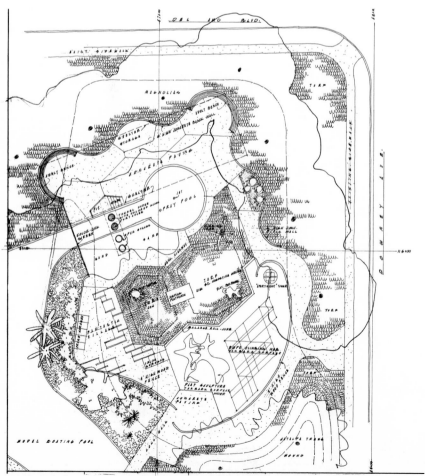

Preschool-age plan

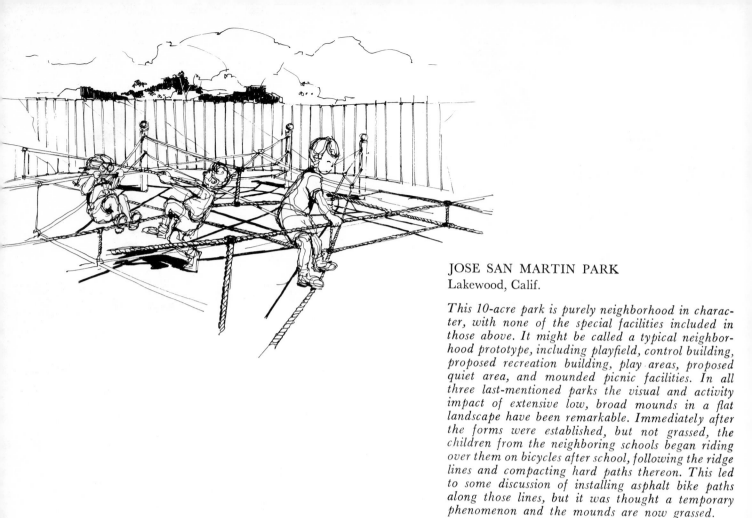

JOSE SAN MARTIN PARK
Lakewood, Calif.

This 10-acre park is purely neighborhood in charac-
ter, with none of the special facilities included in
those above. It might be called a typical neighbor-
hood prototype, including playfield, control building,
proposed recreation building, play areas, proposed
quiet area, and mounded picnic facilities. In all
three last-mentioned parks the visual and activity
impact of extensive low, broad mounds in a flat
landscape have been remarkable. Immediately after
the forms were established, but not grassed, the
children from the neighboring schools began riding
over them on bicycles after school, following the ridge
lines and compacting hard paths thereon. This led
to some discussion of installing asphalt bike paths
along those lines, but it was thought a temporary
phenomenon and the mounds are now grassed.

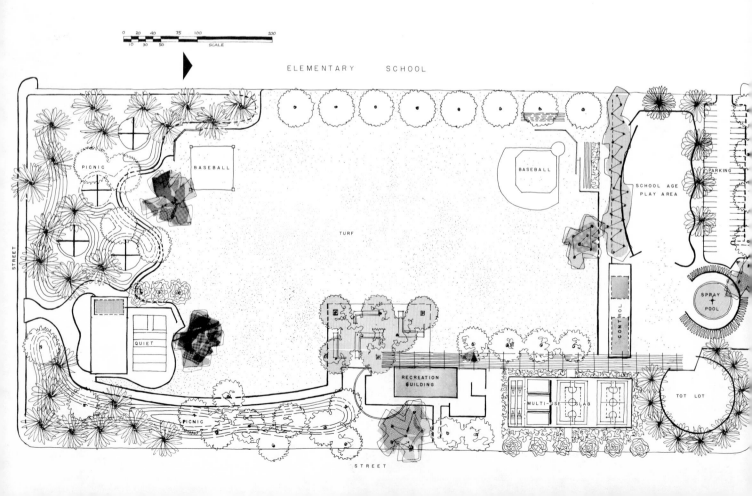

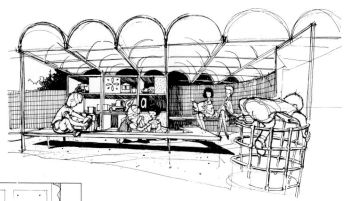

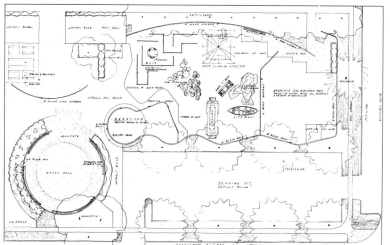

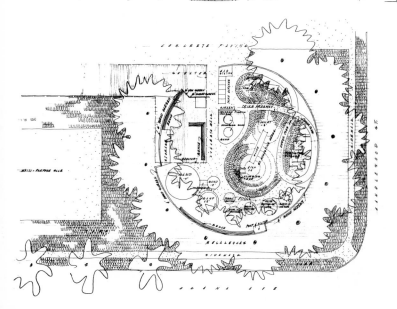

125

EUGENE BISCAILUZ PARK
Lakewood, Calif.

On a small 2-acre site in a small section of the city isolated by heavy traffic, this park was developed to include a softball field, a sheltered picnic and play area complex, designed to overlook the ball field, and an expanded control building with more social facilities. The building and ball diamond are installed; the rest is yet to come.

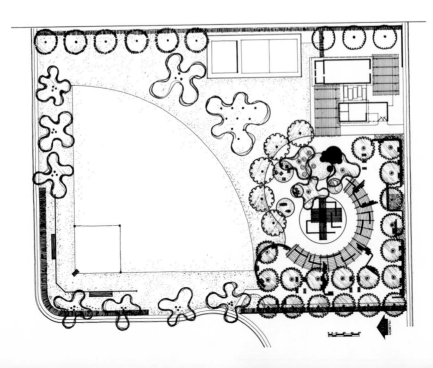

SUNSET DEMONSTRATION GARDENS
Los Angeles County Arboretum, Arcadia, Calif.

Cooperation between "Sunset Magazine" and the Arboretum produced these unique gardens, designed to demonstrate for the average home owner the well-designed use of a great many structural and natural garden materials. Incorporating five gardens—plant collector's, work center, middle income, low maintenance, and entertainer's—the development includes a remarkable variety of paving, screening, and sheltering materials.

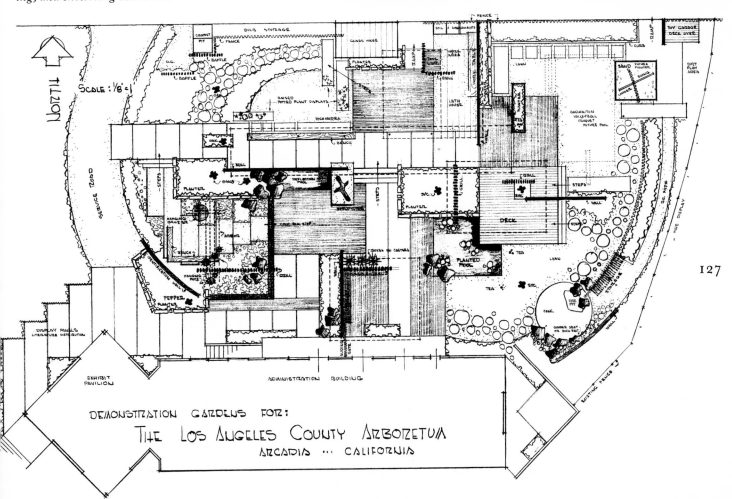

127

MARINA
South San Francisco, Calif.

In addition to the normal boat servicing and storage facilities required by this recently mushrooming activity, this plan provides a complex of other facilities designed to service the entire family, to give alternatives to boating for variety and contrast, and to accommodate lookers as well as doers. These include two restaurants, picnic facilities, 3 par golf, a health club, bowling, and a day park with sunning island, an outdoor gym, volleyball, a dance slab, a tots' seaside-adventure play area, model boat sailing, rental boating, sheltered picnicking, and children's marine zoo.

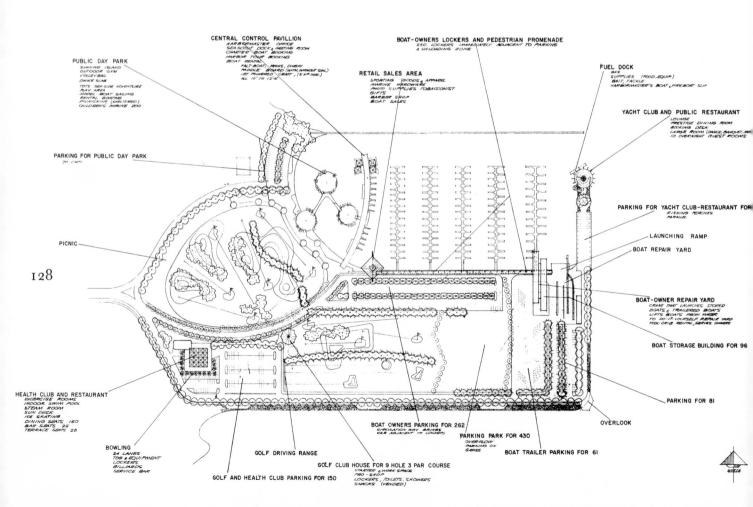

128

PUBLIC DAY PARK
SUNNING ISLAND
OUTDOOR GYM
VOLLEY BALL
DANCE SLAB
TOTS SEA-SIDE ADVENTURE
PLAY AREA
MODEL BOAT SAILING
RENTAL BOATING
PICNICKING (SHELTERED)
CHILDREN'S MARINE ZOO

CENTRAL CONTROL PAVILLION
HARBORMASTER OFFICE
SEA SCOUT DOCK & MEETING ROOM
CHARTER BOAT BOOKING
HARBOR TOUR BOOKING
BOAT RENTAL
SAIL-BOAT, MAWS, DINGHY
PADDLE BOARD (WITH, WITHOUT SAIL)
JET POWERED CRAFT, (IS HP MAX)
ALL 10' TO 12'6"

BOAT-OWNERS LOCKERS AND PEDESTRIAN PROMENADE
250 LOCKERS IMMEDIATELY ADJACENT TO PARKING & UNLOADING ZONE

RETAIL SALES AREA
SPORTING GOODS & APPAREL
MARINE HARDWARE
PHOTO SUPPLIES TOBACCONIST
GIFTS
BARBER SHOP
BOAT SALES

FUEL DOCK
GAS
SUPPLIES (FOOD, EQUIP)
BAIT, TACKLE
HARBORMASTER'S BOAT & FIREBOAT SLIP

YACHT CLUB AND PUBLIC RESTAURANT
LOUNGE
PRESTIGE DINING ROOM
ROCKING DECK
LARGE ROOM (DANCE, BANQUET, MTG)
10 OVERNIGHT GUEST ROOMS

PARKING FOR PUBLIC DAY PARK
70 CARS

PARKING FOR YACHT CLUB-RESTAURANT FOR
FISHING PERCHES
PARALLE

LAUNCHING RAMP

BOAT REPAIR YARD

PICNIC

BOAT-OWNER REPAIR YARD
CRANE THAT LAUNCHES STORED
BOATS & TRAILERED BOATS
LIFTS BOATS FROM WATER
TO DO-IT-YOURSELF REPAIR YARD
TOOL-CRIB RENTAL SERVES OWNERS

BOAT STORAGE BUILDING FOR 96

PARKING FOR 81

OVERLOOK

HEALTH CLUB AND RESTAURANT
EXERCISE ROOMS
INDOOR SWIM POOL
STEAM ROOM
SUN DECK
ICE SKATING
DINING SEATS 150
BAR SEATS 25
TERRACE SEATS 28

BOAT OWNERS PARKING FOR 262
CIRCULATION WAY BRINGS
CAR ADJACENT TO LOCKERS

PARKING PARK FOR 430
OVERFLOW
PARKING ON
GRASS

BOWLING
24 LANES
TOG & EQUIPMENT
LOCKERS
BILLIARDS
SERVICE BAR

GOLF DRIVING RANGE

GOLF CLUB HOUSE FOR 9 HOLE 3 PAR COURSE
STARTER & WORK SPACE
PRO-SHOP
LOCKERS, TOILETS, SHOWERS
SNACKS (VENDED)

GOLF AND HEALTH CLUB PARKING FOR 150

BOAT TRAILER PARKING FOR 61

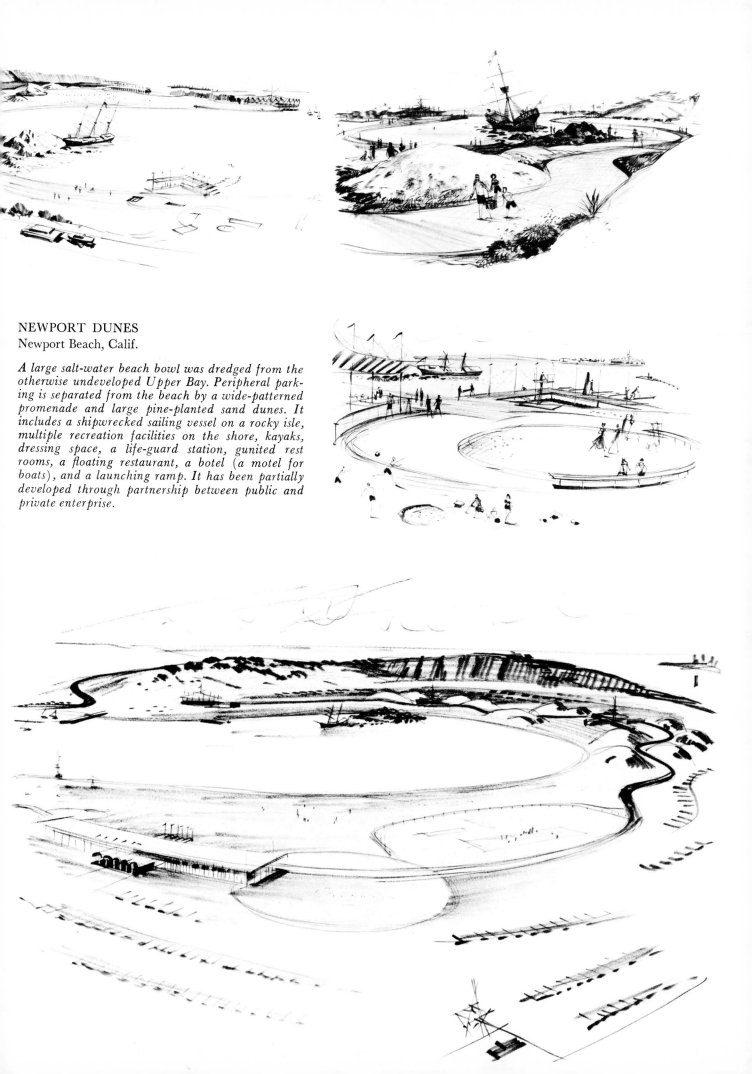

NEWPORT DUNES
Newport Beach, Calif.

A large salt-water beach bowl was dredged from the otherwise undeveloped Upper Bay. Peripheral parking is separated from the beach by a wide-patterned promenade and large pine-planted sand dunes. It includes a shipwrecked sailing vessel on a rocky isle, multiple recreation facilities on the shore, kayaks, dressing space, a life-guard station, gunited rest rooms, a floating restaurant, a botel (a motel for boats), and a launching ramp. It has been partially developed through partnership between public and private enterprise.

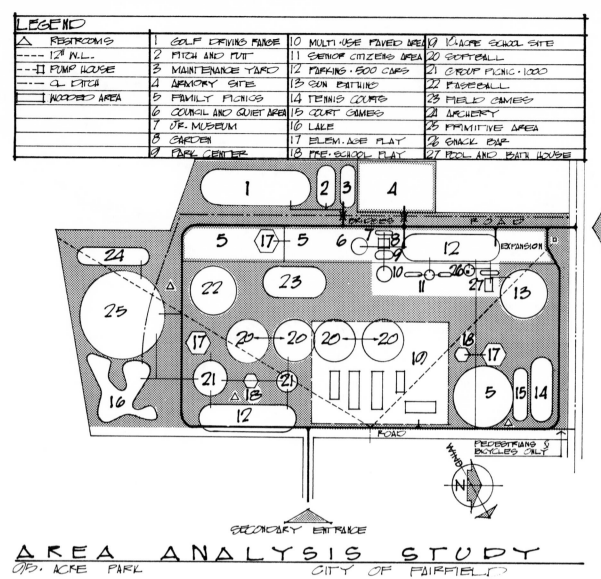

AREA ANALYSIS STUDY

O.5. ACRE PARK   CITY OF FAIRFIELD

FAIRFIELD PARK
Fairfield, Calif.

This is a long-term park project, begun in 1955 with the construction of a swimming pool and bath house. Yearly, as the city budget permits, additions are made in accordance with the master plan. In the second year the kiosk, lounging area, wading pool, and some planting were added; in the third year some lawns and sprinklers. In the fourth year approximately one-half of the remaining site was graded and trees were planted. Water lines were also extended.

The site was flat, barren, and subject to almost continual wind. The basic arrangement calls for extensive windbreak planting to protect the most-used areas and an arrangement of the various areas in relation to wind protection and to each other according to the activities involved. Thus, the principally active areas are along the west side in the lee of the windbreaks, leaving the family and group picnic areas and their related play areas to the east. Open meadows in the center of the park are for free play.

Ground modeling will provide intimacy, separation, and relief from the flatness of the site.

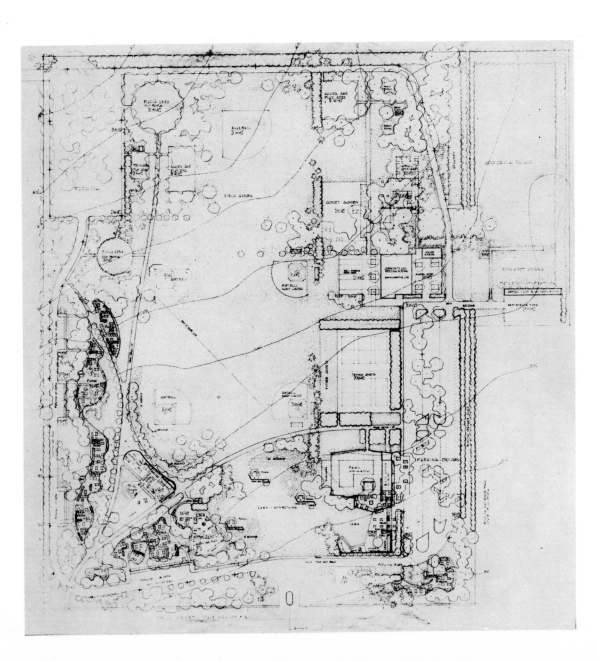

131

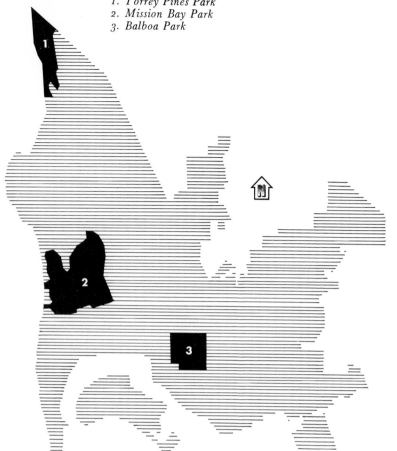

Location of major parks of San Diego:
1. Torrey Pines Park
2. Mission Bay Park
3. Balboa Park

MISSION BAY PARK
San Diego, Calif.

This study is not a technical plan for the park, not a land-use plan, circulation plan, or engineering design. All this basic planning has been done well by the city planning department, city engineer, United States Army engineers, and innumerable city and state departments. It is not an architectural plan for any building, nor is it a site plan for any portion of the park; detailed designs for specific developments have been and will be prepared by city departments, consultants, and the lessees and their architects.

This study is a set of design principles and concepts to guide the integrated development of the whole park. It studies the complete physical environment—architecture, landscape, waterscape. The principles here will coordinate the work of the many designers, technicians, administrators, and businessmen who will have a say in what Mission Bay Park

will be like in the future. Those people will be concerned with a specific part of the park, a certain facility. This study suggests the character and spirit of the whole park which must be far greater than the sum of the parts. It predetermines the general character of the total scene and of the large component areas which can be dealt with as cohesive units.

WHY ARE CONTROLLING DESIGN PRINCIPLES NEEDED?

Mission Bay Park is a huge land area under city control. It is almost four times the size of Balboa Park. It will be central in the San Diego metropolis and will affect and be affected by its surroundings. Like Balboa Park, it will be a symbol of San Diego to the city's millions and to visiting millions. The city has recognized that an area of this size and importance cannot be allowed just to grow. It has initiated this project which calls not only for comprehensive land planning but also for comprehensive visual planning. What people see is their basis for judging the park and the city; what people see in Mission Bay Park will largely determine the kind of time they have there.

Like many other large recreation facilities, Mission Bay Park will be a partnership between public and private enterprise. About 300 acres have been set aside for commercial lease sites—for restaurants, hotels, botels, sports fishing, boat and fishing tackle rental, slip rental, boat storage, repair, launching facilities, and the full gamut of sales and services related to aquatic activities. The lease sites are only 7 per cent of the total land area of Mission Bay, but they are the key to the character, spirit, and quality of the entire park. On these sites will be the park's largest buildings, its most bustling activity, and the most people.

If each of the many small parcels of this critical acreage was subject to strictly independent private decisions as to physical development, the result would be chaos. Three hundred acres of uncontrolled whimsey in building styling, signs, parking, and landscape patterns could produce in Mission Bay Park a visual disaster which would downgrade the entire park. Neighboring Mission Beach is a convenient example of the urban anarchy which could threaten Mission Bay Park.

This problem of architectural control of commercial lease development led to the retention of Community Facilities Planners as design control consultants to the city. But it is impossible to view the design of the commercial lease sites apart from the design of the park as a whole. Private and public facilities together will produce the parkscape. Therefore, private and public facilities alike should follow the basic design principles. Only in this way can the huge park be made an entity with its own very special personality.

Mission Bay Aquatic Park has 4600 acres of land and water, 31 miles of shoreline dredged out from a marshy duck pond to offer recreation for three million people annually by the year 2000. The 12,000 boats which will call Mission Bay their home port will provide a quiet panorama of sails, a mighty spectacle of power boats, an impressive rank of yachts, and a playful covey of paddleboats. The 3 million people will fish from piers for the afternoon, board a commercial vessel for a deep-sea fishing weekend, swim, hike, ride, picnic, play, explore, or watch. They will stay in fancy and less fancy hotels, cottages, trailers, and tents. They will eat at chowder bars or elegant restaurants. They will lie on the beach and watch sand castles under construction or wander about and watch fishing and boats and tides and the plants and animals who like the edge of the water.

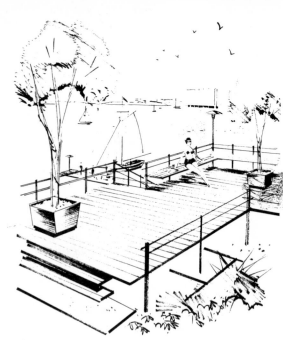

2 *The width and character of the promenade zone should vary.*

3 *Extend platform over the water.*

WHAT WE SEE: DESIGN PRINCIPLES

Surrounded and fringed as it is by urban development which, regardless of use or economic level, has "the monotony of variety" (when everything tries to look different and all ends up feeling the same), Mission Bay Park has both the need and the opportunity to become a great oasis of quietude, calm repose, unhurried meaningful activity, and rich sensory experience of happily balanced relations between land, water, buildings, trees, and paved and green open spaces.

This can be achieved by close control of all physical development, however small or large, with the unified character of the entire park and its various zones and areas constantly and clearly in mind. The visualization of ultimate character must be strongly felt in terms of qualities, forms, materials, and relationships; yet it must remain flexible enough to absorb new creative and functional ideas.

The theme of unity with variety pervades this study. Each is necessary to the other. Unity without variety means simply monotony. Variety without a strong unifying force is chaos. To achieve both unity and variety is the essence of the design problem of the park. The interrelated principles discussed in the following pages do not fall into a simple list.

DEVELOP AQUATIC PARK CHARACTER

Mission Bay Park is a water park. The direction of all its facilities toward water recreation is the dominant theme in the Mission Bay Commission's statement of purpose. There will be water-oriented activities of all kinds for all ages and all skills.

The physical form of the Park has been designed to provide maximum shoreline around its bays, lagoons, basins, and coves. This form makes it possible to orient the maximum number of people toward the water. Mission Bay will be a hub of marine activities for those who come to participate in them and for those who come to watch. The park is also for those who come to relax, to meditate, to enjoy quietly the near-water atmosphere. All facilities must be designed for lookers as well as doers, and substantial areas in the eastern half of the park will be primarily for quiet recreation. That the doers and the lookers will almost always be in view of each other will lend richness to the experience of both.

CONNECTION BETWEEN LAND AND WATER

Water orientation requires physical design for the maximum connection between land and water. Despite the abundance and variety in form of the shoreline, there is little variety in its development. There are but two kinds of land-water relationship in the park now—gradual beach and harsh riprap. (The riprap is the steeply sloping rocky bank which separates and protects the land from the water.) Existing and planned beaches have been designed at uniform slope and width throughout the park. Riprap, with its rocky texture, steep constant slope, and straight lines, tends to divorce the land from the water.

Design should henceforth seek for maximum connection between land and water—variation in width and slope of beaches and riprap, steps, ramps, and piers and platforms out over the water. These connections will make possible movement perpendicular to the shoreline—out from it, or down from it to the water. Perpendicular movement contrasts and balances with the normal parallel movement along the shoreline which emphasizes the unity of the smaller coves within the large bay. This balance of movement perpendicular and parallel to the shoreline will add variety to the experience of both doers—boatmen, fishermen, swimmers—and lookers—tourists, visitors, and the superintending public.

PROMENADE

The single strongest physical element creating continuity between land and water should be a promenade zone where people can walk along all shorelines throughout the bay. The promenade should parallel the top of the riprap or edge of the beach—not rigidly but freely meandering over land, riprap, beach, and water, linking land and water in ever-changing ways, at the same time creating a space for circulation, activity, and relaxation. The promenade zone is not only for walking; it is for sitting, chatting, sketching, watching boats launch, seeing a fish get caught, and possibly even for diving. The width should vary but should not be less than 15 ft.

The walk itself and all its "furniture"—seats, rails, lights, tree boxes, trash receptacles—should be consistent in character throughout the park but variable in color and detail within the areas of the park. For instance, three typical walk treatments might be: boardwalk, pebbly concrete, sandy or gravelly trail; these would be used throughout the park. Seats, rails, planting, and other furnishing elements would be consistent in form but variable in color and detail.

4 *Botel unit and promenade should link land and water.*

5 *Provide a variety of walking levels over both land and water.*

6 *The Promenade—a space for circulation, activity, relaxation.*

7 *To improve the water view, housing should be raised at least one story above the ground.*

RAISED HOUSING

Guests in the hotels, botels, and other bay housing accommodations, should be continually aware that they are in a great aquatic park. Unfortunately, topography and shoreline where present guest housing is situated make it difficult to see the water and its activity from more than a few steps back from the shoreline.

To improve the water view, housing should be raised at least one story above the ground; this will have the added advantage of freeing the ground surface for parking and other uses. Multistory construction will improve views as it goes up, and taller buildings will offset the flatness of water and terrain, creating landmarks visible from afar. Careful location of multilevel buildings will avoid congestion and sprawl. At least 50 per cent of all guest-housing floor area should be at least one story above the ground, and guest rooms and guest-gathering places should be planned with a view of the exciting, everchanging bay.

OTHER LAND-WATER LINKS

Additional measures to improve further the physical and psychological connection between land and water may include the following:

WATER ELEMENTS of all sorts—canals, basins, fountains, pools, lagoons—should be designed and developed throughout the land portions of public and lease areas. These will not only improve the interest and quality of the land developments, but will also provide a comfortable transition in scale and detail to the broad expanses of the bay.

MARINE SYMBOLS—pilings, piers, boardwalks—should be incorporated in land facility developments. Individual designers will be responsible for the maintenance of dignity and good taste, and the avoidance of cliché.

8 *Multistory construction will improve views from within and create landmarks.*

136

Botel units, snack bars, bait stands, benches, shelters, diving boards, and platforms should be provided on extended pier or float areas over the water, to create a leisurely approach to the experience of boats and water, to increase the comfort of boat users, and to provide an observation platform for pierside superintendents.

A variety of walking levels over both land and water, and the possibility of crossing from land to water above the promenate will make it possible for more people to see more activity from more interesting angles.

HOW NOT TO DEVELOP AQUATIC PARK CHARACTER

There is always a temptation in a waterfront setting to copy from the waterfronts of the world, to recreate Italian fishing villages, Paris quays, and South Seas beaches. This approach has been consciously rejected for Mission Bay, for it would lead to movie set design, self-conscious quaintness as contrasted to real and meaningful recreation. This study wholeheartedly advocates capturing the flavor of the world's waterfronts—the excitement and interest, the variety of activities, the beautiful views, the variety of land and water relationships.

UNITY: MAKE THE PARK AN ENTITY

The emphasis on aquatic atmosphere and activities will tend to unify the park. But does the identification of the park stop there? Further means must be used to give the park a visual identity. It is the visual impression that will make Mission Bay a place distinguished from other areas where swimming, sailing, and fishing are available.

Here are some unifying visual factors which can be used to make Mission Bay an integrated unit. Some are subtle, some are obvious. Some will be in the foreground, some will be subconscious. Together they will combine to say "This is Mission Bay Park."

WATER, *the continuity of the horizontal plane surface in the bay waters and in smaller bodies on land, is almost always calm, underlining its unifying effect.*

BEACHES *show the continuity of slope and sand.*

STRUCTURES *include continuity of material and detail in riprap, seawalls, slips, piers, floats, boardwalks and continuity of materials and colors in buildings.*

SIGNS *which have continuity of color, typography, symbol, shape, size, and height limits.*

STREET FURNITURE *should have continuity of detail for street lights, street signs, markings, curbs, gutters, gratings, bridges, railings. These should be of individualized design for the park, softer, more colorful, more informal than the city's standard street furniture.*

PAVING FOR CARS, *again individualized for Mission Bay Park, should be distinguishable from the standard asphalt paving of the world's parking lots. Colored rock rolled into the surface of all park roads would immediately identify the park. For all but the most intensively used parking areas, softer and more parklike materials—gravel, sand, Bermuda grass—should be used.*

PAVING FOR PEDESTRIANS, *the continuity of perhaps three types of "pedestrian paving," includes boardwalk, pebbly concrete, sand or gravel trail. Variations such as brick, flagstone, colored concrete, should be held to a minimum and used only where most effective.*

TREES AND SHRUBS. *The continuity of basic trees—eucalyptus, pine, palm, and rubber tree groupings—and the continuity of color patterns in shrubs and ground covers will draw the park together. These basic species and patterns allow interesting and meaningful variety, but avoid a haphazard and confused impression.*

9 A variety of land-water links: different levels, different activities, different views.

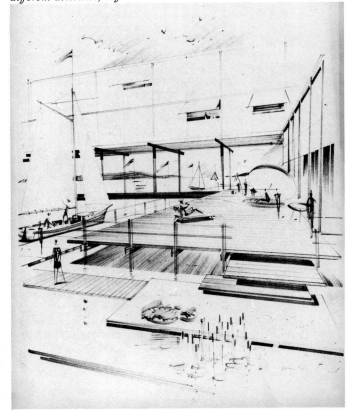

PARK BOUNDARIES

If the park is to be an entity, it must be finite. You should know when you are in it and when you are out, when you are entering and when you are leaving. The park must be gently but firmly separated from the small-scale urban patterns surrounding it.

The park boundary should be marked either by a peripheral road, or by a walkway like the promenade zone proposed earlier, or both.

A peripheral road will delimit the park very clearly. It is obvious which side is in and which is out. Wherever possible, the peripheral road should give a view of the park's water activities. The outer drive on Crown Point is a good peripheral road, affording fine views of the park side. This study recommends extension of this road to the northeast.

A walkway—an extension of the promenade described earlier—can serve as a very pleasant park boundary if carefully planned. Where the park abuts private property, this will be the appropriate device for defining the edge of the park. Even where peripheral roads exist, walkways are needed on the park side. Mission Beach already has the beginning of a promenade zone in the form of a broad sidewalk bordering the Bay beach; this could be extended and developed as a delightful welcome to the Bay.

Seen from the encircling roads or promenade, the distinctive paving material, signs, landscaping, buildings, and special park "furniture" will further notify the visitor that he is in Mission Bay Park.

The idea of through highways traversing the park is diametrically opposed to the principle of making the park an entity. Highways chop up the park rather than unify it. To 60 mph traffic, the park would be 2 min. in a vast urban continuum. At this point, talking about the park as a unified whole, we would only suggest thoughtful reconsideration of where and why traffic must speed through the park and, where through routes are imperative, how to accomplish them gracefully. The section of this study dealing with circulation further analyzes the design problems of through and intrapark traffic.

VARIETY: PROVIDE VARIATION IN PHYSICAL ENVIRONMENT

This is the other aspect of the design problem, the other side of the unity-variety coin.

The millions of people and thousands of boats will bring endless variety to the Mission Bay parkscape. Their activities will be infinitely varied. They will give life to the physical framework. But the physical framework needs to offer variety to the people—not confusion and formlessness, but diversity and choice.

Here are the design variables which, within the

framework of the total park, individualize its smaller areas or zones. These factors should be selected and combined to give each zone or area its own character.

SHORELINE *is the meeting of land and water, abrupt, rough, gentle, smooth; bluffs, palisades, piers, floats, poised boardwalks, marsh, docks, beach, tide pools, caves, river basins, dams, dikes, grassy slopes, rocky abutments, seawalls, buildings extending over the water.*

TERRAIN *can be flat, hilly, sandy, rocky; turf, beach, meadow, cliff, dunes.*

WATER SHAPES *are either channel, inlet, cove, bay, or reflecting pool.*

STRUCTURES *may range from overhang to setback, rambling to high-rise, small bait shack to large hotel. The intelligently limited variety of materials, colors, heights, and forms must be considered.*

TREES *have ample variety in use and selection within the four basic groupings. Variations in size, silhouette, structure, texture, and color are available.*

SHRUBS AND GROUND COVER *include controlled variations in patterns of form, texture, and color.*

By use and by topography, existing and proposed, the park articulates naturally into six major zones. Each will have its special character. The unifying and the variable factors should be planned to develop and strengthen that character. Before describing each of these zones, however, let us discuss in greater detail some of the design subjects touched on above.

These subjects—topography, architectural and tree patterns, circulation and parking, street and outdoor furniture—are of critical importance in establishing the aquatic character of the park and in achieving the unity and harmonious variety discussed formerly.

TOPOGRAPHY: PLAN THREE-DIMENSIONAL LAND FORMS TO CONTRAST WITH WATER

The word for Mission Bay today is: flat. The water is flat. The elevation of surrounding lands and islands is only 5 to 12 ft above water level. The major exception is Crown Point, rising to 59 ft above the water. Cabrillo Island is proposed to rise to 20 ft, and the southeast corner of the park along the floodway is proposed to be 44 ft in elevation. The figures indicate a continued flat and featureless topography. The fine, curving forms of islands and shorelines on the park master plan lead one to expect comparable contoured curves in the skyline profiles of those land forms. What a disappointment to discover that such profiles are not planned and that the islands are merely flat shapes a few feet above the water.

Mission Bay needs three-dimensional land sculpture to contrast with and emphasize the clear plane of the water, to reflect the fine, typically Californian hills north and east of the Bay, and to make more interesting and dramatic relations to the water possible for more people by elevating them above it on slopes or terraces. Compare the view from Crown Point with that from Ventura Point. Compare Lido or Balboa Island, whose flat interior lots have no view and no water character, with Catalina Island where every view, even though far interior, is exciting.

This study recommends strongly that:

1. Cabrillo Island be filled to its maximum elevation. It is possible, with 8 per cent allowable fill slope, to build the Island to heights of 40 to 80 ft above the water.

2. The sides of the bay be built up to their maximum.

3. Tierra del Fuego Island receive enough additional fill to make possible the development of contoured ground forms.

4. Offsite fill be imported during development operations, to improve both soil conditions and ground forms.

All developments and changes in topography must be carefully designed and must be subject to design review. New contours should be scaled to blend with existing contours; a small mound on a large flat site is worse than no mound at all.

ARCHITECTURE AND LANDSCAPING: DEVELOP USEFUL AND BEAUTIFUL ARCHITECTURAL AND TREE PATTERNS

No limitation is to be placed on the architectural style used by any tenant or public agency. Instead, this study establishes standards of land coverage, open space, circulation and parking, colors, materials, and signs. Using these as guides, architects can evolve interesting, beautiful, and functional structures. Following these standards, buildings throughout the park will vary and yet show a family resemblance, a distinct Mission Bay character.

Buildings and plantings should be organized to complete the visual experience of topographic spaces. Buildings and planting working together can achieve environmental control and visual impact impossible for either alone. They can enclose and shelter spaces, separate them from or join them to other spaces; they can enhance, by framing in depth, distant vistas or intimate detail; they can contrast openness and closure, sun and shade, hard and soft light, smoothness and roughness, formality and informality. Tree patterns should supplement architectural patterns; accentuate the topography; humanize roads and parking areas; and create a sense of space, scale, and three-dimensional unity throughout the park and within each zone.

The objective for the park landscape as a whole is the achievement of relationships between continuity and accent. The continuous elements are low buildings, trees, grass, roads, and water. The accents which enliven and enrich the view are tall buildings, engineering structures, steep topography, stony points, and vertical trees. In use as well as physical appearance we are seeking a delicate balance of continuity and accent, flow and interruption, action and reflective pause.

The architectural and landscaping standards have been designed to encourage the balance of continuity and accent. The harmonious colors and finishes, selected for their appropriateness to a waterfront environment, will help to develop continuity; accent will come through special design features, furnishings, and displays. The tree and shrub groups, also selected for suitability in a bayside setting, will help create continuity, while allowing accent in individual selections and designs. Similarly, the coverage provisions are intended to produce both continuity and accent in views of the water and preservation of open space.

139

11

12

13

14

FURNITURE: GIVE ALL STREET, PIER, AND BOARDWALK "FURNITURE" A SPECIAL MISSION BAY CHARACTER

Lighting structures, benches, signs, trash receptacles, telephone booths, fire alarm boxes, and similar items of outdoor "furniture" will appear throughout the park. They are numerous and conspicuous. Let us not overlook these important elements. Let us instead design them especially for Mission Bay Park; let us use them to identify and unify the park and express the marine atmosphere. Many otherwise fine developments have fallen far short of their visual potential because ordinary, standard furniture was used, standard items which are often uncomplementary to each other and to their environment. At Idlewild Airport in New York, by contrast, the soaring, sculptural lighting structures magnificently express their air-oriented location.

The illustrations suggest how these important elements of furniture can be used to identify this great marine park and how, through form, color, and material, they can represent their nautical environment and relate to each other. Each item of furniture can and should be simple, interesting, functional, and harmonious with the park atmosphere. The illustrations are only ideas, not specific designs. This study recommends that a competent design firm be employed to design all these necessary elements to enhance and blend into the park environment.

140

15

16

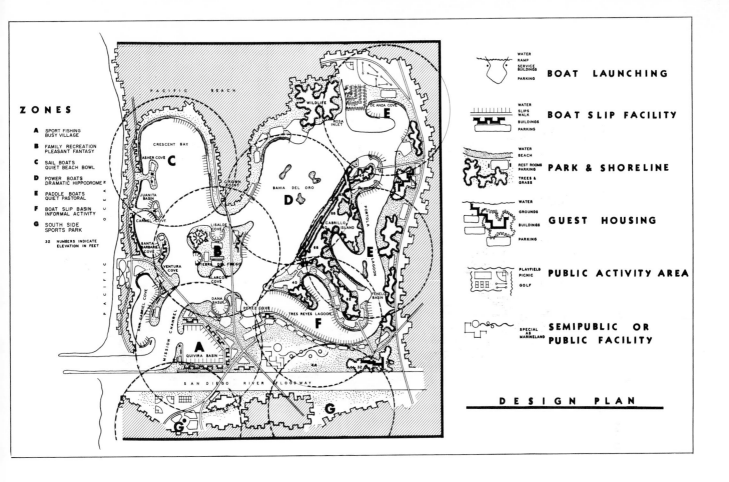

DESIGN PRINCIPLES FOR THE ZONES OF MISSION BAY PARK

Mission Bay Park articulates naturally into seven major zones, based on existing and proposed use and topography. Each can have individual character and atmosphere, yet still belong to the park. Each has its own problems and possibilities. The seven zones with their major use and a two- or three-word characterization of their atmosphere are:

LOCATION	MAJOR USE	ATMOSPHERE
Quivira Basin, Dana Basin, Yacht Club Point, Point Medanos	Sport fishing	Busy village
Tierra del Fuego Island	Family recreation	Pleasant fantasy
Crescent Bay, Santa Clara, El Carmel, and Gleason Points and surrounding coves	Sailing, beach	Quiet beach bowl
Bahia del Oro Cabrillo Island— west side	Power boats	Dramatic hippodrome
Portola Lagoon, De Anza Point and Cove, Cabrillo Island—east side	Paddle boats	Quiet pastoral
Tres Reyes Lagoon	Boat slips	Informal activity
South side, south of floodway	Uncertain	Sports park

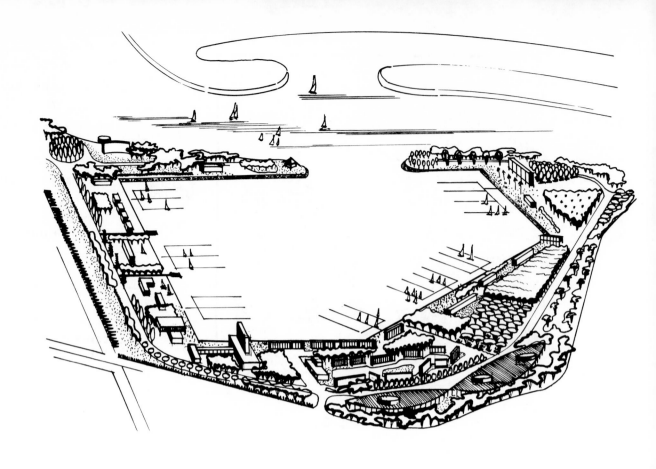

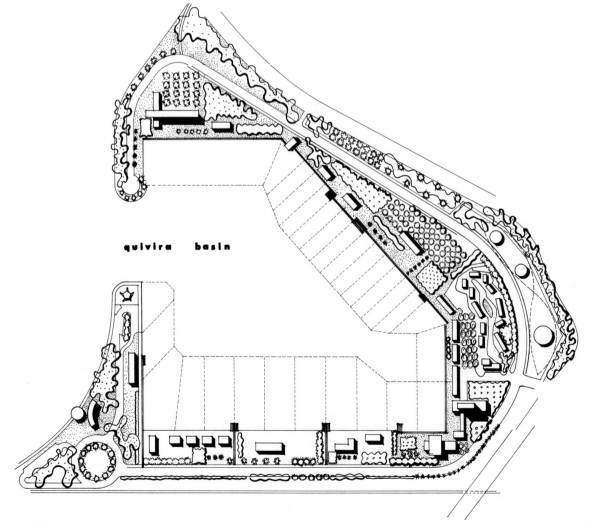

quivira basin

142

PROTOTYPE TREE PLANTING PLAN

17 *Private yacht clubs in a public park have a responsibility for setting an example of quality.*

18 *Pleasant fantasy.*

143

19 *Dramatic hippodrome.*

20 *Quiet pastoral.*

THE OVERALL VIEW

An overall view of planned uses reveals a shortage of community buildings in the park. The one small one on Santa Clara Point will scarcely be able to meet the needs of a developing aquatic center and a growing metropolis. It is urged that community buildings with facilities for various age groups and for community groups with water-oriented interests be developed throughout the park—one in each of the seven zones, if possible.

An overall view of the visual character of the park highlights certain general qualities. To the south and west a waterfront character will dominate with structural connections between land and water. To the north and east a park character will dominate with a more gradual and natural meeting of land and vegetation with the water, using such elements as topography, rocks, and perhaps streams. Scale—by which we mean the apparent size of the various parts and the whole picture in each area—will vary from small and intimate along the west coves and east lagoons to broad and dramatic in the power boat and sail boat areas.

Time-scale, or the rate of speed at which an observer proceeds through and experiences the park, is a complex quality. The landscape must be designed to provide pleasant experiences for pedestrians as well as for those traveling on horses or bicycles and in small boats, sail boats, power boats, and motor vehicles.

THE QUALITY OF RECREATION

Wayne R. Williams

To fulfill the park's potential, to live up to the quality of design which this study envisions, the whole quality of recreation in Mission Bay Park must be very special. Present land-use plans for the park indicate that recreation will be water-oriented and varied—two qualities which we have used as design principles as well. What beyond this?

Mission Bay Park recreation can be a meaningful experience, as well as a form of relaxation and a change of environment. The beauty of the environment contemplated in this study will help to create such an experience. A meaningful recreation experience is one which involves the individual, enriches his personality, has carry-over values in learning, growth, and health throughout the week and year.

Let Mission Bay recreation not suffer from "spectatoritis." There will indeed be an abundance of things and events to be looked at and absorbed, from water skiing contests, power boat races, and model yacht regattas to quieter spectator sports like watching children on the beach and seeing the sport-fishing boats come in. Let there also be abundant opportunity for people to participate together in creative, enriching, interesting recreation; let there be a chance to give, to express, as well as to take. Disneyland is a feast for all the senses. It is a marvelous place to walk or to sit; the variety of vehicles and environments to sit in is incomparable. But the opportunity to be involved, to create, express, and participate, is limited.

Mission Bay Park must offer meaningful recreation to "all the citizens of San Diego and visitors from outside communities," states the Park Commission. This means all age groups. This means women and girls as well as men and boys. Each age group and each sex has its own recreation needs and preferences and the park's facilities and programs should be specially planned to provide for them, such planning to develop out of a deep and subtle understanding of what those needs and preferences are.[1]

To fill out the recreation program and facilities offered at Mission Bay Park, the resources of all kinds of groups, clubs, societies, and agencies should be tapped, as well as the resources of governmental departments and business interests.

The policy of partnership between public and private enterprise has already been established. This concept can be broadened to encourage a boat dealer, for example, to offer instruction in boat handling at the park.

Every public park has had to face the "problem" of community groups. The question seems to be: do such groups constitute private interests incompatible with the public nature of the park?

These groups are one of the most discussed aspects of modern American culture. People today form groups for companionship, to be more effective, and for diverse other reasons. Additional leisure time has multiplied the number of clubs, committees, societies, and associations interested in a thousand different subjects. They are special interest groups in that the members share a special interest. But who are the members? They are the public—organized.

These groups can contribute in many ways to meaningful recreation and can enrich the park's program and facilities. They may give instruction or stage exhibits and demonstrations. Since these groups are usually trying to get more people interested in their subject, many of their activities have appeal for the general public as well as their own members. The fly-casting club can offer demonstration and instruction (perhaps using equipment provided by a sporting-goods store). This is fun not only for those who come to learn but also for those who instruct, sharing their skill with others. All parties are involved. An incidental benefit of welcoming these special groups and making them a part of the park is that, through their activities, they can carry some of the recreation-programming load that would otherwise fall on overburdened city recreation personnel.

A superb example of the advantages of a government-business-community group partnership is the Los Angeles State and County Arboretum. The arboretum features shrubs and trees from all over the world and carries on plant research. It is also a historical preserve and a bird sanctuary. Its acquisition and development has been a joint effort of state and county governments. There are gardening classes conducted by volunteer professionals and amateurs. Planting and classes are conducted by the local herb society chapter. The Orchid Society meets there and arranges displays. There is also a unique garden for the blind. School classes and scout groups use the Arboretum for various projects. A few years ago, "Sunset Magazine" established its famous "demonstration gardens" there with the cooperation of many manufacturers of all sorts of construction materials; these are used by landscape architects and other professionals as well as by the lay public. The Arboretum's facilities are open for meetings of various community groups.

The stimulating array of facilities and activities offered at the Arboretum could only have been achieved in the few short years of its operation by this enthusiastic and cooperative partnership of diverse interests. It is far more than an unusual park to visit. It is a place to explore in all weathers and seasons; it is a place to participate in; a place to visit often because it is constantly developing.

Mission Bay Park has the unprecedented opportunity to provide a similar vital facility for everyone—the highest quality water-park in the world.

There are two methods of creating a "perfect" aquatic park:

1. Have unlimited funds

2. Have a detailed master plan of needs, showing which of these needs can be provided by public agencies and which needs must be satisfied by other sources. The park commission then can refer to this master plan to select individuals and groups who will provide the needed services. And in fact, the park commission should initiate an aggressive program to obtain the needed services and programs.

In summary: the many community clubs, business organizations, and groups interested in aquatic activities and studies should be welcomed to Mission Bay Park and urged and aided in every way to enrich the park through their efforts. This approach has been implicit in the city's master planning to date; the detailed plan referred to above represents a logical outgrowth.

---

[1] The book *Recreation Places* by Wayne R. Williams (Reinhold Publishing Corporation, New York, 1958) has an excellent chapter on this subject: "Needs of Different Age Groups."

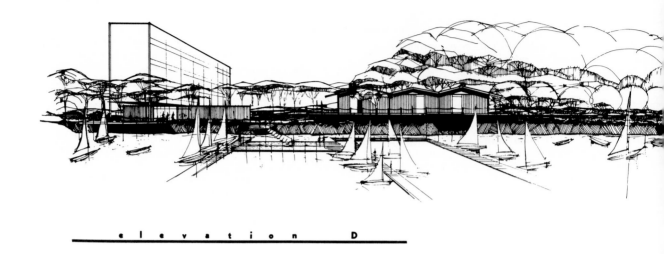

elevation D

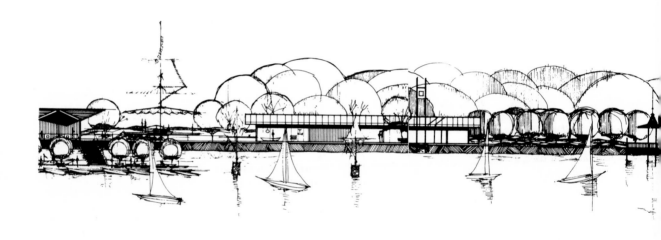

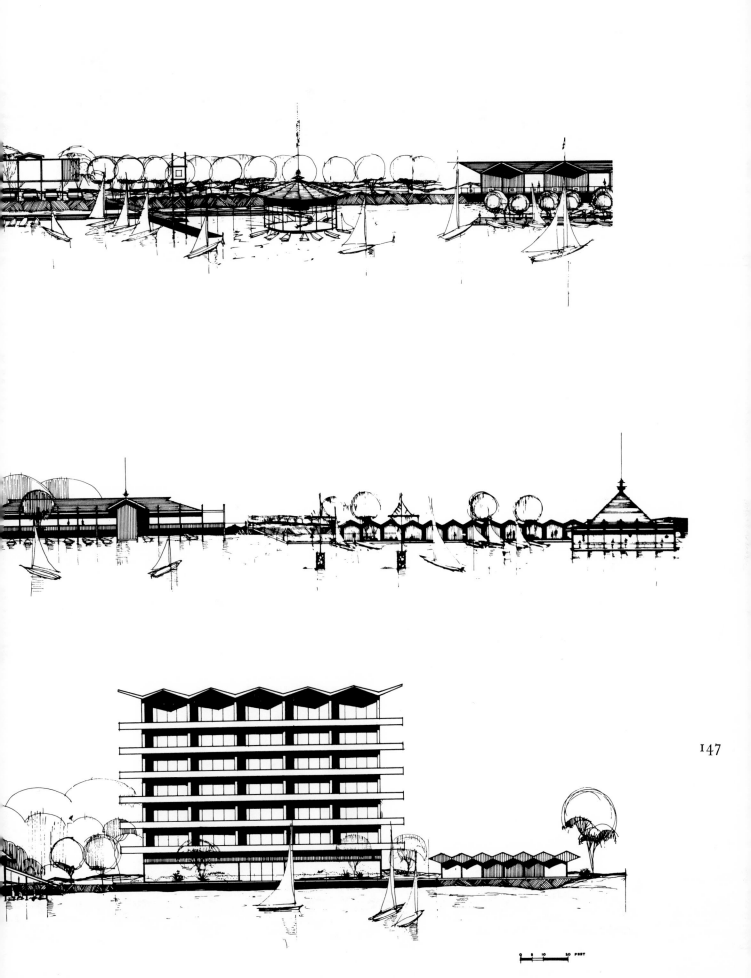

147

0 5 10   20 FEET

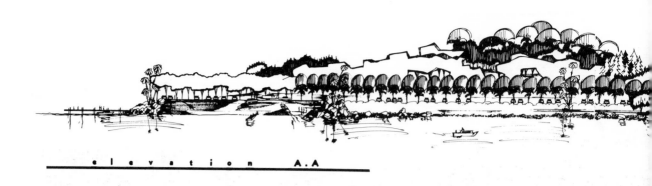

elevation A.A

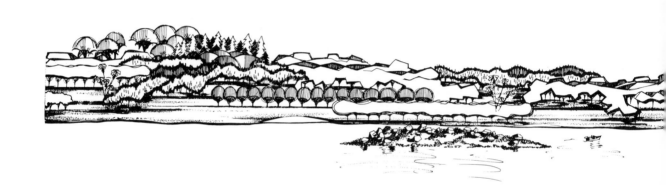

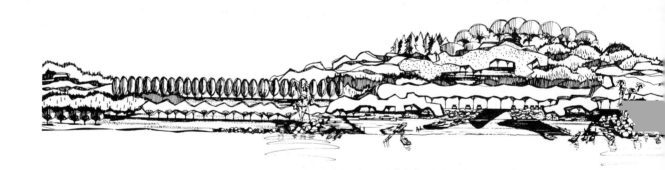

148

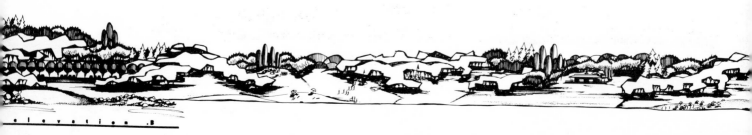

elevation B

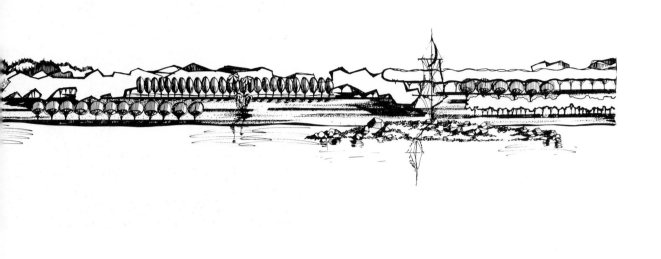

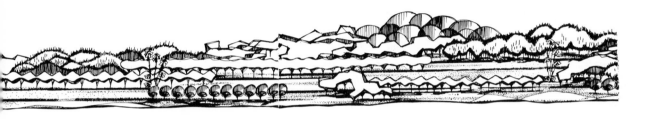

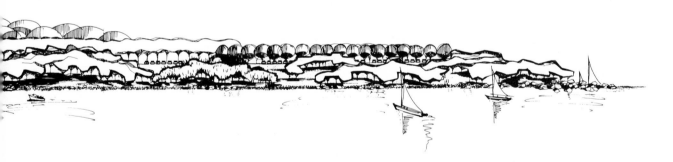

149

elevation .c

A CHECK LIST OF HOW MISSION BAY PARK MEETS ALL RECREATIONAL NEEDS

BIG MUSCLE ACTIVITIES

Walking and riding
  (bicycle and horse) — *Many types of experiences, across water, alongside of water, above looking down, etc.*

Boating — *Two kinds of areas, one for competitive (either power or sail) and another "mood" boating area for people to work on their own boats.*

Swimming
  Above water — *Quiet warm water for infants and senior citizens as well as for the adventuresome adult.*
  Under water (skin diving) — *Weird world of underwater. Human aquarium—safer than in the ocean (no sharks), therefore beginners can enjoy and learn.*

Outdoor gym — *"Muscle beach" atmosphere, space, and seating (maybe) for people watching informal muscle activities or a meet.*

SOCIAL ACTIVITIES

Picnicking — *Picnic areas for large groups as well as intimate scaled areas for very small groups.*

Social events
  Outdoor — *Outdoor areas for special events—level, relatively unobstructed—power source for special lighting requirements. Some area close to the water; another area away from the waterfront and protected from wind.*
  Indoor — *Community buildings should be provided. Buildings might be expected to be found adjacent to water and away from water.*
  Combined indoor-outdoor — *Buildings and surrounding space should be designed for flexible indoor-outdoor use.*
  Social events related to boating races, etc. might extend to the whole event. Hippodrome—flags heralding outdoor assembly of contestants. Indoor areas for judging, victory dances, films of events, etc.

GAMES — *Indoor and outdoor games; volley ball, shuffleboard, quiet games.*

MUSIC AND RHYTHM

Informal music — *Mounds—outdoor perches as places near teen-age areas, perhaps near "muscle beach," for bongo groups and other informal amateur bands. Places indoors for amateur music, for dancing.*

Formal — *Band concerts, professional band playing for special events in the grandstand of Hippodrome, or on a float, or upon a bandstand that has been carefully placed in the total park to become a focus. Formal band playing for dances.*

Natural sounds — *Planting trees that point up the sound of wind in leaves. Sensitive recognition of rhythm of water and tides against sea walls—slapping under buildings that are built over the water.*
  Hanging bamboo chimes for wind sounds.

HAND-INTELLECT ACTIVITIES — *Boat building and repair area to serve this basic need for manipulative activity. Model boat building area as well as sailing. Marine-related crafts, fishing poles, lines, shell jewelry.*

CREATIVE PLAY ACTIVITIES — *Sea "adventure playground," boats children can dream on, paint on, and imagine on. Sunken boat. Historical sea events locale; teen-agers' and adults' version of imaginative play is to be involved in the planning and design and production of park areas and facilities, not just the use of them.*

NATURE SCIENCE LEARNING ACTIVITIES — *Establishment of a marine coastal zoo and arboretum.*
  Classroom lecture halls, laboratory space plots, marine-related science study areas (indoor and outdoor).

ANGLESEA, N.J. OCEAN CITY, MD. REHOBOTH, DEL. WILDWOOD, N.J. SEA ISLE CITY, N.J. CAPE MAY, N.J.

MENTAL ACTIVITIES

High level—college and graduate work level

"University by the Sea" for seminars, institutes—involves an atmosphere of serious study, contemplation—open plaza spaces. Housing required for people coming a long way—invitational, like Asilomar or Arrowhead or Aspen.

Public school level

Public schools should have a headquarters here. For all outdoor learning activities—this would parallel and augment San Diego School camping program in which they are leaders.

Public level

Day camp for character building, organization classes, adult education; or sponsored by community organizations in sailing protocol, fishing techniques, boat making—all marine learning situations.

COLLECTING

Collecting, though less important today than in grandma's day, still important recreation need to be met.
Places should be provided for displays by collectors and for working with the collection, perhaps in the community building. Some collecting is closely related to the nature science area—collecting specimens: birds, plants, rocks, shells, etc.

SERVICE

Helps environment if users also serve as committee members or workers in the producing and servicing areas and facilities, and as programmers and leaders, because through close identification comes a respect for the place, hence less drain on public personnel.
Serve as judges, board members, resource people (consultants), guides, philosophers, initiators.

RELAXATION AND SOLITUDE

Areas must be provided, and always protected from encroachment, that offer the user freedom from competitive and action-inspired activities.
Places to be lazy in, repose, contemplate. This means control of the sights and sounds of active sports, all without the loss of a water-related environment. Environment should be provided that allows the individual to have a place.

REFERENCES FOR CHECK LIST

National Recreation Association
American Recreation Society
California Committee on Planning for Recreation Park Areas and Facilities
Metropolitan Recreation and Youth Services Council, Los Angeles County
National Advisory Council on Regional Recreation Planning

VII

STREETS AND SQUARES

Parks and multiple building projects up to several hundred acres or more are about the largest single specific design and development jobs normally undertaken by architects and landscape architects. The occasional new town built from scratch must be considered separately. While some projects, particularly in the urban renewal area, may include sizable segments of cities, the complete, balanced community landscape is a still larger problem. Access to it, and connection between the various projects and the multitude of private structures which make up the community, is through the public rights-of-way, the streets and highways. This is the community landscape within which the average citizen spends important segments of time.

We might say, taking the liberty of oversimplification, that there are two typical kinds of street landscape in America. One, found in a few of the older cities of the Eastern seaboard—Boston, Charleston, New Orleans French Quarter—stems from the irregular, small-scale, unpredictably variable, charming, and natural European prototypes described by so many travelers. This we might call the preindustrial pattern—there is precious little of it in these United States. The other, the postindustrial, the product of practical engineering and surveying, T-square, triangle, and transit, the opening of the West via the Homestead Act and the large-scale subdivision of the whole continent, and the subsequent constantly mounting pressures of wheeled traffic and land speculation, is all too familiar to us. The gridiron plan, universal, all-encompassing, endless, all things to all men, allowing the most access to the most separate parcels of land, the most flexibility in their sale and resale, changing uses, development and redevelopment—this has been the American contribution to city planning and urban development. Subsequent improvements—development of the major highway grid on mile squares with service roads, the minor highway grid on alternate half-mile squares, the intermediate quiet streets which have ingenious patterns for not going through—have not changed the essential nature of the gridiron. Whether curved or straight, whether bending with the contours or cutting straight through them, the essential nature of the grid is that it reverses the historical dominance of streets by buildings and open spaces. With the Indus-

trial Revolution and the motorized traffic and urban congestion which it spawned, the street took over, as circulation for vehicles, with pedestrians strictly secondary. It now dominates our cities. When Haussmann cut his boulevards through Paris to control the city, he little realized that this was the beginning of a plague that would destroy cities yet unborn. The great architectural concepts of boulevard design, which give Paris its magnificence, seem foreign to the practical American mind. (Century City in Los Angeles will try to introduce them.) The implied responsibility of street dominance of the urban landscape is that streets should be made the most meaningful human experiences in the city. Instead, they remain places of regular hazard, occasional catastrophe, and sudden death.

The landscape of the street is bounded, not by the right-of-way lines, but by the buildings which front on it. Wall Street is a multistoried canyon whose paving rarely feels the direct sun; the typical suburban street, lined with one- and two-story castles of Cinderella, modern, or ranch house persuasion, includes landscaped front yards and street façades, vistas down unscreened side yards and driveways, and the tree-tops which may appear in the rear above the roofs. On all sorts of streets, wherever space permits, street-trees lining the parking strip have embodied the community effort to offset and harmonize the play of individualism in front yards and driveways. Many an Eastern and Midwestern town, not yet sufficiently urbanized to lose its old trees, is saved visually and climatically by the canopy the trees spread over it during warm weather. Modern designers, frustrated by the monotony and confusion of most American streets, view with longing the European and Latin tradition of urbane street-fronts combining quietly elegant row-house façades and neutral garden walls with handsome gates and fascinating, grilled glimpses of lush interior gardens. But any existing situation can be solved as a design problem if it is recognized as such, rather than as a collection of disconnected miscellanea.

The modern street dominates our communities everywhere by virtue of the hazard from stray speeding cars which it may carry anywhere. We stop, look, and listen before stepping off the curb into any street, if we want to live out our three score and ten.

1

2 *Welwyn Garden City, England—before.*

Autos and pedestrians are always incompatible. The modern street dominates our communities visually whenever its width from building to building exceeds about twice the height of those buildings (Sitte),[29] as it does in most outer urban and suburban areas. When this occurs, the only salvation for the ubiquitous standardized asphalt and concrete is trees. They must be a size which will grow tall enough or broad enough to dominate the street—there are multiple variations of this combination. Trees of such size need adequate root space, roughly comparable to the volume of the top, and ground area, perhaps half the spread or the height, whichever is greater. Few parking strips are equal to this demand. Hence, the great search for the neat, narrow, nontroublesome tree which will conform to the city's requirements, based on no consideration of trees whatsoever. Seldom will such ideal trees attain the height or spread needed by the street. Rational and cultured city planning, if it accepts trees as land-use elements, will begin to think in terms of adjusting the city to the desirable tree, rather than adjusting the tree to a mechanical street formula based on narrow economics and rigid nonthinking rules.

It is, of course, possible to plant street tree patterns in front yards, with greater freedom in selection and arrangement, if the cooperation of property owners can be guaranteed, or if the front yards become part of the street by specific easement for trees or by general title. The problem of responsibility for maintenance will have to be solved in either case.

In addition to providing adequate space for trees, it is necessary to coordinate underground and overhead utilities and street lights in order to avoid conflicts which may eliminate the trees. This is easier to say than to do, but persistence, determination, and cooperation between engineers and tree men can solve the problem. Other objections to street trees—litter, falling leaves and branches, dripping, cutting off too much sun and light—can be solved by combinations of careful selection of species, efficient mechanized maintenance, and adequate continuing communication between authorities and citizens. The Greenway concept, developed under Edmund Bacon in Philadelphia for urban continuity, is a creative recognition of the structural potential of trees.

With or without street trees—although much less

with—the modern street remains a visual problem. It has no beginning or ending, only sides which are rarely adequate in scale or interest. Even if adequate in scale, the regular alignment of façades forced by zoning setbacks and intensity of land-use produces a monotonous continuity which is rarely offset by detailed quality. Our most interesting and pleasant streets are those in downtown or well-to-do residential areas where architectural scale and detail, and landscape richness, combine to offset the basic two-directional continuity of the street. Most streets are boring slots through which we hurry, with varying danger to pedestrians, cars, and ourselves. Every intersection is a hazard and a source of visual confusion and stagnation, as one endless vista crosses another.

Gridiron patterns are at their worst on flat land, or land of constant slope. Irregular topography, even if gentle, will immediately introduce variation in scale and vista, unpredictability, and visual interest and stimulation. This will be true even if the gridiron refuses to recognize the contours, as in the classic example of San Francisco. Great urban landscapes such as this too often seem to result from the persistent influence of great natural land forms surviving the muddling processes of development, more than from any widespread human sensitivity or genius. It is only when we find great conceptions on uninspiring land—as Washington or the Chicago lake front—that our faith in the potential of human creativity revives.

It is clear that industry, the auto, and the modern city are here to stay. What is done is done. Problems begin with the conditions which exist. We are not going to embark on a foolish and fruitless effort to turn back the clock to the quiet and picturesque scenes of Medieval and Renaissance Europe. However, those scenes contain healing qualities which we have lost. Consideration of them, in relation to our monumental and staggering urban problems, may help to provide a key or an insight. For instance, Sitte points out in detail how successful urban spaces are produced by nearly complete architectural enclosure, with street entrances so arranged as to be at right angles to normal lines of vision.[30]

There are some interesting detailed aspects of the impact of street and highway design on the land-

3 *Welwyn Garden City, England—after.*

4

scape. One is that their details—curbs, gutters, sidewalks, paved cross section, fire hydrants, lights, trash containers, benches, mail boxes, fire boxes—are among the most standardized elements around the world. One hundred years or more of functional engineering design, with little regard for visual quality, has produced a system of street furniture and detailing which is quite similar in quality, if not in precise detail, wherever we go. This system is reliable and functional, but completely lacking in possibilities for subtlety, variation by district or neighborhood, or emotionally appealing sensory qualities. Perhaps this would be asking too much, but I for one would like to feel that the serpentine sidewalks of Rio are not the last word in street enrichment, and that the new starred terrazzo sidewalks of Hollywood Boulevard are not typical of our new civic taste.

Active traffic planning makes major changes within and in the gridiron. Major highway streets, separated from service streets by 10- to 15-foot planted dividing strips, create maximum planting installation and maintenance costs for minimum visual satisfaction. Here again, the form of the vegetation is a by-product of engineering design, rather than an integrated part of total street design. Major highway streets, with residential lots backing up to them, are apt to become a visual shambles. Rear lot lines are enclosed with a great variety of cheap, shoddy, improvised fences and walls which turn their worst faces outward. The 5- to 10-foot parking strip between curb and lot lines is apt to be left to weeds and trash. Once again, responsibility for landscape quality falls between private ownership and public authority. We have already mentioned the likelihood that major freeways will take curving forms which are both antigridiron by virtue of their own functional needs and anticommunity because of arrogance or apathy, or both, on the part of the public authorities. Too often, freeway systems, with their sculptural forms, exciting bridge and ramp structures, and wide rights-of-way, will miss the opportunity for planting design of comparable scale and inspiration through narrow-minded penury on the part of the puritanical guardians of the public purse.

Visually our streets need:

1. Visual terminals at reasonable irregular intervals in both directions, achieved by adjusting hori-

5

6

7

155

8

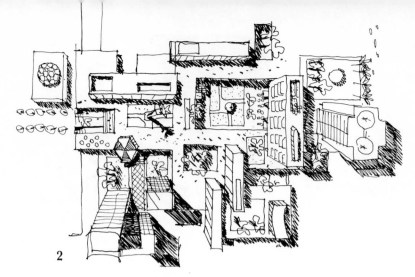

1　　　　　　　　　　　　　　　　　　　　　2

zontal or vertical alignments. While this may shock the traffic-must-go-through-at-all-costs school, it happens fairly often by accidents of topography, real property, or disconnected subdivision, with more or less pleasing results. Displacement of a street by its own width will achieve this potential. Traffic flow can be returned to its original smoothness by angular connections extending a half block in either direction. There will remain, of course, the problem of establishing a physical element at the point of change which will justify its important position. All these things can be accomplished if the will exists. Much more brutal changes in urban patterns are pushed through for more limited objectives.

2. Enclosure at the sides by buildings, trees, or open space adequate in scale to the width of the street. Open space, with a pleasant distribution of trees, ground forms, and/or structural elements, will function as visual enclosure. The country road through varied pastoral landscape does not require lining with trees. Together with the problem of enclosure will go the designed control of some cross street openings. This might be accomplished partly by street closure, partly by tree selection, partly by construction of arches or second story bridges, depending upon the situation.

3. Breaking up and irregularizing the rigid alignment of street front construction along setback lines. As can be seen in older and less developed or controlled neighborhoods, or in downtown areas where old buildings have been torn down to make way for parking lots, every step in this direction improves the street landscape by opening up unexpected spaces and vistas at irregular intervals and reducing the monotony of the continuous unbroken wall of building façades. This can, of course, be done much better by design than by accident. It will also be done better by cooperation among property owners than by directives from City Hall. But community cooperation for the benefit of all is larger than either of these.

The visual design of street sides must, of course, be adjusted to the speed for which the street itself is designed. This will vary from the 15-mph intersection and school crossing limits through the 25-mph urban and residential limits, the 35-mph suburban- and 45-mph exurban-highway limits, to the 55-mph

or more of the open road. Each speed zone may be said to have its own required scale of enclosure design. Of course, in actual practice, speed zones are derived from the nature of the enclosing elements, and are designed to protect those who use them. This is as it should be. Streets should be subordinated to the pedestrian spaces they serve. Only when we reach the scale of planned throughways, highways, turnpikes, freeways, and parkways does the sculptural form of the roadway and its enclosing elements assume primary design importance. This problem has received absorbing and detailed study by Boris Pushkarev, student of Christopher Tunnard.[31]

The street which serves pedestrian land-uses along its entire right-of-way should be designed as a reciprocal relationship between the needs of pedestrians and those of people in vehicles. As access to the right-of-way becomes more limited, the design of the road space becomes more an end in itself. But, aside from wilderness and large-scale farming areas, there will always be pedestrian uses adjoining the right-of-way, and reciprocal visual and functional relations will exist even if physical access is limited. In fact, the more limited the access, the greater the impact of the right-of-way upon the community or countryside through which it cuts. Good design processes will redesign the disturbed peripheral areas parallel and integrated with the design of the right-of-way development. (See Gruen on pedestrian oases.[32])

It is in the relationship between auto living and pedestrian living that the problem centers. While there is a good deal of living in cars by young adults, Sunday drivers, drive-in movie and restaurant patrons, campers and trailer towers, the auto is primarily a transportation and communication element. It stretches our lines of contact between the principal points of daily and weekly life enormously, compared to any previous period. Home, work, and recreation can now be a triangle with sides up to 50 miles long, compared to 5 for a pedestrian community. The weekend region can have a 300 to 500 mile radius for hardy drivers, compared to 25 for good walkers. The substitution of horse for pedestrian community reduces the contrast by only a fraction. We are, of course, disregarding the fact that the auto citizen also has more leisure time than the pedestrian or horse-riding citizen.

3

4

The extension of contact lines between points of principal living has eliminated the necessity, and thus made it possible to ignore the responsibility, for planning them in functional and organic relations to one another. Housing, work places, and recreation facilities need no longer be close to each other for each individual. This has produced a certain whimsical mobility in all three. We live where we please, the employer provides work where he pleases, and recreation is where we find it. Convincing and persuasive presentation of originally planned community patterns which would reduce car time (or other transit time) in getting from point to point, would establish the existence of a clear alternative to this aimless pattern. This is more than an alternative to whimsy. Without it we may all smother in smog in the last great traffic jam on the final obsolete freeway. As Albert Wohlstetter has said:

There are, however, critical points at which private aims become a public concern. For example, as individuals we decide where to live, where to work, and how to travel to and from work; but without public guidance these decisions are not likely to be compatible at all. In fact they have brought about an intolerable congestion and an urban sprawl desired by no one.[33]

There is a general consensus among planners and designers on the need for much greater separation of cars and pedestrians, and for greater and clearer articulation and separation of local, intermediate, and through traffic, than we have today. With some isolated beginnings at designed exceptions, we are still living and planning with a preindustrial concept of traffic so slow as to need no articulation. The physical symbol of the need for separation of cars and pedestrians is the superblock, a half mile or more across, in which there are no through streets. Expansion in scale and diversification in detail of the street pattern makes possible the development of pedestrian oases of a scale adequate for quietude, greenery, and relief from the imminent roar and mayhem of traffic. Of course under standard subdivision practice this same expansion makes possible a worm's-nest type of street pattern in which one is easily lost with no resultant change of scale or release from noise and confusion.

Squares. G. E. Kidder Smith in *Italy Builds* said:

The square for too many planners has meant only an empty area in the city about which traffic circulates, its rigid shape determined by the blocks that hem it in and its spatial qualities by the fortuitous buildings of its four sides. A square, however, is more than a hole in a city. . . . The square, or piazza, in Italy is far more than so many square feet of open space; it is a way of life, a concept of living. . . . The square, the street and the sidewalk are their living space. . . .[34]

Sitte's examples and studies are primarily of the most concentrated urban spaces, dominated by fine architecture and kept open for the display of good sculpture and fountains and the circulation of crowds of people. These spaces serve as relief, outlet, and focus for crowded and congested dwellings, shops, and workplaces around them. This follows the Renaissance ideal of the city as an architectural organism, separated precisely from the natural and rural countryside around it. This concept was excellent for the townscape of the times. Our problems are immensely expanded horizontally and vertically, more complex, confused, a peculiar blend of rigid gridiron lot-and-block land planning and the inclusion of a vast miscellaneous collection of natural, agricultural, industrial, commercial, and residential elements within its hopscotch pattern.

The highly developed architectural square is relevant to the most concentrated centers of urbanized activity. There is little room in this concept for the free elements of nature. Sitte speaks of:

. . . a clash between nature and stylistic monumentality . . . the charming result of bringing rustic beauty into the midst of a great city where nature's work and man's architecture can be seen in fascinating contrast . . . the more green open space the better. But if art is to be taken into account, we must give some thought to where and how the green open areas should be located. . . . What is the value of a plaza, created especially to provide a view of a building, if we permit vegetation to obscure the view? . . . Just as we have no suitable plazas for monuments, we have none for trees. In both cases the deficiency is due to the "block" system of planning.[35]

While our limitations today are rigid and frustrating, behind them, in the wealth, extent, and energy of our physical development, there is a potential for a wide richness of landscape, inconceivable in Renais-

157

sance times. The concept of a conflict or contrast between pure architecture and pure nature, traditional in urban thinking and reinforced by the separation of architectural and landscape design thinking, is too narrow and limiting for the multiple diffusion of our problems today. Certainly, pure architectural open space without landscape elements, and pure natural landscape without architectural elements, are both relevant to humanized landscape design today. But much more generally relevant is the wide range of variable combinations which now spans the former gulf between these two theoretical extremes. We are capable of producing infinitely richer relations between fine architecture and sculpture on the one hand, and fine plant, ground, water, and rock forms on the other, than were conceived in any historical prototypes. To requote Lucio Costa, ". . . the modern concept of urbanism . . . abolishes the picturesque by incorporating the bucolic into the monumental." [36]

Paul Zucker traces the relation of square to town much more comprehensively as "the artistically shaped void" from antiquity to early America.[37] Since then we have done little with the idea. European influence on the Eastern seaboard, and Spanish influence in the Southwest, made little headway against the vast, narrow-minded practicality which subdivided the heart of the country, Middle West and West, into a gigantic gridiron. Recent years have seen renewed efforts by architects, planners, and designers to introduce square and plaza space into the rigid block-and-street patterns of our cities. Whether as architecturally enclosed open spaces, or as open settings for buildings, sculpture, or fountains, they are demonstrating anew the potential and the need for variation and enrichment of pedestrian experience on our streets. And they are demonstrating that, in spite of gridiron patterns and high-density psychology, when it has the will, design can find the way.

The examples shown here are not all urban or high density. The line at which square becomes park, whether in terms of degree of architectural enclosure, size, or relations between structural and natural materials, is as debatable as the line at which patio becomes square. Definition can become a vice and categorizing a sin. But we might perhaps say that squares range from spaces whose quality is determined absolutely by the architectural enclosure, through those whose enclosure is more modest and whose quality comes more from elements within them, to those whose quality comes almost entirely from architectural or sculptural elements within them. Parking lots and playgrounds are open spaces set aside for special functions, and parks are open spaces dominated by vegetation in which structures are minimized. However, such definitions ignore, and tend to eliminate, those spaces of intermediate nature which may have maximum validity. Equilibrium between open space and architectural enclosure, between structure and sculpture or greenery, between elements within and elements around, between vehicles and pedestrians, is a peaceful objective seldom

conceived in the battles between architectural, sculptural, landscape, traffic, or parking dominance.

It should be clear by now that these general divisions of landscape spaces and elements into various categories are arbitrary, overlapping, and somewhat interchangeable. This is true of most efforts to categorize the unbroken continuity of the landscape. In addition to the relations already discussed there are many others: between patios and buildings (the latter shape the former), between patios and squares (smaller and larger, shaped by single or multiple buildings), between building groups and squares (the former shape the latter), between streets and squares (both shaped by buildings, varying proportions and relations between pedestrians and vehicles), and between squares and parks (smaller and larger, less or more green?). These are categories for convenience, but their elements are real and they are useful. Their usefulness will vanish with any effort to formalize or institutionalize them. As used here, they demonstrate continuity in expansion of scale from individual to community spaces, and the need for richly variable sequence in this two-way hierarchy of landscape space-scale. From a landscape point of view, actual development projects fall naturally into these groupings which make possible the construction of a bridge from isolated single-site design to inclusive community design. Thus they make a useful, but not the only possible, framework for discussion and work.

Emphasis on the continuity of reciprocal relations between individual and community scale will make an effective brake on two constant tendencies: one, to focus down on isolated itsy-bitsy corners of charm where we forget the jungle around; and the other, the grand and sterile gesture of the big-time planner who sees the crowd only as a faceless and shapeless mass of undifferentiated humanity. Finally, we see that the landscape of neighborhood, community, and region is a continuity which includes all the elements we have discussed and many more. These are united visually and geographically no matter how glaring the conflicts between charm and brutality, clamor and quietude, gaudiness and monotony, or apathy and aggressiveness may be. Any community landscape is a whole, greater than the sum of its parts; but the unprecedented disorder of twentieth century urbanism produces the most indigestible wholes in the history of man.

1

KERSEY KINSEY OFFICE BUILDINGS
Studio City, Calif.

This is a series of relatively small one- and two-story office-store buildings acquired over the years and remodeled to accommodate various tenants. A continuous new façade and a row of existing palm trees tie the buildings together. A new paving pattern and smaller scale planting beds along the curb increase the sense of unity and the pleasure of passing through, rather than by, the office fronts. A central parking entry makes a break in what might otherwise be a monotonous façade. Next to this drive entry a small sitting area provides the pause that refreshes for tenants and passers-by.

1 *Parking entrance.*
2 *West office block.*
3 *East block meeting neighboring stores.*
4 *East block at parking entrance.*

2

159

3

4

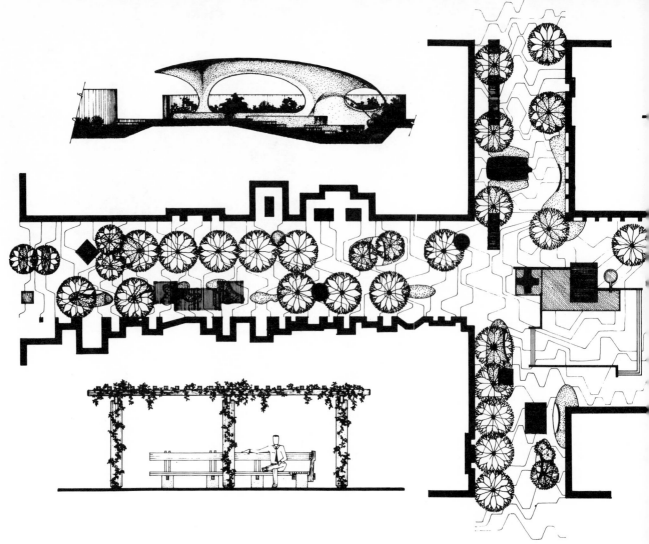

FRESNO DOWNTOWN MALL
Fresno, Calif.

The pedestrian mall has come forward increasingly of late as a means to help tired downtown districts compete with new suburban shopping centers. Kalamazoo, Pomona, Miami Beach, and Rochester are well-known examples. But the first three never escaped from preconceptions about the street that they were intended to replace. The last incorporates the street within a larger and more revolutionary building, which recognizes the climatic limitations of the Northeast. The Fresno Mall will overcome the limitations of the streets it will replace, while taking advantage of the desert hothouse climate of California's Central Valley.

Several years of hard work and careful planning by leading citizens, the Downtown Business Association, the city government, and Victor Gruen Associates have made this new mall possible. The enthusiastic support for the idea, the program, and the most refined design projections are heartwarming to the designers' morale. The vehicle for the program is an Improvement District, supported by the DBA, which will take over the redevelopment of six blocks of Fulton Street, Fresno's main street, and four blocks of side streets. Six more blocks of side streets are to be closed later. In addition, a widening at the main street crossing to create a central plaza, and at the two ends to create better entrances, will take place later under Redevelopment Agency auspices.

The mall right-of-way is 80 ft wide, and the bounding buildings, of typical miscellaneous design, average 30 to 40 ft in height. A substantial percentage are a good deal higher—The Security Bank Building, at the main central crossing, is 240 ft high. From a third to a half of the buildings bounding the mall are subject to redevelopment.

The mall design incorporates a number of basic concepts:

• New paving from wall to wall, concrete with freely curved pebbly header strips crosswise to reduce length and promote leisurely cross circulation. All elements are of curvilinear form within this total paving pattern to promote easy circulation.

• A continuous but irregular tree pattern to provide shade during the three hot summer months, and the six warm spring and fall months. Trees to be a balance of deciduous and evergreen, with a concentration on the clear fresh green, which are least common among California trees. Most trees to be set in open paving, with 4- to 6-ft circles of porous terra

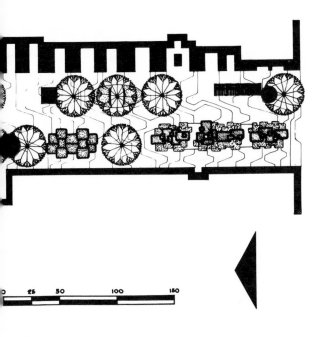

cotta slabs around them, and with provision for underground irrigation and aeration within the ultimate drip line area. Trees are reinforced with pergolas of wood and concrete.

• A system of small but potent planting islands, incorporating shrub areas, sheltering seats, lawn panels, and flowers in beds and boxes.

• A fairly complex pattern of water features, including simple round and oval basins with jets, clusters of interlocking round-cornered square basins at different levels with water gushing forcefully from top to bottom, and larger free form pools incorporating more elaborate fountains, sculpture, fish, and waterplants.

• An art program which includes three major sculptural elements in the general contract, and 39 smaller elements of sculpture and mosaic or mural, to be provided by private sponsors outside the contract.

• Comfortable seats with backs, distributed

throughout the mall in careful relations to trees and shelters, planting, water, and sculpture.

• Careful coordination of all other furnishing elements—trash receptacles, drinking fountains, directional signs, street, garden and pool lighting, telephones and fire alarms, speaker system, and utility centers. A control system for private signs will be recommended.

• Utilities will be provided for a future system of rest rooms and free-standing kiosks.

• A central plaza with sunken seating area bounded by water and sheltered structurally, raised terrace for outdoor eating, bandstand, movie screen and news tape.

• Two children's play areas with special play sculpture, spray pools, and shelter shell.

• A host of complex engineering problems, such as numerous private basements under the public right-of-way, are being solved with great dispatch by the Victor Gruen Associates engineering staff.

161

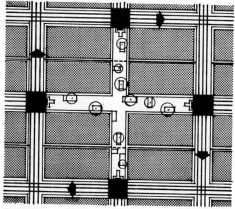

TYPICAL LAYOUT- FOUR BLOCK AREA

ELEVATOR

TYP. PLAN - PARKING
STRUCTURE

0 10 20 30 40 50

TYP. SECTION - PARKING
STRUCTURE

0 50 100 200

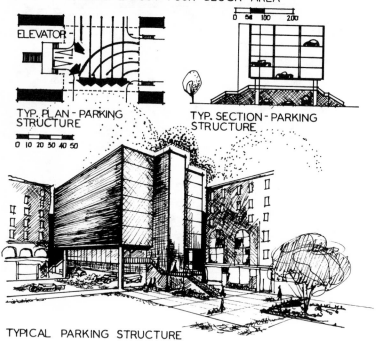

TYPICAL PARKING STRUCTURE

STREET STUDIES
Seattle, Wash.

Sketch proposals for salvaging pedestrian space from downtown gridiron street patterns by setting parking structures over intersections and closing the streets beyond. Traffic would flow under the structures, so that pedestrian malls could develop new dimensions of space and comfort for shopping.

Small spaces such as this for pedestrian rest and relaxation can be developed in many odd, wasted patches of urban land in high- and medium-density areas.

162

THE TEXAS SCULPTURE ENTRANCE PLAZA
The First National Bank, Fort Worth, Tex.

The entrance plaza to the First National Bank was designed to show off the bank building, to afford an interesting and inviting approach to the bank, and to give people driving along Seventh Street the feeling that they are going through a corner of a park, since they will have the bank plaza on the left and Burnett Park on the right.

In the summer of 1959 when the project was first discussed, Noguchi said that he wished to use two kinds of stone, both of which were obtainable only in Japan; the stone to be carved was a gray granite with a very slight greenish cast; there were also natural boulders of green. These particular materials were felt to be important both by him and by the architects to the overall color scheme of the building and the pavement of the plaza. He also said that it would be better to cut the stone in Japan, where more craftsmen were available. In this country there remain less than half a dozen competent stonecutters who still use hand tools, which Noguchi considered necessary to the work. These few are kept busy, and it is difficult to have them available for a project of this size.

Noguchi went to Japan in April, 1960. The 15 natural green stones, used in their original shape, were chosen by him on the island of Shikoku, inland from the town of Tokushima. They were found in deep ravines in the mountains of this area "in or near swift clear water." They are a metamorphic schist with striations of quartz; the green color is from the chloritic content of the material from which the stone was formed.

All the sculptured pieces came from one huge granite boulder. This boulder was located half way up a mountain above a village 65 miles north of Tokyo on the island of Honshu. The name of the mountain is Tsukuba, and the name of the village is Makabe. According to Noguchi, this source for granite was not discovered until 1958. Usually granite in this size comes from a quarry, but these granite boulders on this mountainside are the only ones known that furnish this particular color and grain. The granite was cut and moved down the mountain with primitive equipment. No mechanical hoists or cranes were available; hand-operated winches and primitive jacks were used. The great pieces of granite were cut and shaped into the sections for the sculpture by Noguchi and a number of Japanese workmen under his supervision. On those parts of the sculptured pieces where the surfaces were left as they were split, the marks of the handtools are an essential part of the sculpture's character; they heighten the contrast between the rough and the honed surfaces.

The eight sections of granite which comprise the three sculptured pieces were shipped from Yokohama and the green stones from Kobe.

In addition to the 8 crates of granite, there were 15 crates holding the natural stones; all weighed a total of 130,000 lb. Some of the crates were made of 10 by 10 timbers, held together by steel re-inforcing rods at both ends.

The plaza is paved in Acme Brick's red "half-pavers." It contains three planting areas: two areas to the east contain live oak trees, Camellia sasanqua, scrub elm, and dwarf pine; the ground cover is Festuca glauca that grows in mounds of blue-gray blades. This planting is reminiscent of East Texas;

163

its merger with Central and West Texas is symbolized by the mesquite tree, which with the two live oaks are the tallest planting in the plaza. The raised rectangular planting bed with its coping of black granite is a West Texas garden. It contains ocotillo, both red and white yucca, devil's pincushion, and mushroom cacti. The smallest piece of sculpture, 6 ft high, is in the middle of the arid garden. The middle-sized piece, 12 ft tall, is just to the west of the front entrance. The third and largest is in the center of the triangular plaza. Comprised of four sections, it stands 20 ft tall. It has the look of a giant Joshua tree or organ cactus. It is also like an asymmetric North American Indian totem pole. Noguchi has spoken of it as an energy symbol, something that symbolizes the activity and energy of Texas and the Southwest, energy that comes from both the food and the fuel that the land produces. He calls attention to the fact that it is L-shaped, which repeats the silhouette shape of the side view of the building.

Noguchi has also said that whereas formerly banks had heavy solid doors and heavy stone walls with grills over their few windows, nowadays banks have an open, more welcoming appearance; however, people are still interested in the soundness of the place where their money is kept. Noguchi hopes that his sculpture, by its great solidity, is symbolic of the solidity of The First National Bank and that the strength and durability of the granite will also make people think of the bank. The sculpture is "On the Square and in Balance."

Noguchi refers to the entire plaza as one piece of sculpture: the space and its shape, the planting areas, the natural stones, the plants and trees, and the three carved pieces.

Only in Texas could there have been this space and carved pieces of this size to put in it. The individual pieces are symbols of energy, of man, of the bank—but they have no names. The whole thing is "The Texas Sculpture."

164

RICH'S DEPARTMENT STORE
Knoxville, Tenn.

In designing this new store, the architects preserved open space 50 by 250 ft along both of the principal façades of the building. This made possible the creation of urban open spaces with trees, shrubs, flowers, grass, quiet seats, and a fountain. The north side takes on the character of a small park, the south that of an open tree-shaded plaza. The slope of the land from east to west created interesting problems of transition from slope to level by means of steps and walls. The paving pattern reflects the divisions in the building façades.

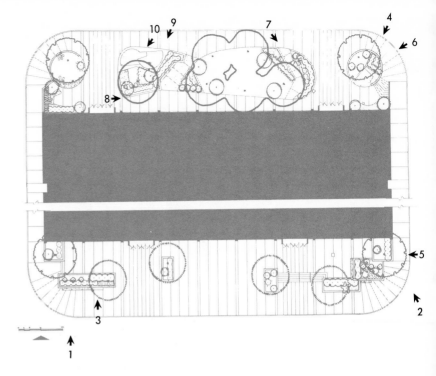

2

3

5

4

6

7

8

9

10

BUSINESS & TECHNICAL DIVISION
Long Beach City College, Calif.

This important and sizable institution fronts directly on the very heavy traffic of Pacific Coast Highway. Constant noise, fumes, and movement were difficult distractions for students, faculty, and administration. A system of earth mounds averaging 4 to 5 ft in height was developed across the entire frontage. These were heavily planted with shrubs and ground cover, backed up with trees. While it is difficult to measure the actual reduction in transmission of sound and fumes, movement is screened out almost entirely. A sense of seclusion and quietude is developed, greatly improving the general atmosphere. A psychological barrier has been erected against the roar of traffic. Street and campus are connected by winding paths which slip through baffle patterns in the berms.

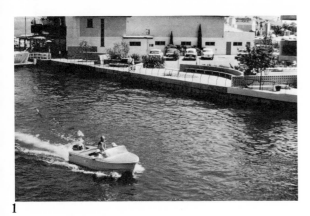

1

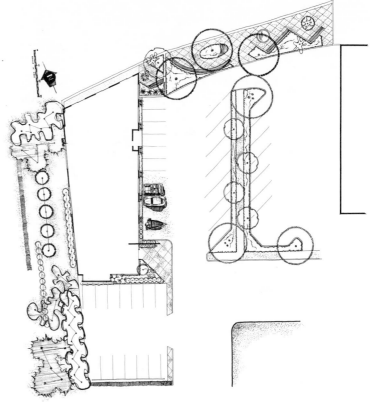

WATERSIDE PROMENADE
Newport Beach, Calif.

This 25- by 130-ft strip of land along the waterfront is surrounded by a city-owned parking lot and two downtown buildings. It was salvaged and developed into an urban amenity through the public spirit and enterprise of George Buccola, owner of one building. Paving, seats, railing, fountain, and planting beds add up to a pleasant space from which to watch the boats go by.

2

1

2

3

SATHER GATE ENTRANCE COMPLEX
University of California, Berkeley

*With the construction of a new student-union build-
ing across the street from the main administration
building, it became possible to close off one block of
the old Telegraph Avenue to provide a main entrance plaza. This provided a major expansion of the
main pedestrian entry space to the university, extending the plaza recently developed within Sather Gate
between old Wheeler Hall and new Dwinelle Hall,
both classroom buildings. A constructive rollback of
street asphalt, recapturing space for pedestrians.*

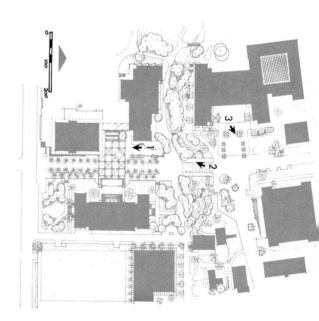

OMEGA, VÄLLINGBY
Stockholm, Sweden

The ground of Omega belongs to the city of Stockholm, which rents it on a lend-lease basis to this small society of 24 home owners. Each house has a small, enclosed private garden, while the remaining land is a common. The terraces outside each living room have only hedges to separate them from the neighbors. The terraces overlook the woodland area and no extra horticulture is allowed here. The central lawn area is the favorite playground of the small children, while the older children prefer the woodland or the fields in the parks of Vällingby.

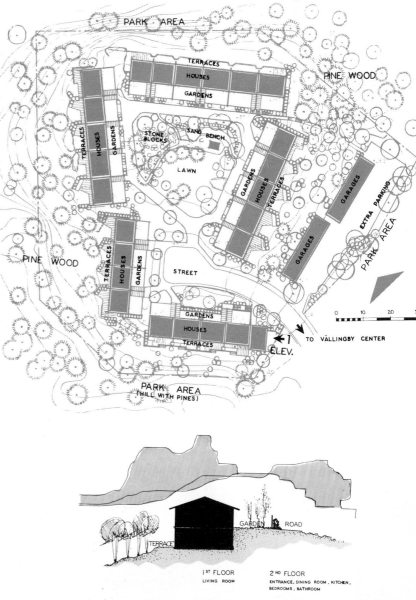

1

LONG BEACH CITY COLLEGE
QUADRANGLE
Long Beach, Calif.

A space of approximately 300 by 400 ft formed by the college auditorium, library, cafeteria, and life-science buildings. It had functioned as a faculty parking space, but was recognized by the college as a potential focal area of campus life. The plan recognizes likely circulation patterns and incorporates them in a three-dimensional structure of paving, grass, trees, seats, and walls which creates a sequence of variable sitting, walking, gathering, socializing, relaxing, or contemplating experiences. Here our patio concept expands to include a plaza or small park.

2

3

4

5

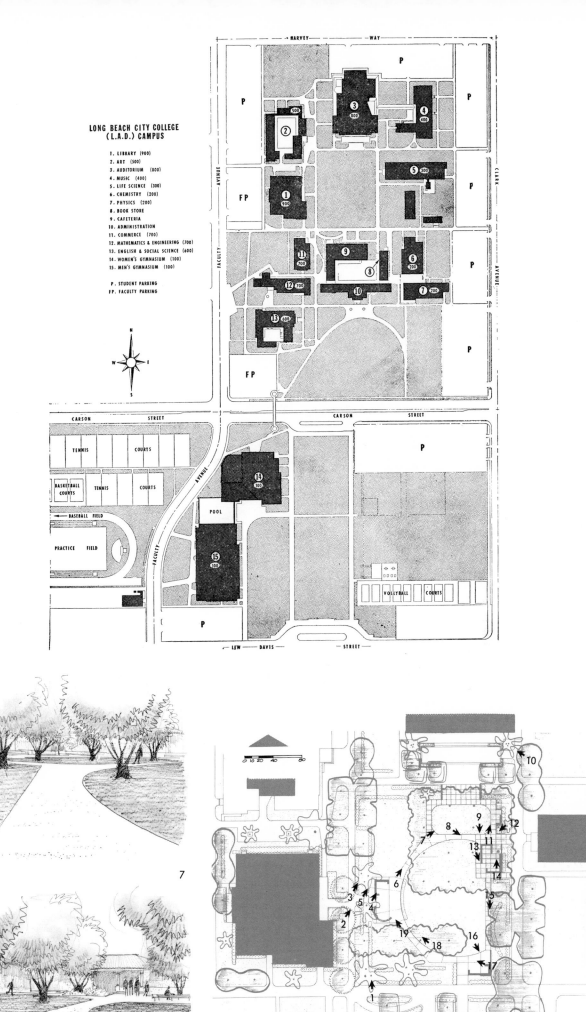

LONG BEACH CITY COLLEGE (L.A.D.) CAMPUS

1. LIBRARY (900)
2. ART (500)
3. AUDITORIUM (800)
4. MUSIC (400)
5. LIFE SCIENCE (300)
6. CHEMISTRY (200)
7. PHYSICS (200)
8. BOOK STORE
9. CAFETERIA
10. ADMINISTRATION
11. COMMERCE (700)
12. MATHEMATICS & ENGINEERING (700)
13. ENGLISH & SOCIAL SCIENCE (600)
14. WOMEN'S GYMNASIUM (100)
15. MEN'S GYMNASIUM (100)

P. STUDENT PARKING
FP. FACULTY PARKING

6

7

8

9

10

11

12

13

14

15

16

17

18

19

20

VIII

NEIGHBORHOOD, COMMUNITY, AND REGION

As we travel from multiple-building projects and parks through the streets of the city we come gradually to sense the problem of the continuous landscape of neighborhood, community, metropolitan area, and region. This is no more, and yet much more, than the harmonious linking of private landscapes over their alienating boundary lines, the linking of street landscapes with the landscapes within all the blocks which they bound, and the linking of those blocks across the streets. It is no more than these because all landscapes are viewed and experienced through individual human eyes, carried on similar physical and psychological frameworks, moving about through space on feet or wheels. People force continuity of scale on landscapes, by requiring connections and transitions between their constant scale and the variable scale of the world. The problem is much more than the mere linkage of many parts, because communities are geographical and social entities with distinct spirits and symbolic qualities.

Normally this spirit and quality are repressed and frustrated by a thin and soulless confusion, counteracted spasmodically by hasty gestures of mechanical regimentation. They can be expressed in articulated physical structures, by the process of assembling and arranging the composite elements of the community landscape. Relationships between circulation and land-use patterns, topography, water and geographical setting; between building patterns, tree patterns, paved and green open spaces, vehicular and pedestrian movements; between home, work, and recreation; between home, school, and shopping; between home, health, and cultural facilities; between civic centers, religious centers, commercial centers, and industrial centers; between all of these and the service and administrative facilities of the community; between the various economic levels of housing, from slum to mansion, and the various densities of housing, from exurbanite to tower apartment; between schools, colleges, parks, and cultural facilities; between mass culture expressed in television, billboards, and autos, and special culture expressed in art galleries, little theaters, and chamber music; between the morality of church and editorial, and the reality of street, shop, and office; all of these are contributory to the spirit and quality of the community landscape.

Neighborhoods, as clusters of housing related to school, shopping, church, recreation, and park at the local scale of $\frac{1}{4}$ to $\frac{1}{2}$ mile radius, make up the majority of the area of villages, towns, cities, and metropolitan areas. In the ideal neighborhood prototype we find the local facilities clustered in a neat parklike core, connected to the housing by pedestrian-ways, radiating through finger parks, while on the outside, the housing connects with the world through dead-end or loop streets leading to the traffic-ways which bound the neighborhood. The average reality is, of course, nothing like this. In older sections it is a gridiron of nearly equal streets lined with housing through which miscellaneous facilities are scattered at random. In newer sections, more order appears. The grid is articulated in half-mile and mile units, with more irregular patterns within, and with the neighborhood facilities spaced somewhat more functionally and rationally. In both, the streets still dominate. The parklike potential for neighborhood landscape has yet to come to fruition beyond such isolated spots as Radburn and Baldwin Village.

There are three main levels of housing: detached one- and two-story houses in the currently favored and exploding suburban tract patterns, low-rise two- and three-story row and apartment housing typical of our older cities, and high-rise multistory tower housing originating in downtown congestion. Each of these has its parallel range from frustration to fruition; from entrapment in speculative, intense-use, gridiron concepts leading to congested building which destroys architecture, open space, tree potentials, and the health of those forced to live there, to escape from the street net into superblocks of free parklike environment in which air moves, sun shines, vegetation grows, architecture sparkles, and people thrive.

The community—an arrangement of neighborhoods or accumulation of residential areas around certain workplaces, shopping, cultural, educational, health, and administrative facilities essential to most neighborhoods but beyond the resources of one or a few to support—is the level of urban development at which its cultural potential may begin to emerge. Surrounded by a rural and/or primeval hinterland with which it enjoys close reciprocal living relations, the community centers sufficiently on certain specific facilities and interests to have a sense of identity and common purpose. This can lead to rich physical expressions in architectural, engineering, and landscape elements—civic and cultural centers, educational and health institutions, fine residential neighborhoods, parks, bridges, dams, and highways. Few existing communities will have more than a few of these, but most will want more. The examples plus the urge supply the potential for raising larger and larger sections of community landscape to the level of the best, through processes prototyped as "urban renewal." However, the high-quality community landscape of consistent integrity and a character which is more than an accumulation of urban parts will not result from any such fragmentary processes. Community form results from community design.

The heavy construction of urban concentration has produced, in the past, the drive for urban parks as "natural breathing pores" within the naturally ugly city, and in the present, the vast scattering to the fresh air and vegetation of the suburbs. Experience indicates that the optimum urban landscape will include balanced and imaginative relations between buildings, trees, streets, ground forms, and all the other elements which complete the landscape. If urbanization is to mean maximum humanization and civilization, rather than mere concentration of construction and commercialism, these balanced relations will include low as well as high buildings, green space as well as paved space, pedestrians as well as vehicles, agriculture as well as industry, sports as well as culture, and modest neighborhood scenes as well as vistas, panoramas, and landmarks. The basic triangle which connects home, work, and recreation in the average citizen's life must be basic to urban design processes. The scenes experienced by most people most of the time are the most important scenes. They should receive the most careful and sensitive attention. We cannot continue to slough them off in routine and sterile patterns, while trying to compensate for this failure by designing special scenes experienced by some people some of the time.

Architectural and landscape design thinks normally of sequence and continuity of spatial and sensory experience; relations between simple, regular, and special elements; the repose of unity and the sparkle of variety; small and large spaces, low and high, narrow and wide, long and short, regular and irregular, precise and soft, dark and light, warm and cool, neutral and colorful, simple and complex; the reliability of balance and rhythmic repetition, the stimulation and inspiration of freer, more dynamic, and less stable arrangements; the richness of combination and contrast of varying materials, textures, colors, and forms. Application of such thinking and feeling to the urban scene will come immediately into conflict with the vast sterile oversimplification of the gridiron street block system; with the domination of all circulation routes by motor vehicles, and the consequent loss of pedestrian experience; with the monotonous variety of construction along most streets; with the exaggerated contrasts between formal civic centers and busy downtown commercial areas, large parks and congested housing districts,

broad streets and low buildings, vast parking lots and important buildings; with the inexorable tendency of real estate and finance to segregate all neighborhoods by use and economic status; and with many similar forces tending toward sterilization, mechanization, standardization, and dehumanization. Reversal of such forces will require concentration on sympathy with the continuity of human experience as much as on rocket ships, geodesic domes, and hyperbolic paraboloids.

Paul Rudolph has said:

Technically we can do almost anything, but this actually makes it more difficult since the choices are multiplied. There are at least four reasons why we are not improving the environment (except possibly for landowners). . . .

First, the Ecole Des Beaux Arts' principles and theories which dominated the nineteenth century proved inadequate for the twentieth. Modern architecture has produced brilliant theories for individual buildings but so far has thrown little light on how to relate one building to another or to the street or city. We build endless streets leading on, on, on, with advertisements shouting stop, stop, stop. We build incoherent assemblages of structures, each crying for as much attention as possible. . . . One way towards a more comprehensive New York is for each building at least to respect its neighbor.

Secondly, if we are to avoid building atrocities we must revaluate our hierarchy of building types and suitable techniques of expression for them. Traditionally the gateway to the city, the place of worship, the governmental building, the palace, the institutional building, and the meeting places of the people became focal points. These buildings were given status by their prominent siting, by the ample space left in front of the building to allow comprehensive viewing, by the manipulation of the angle of vision, by the abundant play of light and shadow, by their dominant silhouette, by the stepping up of scale, and by sculpture, painting, fountains and landscaping. These focal points were carefully juxtaposed to much quieter building types such as housing, office buildings, shops, all of which were usually restrained in design, and certainly did not dare to assert themselves in the presence of the important symbols of the culture. This careful hierarchy was bound into a whole by plazas, courts, loggias, places, arcades, promenades, and grand stairways for the pedestrian only.

Today there is no hierarchy of building types. Hot dog stands assimilate opera houses, institutions look like factories, apartment houses like office buildings, churches like over-sized cottages, office buildings are packages of air-conditioning and other mechanical marvels (whatever space is left over is used by humans).

The appropriateness of this or that technique tends to elude us. The revenue-laden multi-storied office building dominates the cityscape by size alone. . . .

Thirdly, if New York is to become physically more dynamic it will learn anew how to protect its unique spaces and to dispose its new buildings to create different kinds of space. The quiet, enclosed, isolated, shaded space, such as the Cloisters; the hustling, bustling space pungent with vitality such as Times Square (it is best at night because the architecture has disappeared and crude, bold, unsubtle but dynamic artificial light is in command giving us a touch of the future); the paved, dignified, vast, sumptuous, even awe-inspiring space, such as the Western approach to Columbia University; the mysterious space

that one finds in the Wall Street area, under bridges, and in Greenwich Village; the transition space which defines, separates, and yet joins juxtaposed spaces of varying character such as the plaza in front of the Plaza Hotel. We need sequences of space which arouse one's curiosity, give a sense of anticipation, which beckon and impel us to rush forward to find that releasing space which dominates, which climaxes and acts as a magnet and gives direction. This is well illustrated by the Fifth Avenue entrance to Rockefeller Plaza, where one strides forward in anticipation of seeing the sunken court and its activities. Most important of all we need those outer spaces which encourage social contact, again well illustrated by Rockefeller Plaza. . . .[38]

Edmund Bacon has said:

In urban design, if we uncover the nature of the essential with the same clarity that we have used in defining the constitutional framework of government, then the remaining area will be one of liberty, and we will avoid the pitfalls in urban design of trying to control everything.

This paper attempts to consider the determination of the essential from the non-essential in relation to the three principal conditions necessary for urban design.

1. The individual buildings must be related to each other and to their surroundings by a clear space organization system.

2. The area must be subject to continuing guidance from some agency competent in design.

3. The architectural expression of individual buildings must have a reasonable relation with each other and with their surroundings.

Gordon Stephenson . . . says, "There should be a clearer distinction between private and public space. The latter should be provided in an open space system running through the whole scheme." . . .

We have titled our method "The Greenway System," and add to Gordon Stephenson's ideas the concept of planning the open space system so as to bring out important local institutions and landmarks as focal points in the system, and further that the system become the control determining the location and general form of the principal buildings in the various redevelopment projects. When these are once determined there can be complete liberty in the design of the bulk of the project; . . . .

. . . there is need for some sort of coherence in the architectural expression of the principal buildings that make up the core or cores of the over-all development.

This is a very sensitive area of inquiry . . . we did finally arrive at a principle which safeguarded the individual architect's freedom of expression.

. . . such problems exist . . . buildings utterly unrelated to other new buildings in the same redevelopment area, . . . buildings which destroy the effect of public monuments, squares or fountains adjacent to them, and . . . buildings which tear down the established architectural atmosphere of a section of the city.

If we survey the building compositions which people in general have come to accept as being the greatest that man has produced, we note that many of them are the joint product of the work of several or many designers. . . . I am reminding you that many of the most soulful compositions of history were the product of joint effort.

I . . . list below some of the elements of design which may or may not play a major role in securing harmonious relationship between buildings. . . .

1. Materials of construction

2. Color

3. Land treatment, paving materials, surface tex-
tures, planting, etc., the platform on which the build-
ings sit

4. Character of shape; prismatic, pyramidal, pro-
jecting wings, etc.

5. Over-all height

6. Floor heights

7. Rhythm of design, fenestration, directional em-
phasis, etc.

8. Way in which buildings meet the ground

"In essentials, unity; in non-essentials, liberty; in
both, charity." [39]

Catherine Bauer Wurster, speaking on "Architecture and the Cityscape," has said:

. . . we are in an era of dynamic urban growth
and reconstruction, with rising incomes, leisure and
education; with increasing concern for quality and
distinction in our environment, and with the means
to pay for it. We have many of the public powers
and policies that we formerly lacked, and will prob-
ably soon acquire additional tools. And meanwhile,
a great architectural revolution has swept the field
in total triumph. Together, these factors are the his-
toric formula for a great period of city building.

But there is a spreading sense of uneasiness and
uncertainty. The opportunity is here, but do we
really know how to build great cities? . . .

Among the architectural elite today, functionalism
has long been dead and there is little interest in
urban design as such in any terms. Abstract personal
aestheticism is riding high, and the fashions have
shifted rapidly from Mies to Corbu to newer inno-
vations. . . .

Architecture as the art of giving significant three-
dimensional form to cities, never more important
than today, has never been given less attention. . . .

If a poll were taken as to the best-designed mod-
ern cities, in terms of visual enjoyment and distinc-
tion, I suspect that most experts and laymen alike
would nominate Stockholm and Copenhagen. . . .
they are essentially as new as our cities, and it is the
recent development that dominates the scene.

Stockholm has a dramatic site, but Copenhagen
is as flat as a prairie town. Both cities, however, have
used landscape and waterscape with great perspica-
city, for all kinds of recreation, fine views, effective
siting of new and old buildings, and to enhance the
sense of basic geography and urban structure. By
comparison, all American cities have neglected their
natural resources for urban design. [40]

In 1954, Sydney Williams, San Francisco city planner, analyzed the esthetic characteristics of cities as
based on several categories of three-dimensional
form. The categories are: urban site forms—level or
gentle slope (sloping to hills, valley or gorge), amphi-
theater or fan, bowl, ridged or hilltop; urban textures—"the relatively uniform mass of buildings,
streets, trees and yards of which the greater part of
the city is composed"; [41] green areas; circulation
facilities; paved open spaces; individually significant
architectural masses—vertical, slab, massive, horizontal. Williams also suggested the following categories
of perception of city form: panorama, skyline, vista,
urban open space, and experience in motion. In
1958 the Joint Committee on Design Control of the
New York AIA-AIP, after quoting Williams, went
on to emphasize as elements of overall urban form
the following: geometric patterns, linear features,
landmarks, lookout places, and areas of distinctive
character. [42]

In 1960 Kevin Lynch analyzed the following principal elements in *The Image of the City:* Paths—
"the channels along which the observer customarily,
occasionally, or potentially moves. They may be
streets, walkways, transit lines, canals, railroads."
Edges—"the linear elements not used or considered
as paths by the observer. They are the boundaries
between two phases, linear breaks in continuity:
shores, railroad cuts, edges of development, walls."
Districts—"the medium-to-large sections of the city,
conceived of as having two-dimensional extent, which
the observer mentally enters 'inside of', and which
are recognizable as having some common, identifying
character." Nodes—"points, the strategic spots in a
city into which an observer can enter, and which are
the intensive foci to and from which he is traveling.
They may be primarily junctions, places of a break in
transportation, a crossing or convergence of paths,
moments of shift from one structure to another. Or
. . . simply concentrations, which gain their importance from being the condensation of some use or
physical character, as a street-corner hangout or an
enclosed square." Landmarks—"another type of
point-reference, but in this case the observer does
not enter within them, they are external. They are
usually a rather simply defined physical object:
building, sign, store, or mountain. Their use involves
the singling out of one element from a host of possi-

bilities. Some landmarks are distant ones, typically seen from many angles and distances, over the tops of smaller elements, and used as radial references. . . . Such are isolated towers, golden domes, great hills. Other landmarks are primarily local, being visible only in restricted localities and from certain approaches. These are the innumerable signs, store fronts, trees, doorknobs, and other urban detail, which fill in the image of most observers."

The image of a given physical reality may occasionally shift its type with different circumstances of viewing. Thus an expressway may be a path for the driver, an edge for the pedestrian. Or a central area may be a district when a city is organized on a medium scale, and a node when the entire metropolitan area is considered. But the categories seem to have stability for a given observer when he is operating at a given level.

None of the element types isolated above exist in isolation in the real case. Districts are structured with nodes, defined by edges, penetrated by paths, and sprinkled with landmarks. Elements regularly overlap and pierce one another. If this analysis begins with the differentiation of the data into categories, it must end with their reintegration into the whole image. . . .

For most people interviewed, paths were the predominant city elements, although their importance varied according to the degree of familiarity with the city. People with least knowledge of Boston tended to think of the city in terms of topography, large regions, generalized characteristics, and broad directional relationships. Subjects who knew the city better had usually mastered part of the path structure; these people thought more in terms of specific paths and their interrelationships. A tendency also appeared for the people who knew the city best of all to rely more upon small landmarks and less upon either regions or paths.[43]

This brief sampling of three careful studies should, of course, be expanded by more detailed examination of the originals. If we regroup these various elements in terms of the continuity-and-accent relations which create the basic structure of any landscape at any scale, we find that urban site forms have continuity within themselves in each category; they may be continuous or in contrast with the regional topography. The city as a whole is, of course, an accent in its region. Urban textures, geometric patterns, panoramas, skylines, and experiences in motion are elements of continuity. So also are circulation facilities, linear features, and paths. Green areas, paved open spaces, vistas, significant architectural masses, landmarks, lookout places, edges, and nodes are accenting elements. Districts and areas of distinctive character have continuity within themselves although they are recognized by contrast with the different textures around them.

If, perhaps, one grows a little weary of concentration upon the formal aspects of the urban landscape, feeling the need for connection with the social content which produces and conditions them, there is, of course, a considerable literature of urbanism to which we can refer. Such names as Geddes, Stein, Mumford, Tunnard, Gallion and Eisner spring readily to mind. A refreshing discussion of the relations between form and content is *Communitas*

1

2

1

2

by Paul and Percival Goodman, published in 1947, and republished in 1960. This is a condensed, precise, subtly satiric discussion of the forces which shape cities and of various theoretical proposals for improving them. Its concluding paradigms (examples!) suggest: first, a city which gives expressive, coherent, and magnificent form to "the tastes and drives of America that are most obvious on the surface—its high production, high Standard of Living and artificially induced demand, its busy full employment"; second, a city of "planned security with minimum regulation," in which the production and distribution of a guaranteed minimum subsistence level for all citizens is guaranteed by the community and removed from the area of free enterprise, leaving to it complete freedom in the production and distribution of all those commodities which are "not, perhaps, absolutely necessary"; and third, a city which eliminates "the difference between production and consumption . . . where the producing and the product are of a piece and every part of life has value in itself as both means and end; where there is a community tradition of style that allows for great and refined work, and each man has a chance to enhance the community style and transform it." The first centers on a downtown area which is one giant enclosed department store; the second integrates housing, recreation, industry, and agriculture in functional patterns; the third centers on definitive enclosed piazzas which integrate "work, love and knowledge," housing, factory, and culture.

It is doubtless no surprise to find a landscape architect advocating trees in cities, while an architect says, "Urban beauty does not require trees and parks . . . the urban use of trees is formal . . . when finally, as in the Ville Radieuse, the aim is to make a city in the park, a Garden City, one has despaired of city life altogether." [44]

As the psychologists tell us, conditions create attitudes, rather than vice versa. Christopher Tunnard, landscape architect and city planner, speaks of trees in cities. He points out that green forms were absent in urban planning until the seventeenth century because cities were considered separate entities set apart from wild nature; they were still small and the countryside accessible; streets were narrow and buildings high enough to shade them; and the new art of city planning had a definite esthetic of perfectly controlled forms. "Green space as part of the organic structure of the city comes with the seventeenth century and the establishment of new forms based on changing social behavior." Tunnard concludes that:

Green forms will be always necessary and an integrated part of the urban pattern. . . . The plea is thus for realistic urbanism, rather than neo-romantic disurbanism. . . . Open space in cities . . . given a form complementing and increasing enjoyment of architecture . . . to satisfy the needs of all members of the family.[45]

Finally, we are happy to note that the Goodmans do show trees in their sketches for two piazzas in their ideal commune which is "utopian . . . in the child-heart of man."

Lewis Mumford makes the inclusive statement:

What I have been saying about the social function of open spaces can now be briefly summed up. For weekend recreation we must treat the whole region as a potential park area and make it attractive at so many points that the hideous congestion of weekend traffic that goes on everywhere will be minimized, or disappear entirely. As for daily use, the same requirements for open space apply to both the most congested cities and the most sprawling suburbs: for the first must be loosened up and the second must become more concentrated and many-sided. In the cities of the future, ribbons of green must run through every quarter, forming a continuous web of garden and mall, widening at the edge of the city into protective green belts, so that landscape and garden will not be rural monopolies but will likewise be an integral part of urban life.[46]

Metropolis and Megalopolis. As communities grow, destroy their hinterlands, and merge with one another in spreading blankets of urbanism, metropolitan areas emerge in which urban order, political reason, and human scale are lost in vast confusion. In spite of this, New York, Chicago, Los Angeles, Philadelphia, and Boston produce unprecedented expressions of cosmopolitan urban culture. Vertical skyline, broad lake front, geographical sprawl, the battle of old and new, great educational, cultural, and civic institutions—the high points and special qualities of great cities—could never have been produced without their concentrations of wealth and energy. Some will say that the price, in slum, blight,

1

2

delinquency, crime, clamor, and confusion is too great. Certainly the projection, development, and control of rationalized, articulated, humanized landscapes in vast urban belts such as those which will soon be extending from Maine to Virginia and from Santa Barbara to San Diego are among our greatest challenges in this latter half of the twentieth century. From the ideal town-country relationship of the sixteenth century we have moved through a series of plateaus, each one marking a revolutionary qualitative change in comprehensible urban form and structure—the image of the city. From the tangible and sensible balanced community of less than 100,000 through the indiscriminate merging of several or many in metropolitan areas of up to 5 million—Chicago, Philadelphia, Washington, Berlin, Los Angeles, the San Francisco Bay region (partially saved by its topography), to megalopolitan monsters in which giantism is rampant—New York, London, Tokyo, Moscow—we have experienced three plateaus. On each of these we have been able to distinguish, with increasing difficulty, comprehensible units or structures of urbanism. This is true regardless of the contrast between the relative formlessness of the developments which exist and the ideal forms which have been projected on paper by planners and urban designers. But what shall we say of the new tyrannopolis (with apologies to Mumford) which the real estate–chamber of commerce fraternity anticipates with joy as blanketing our Eastern and Western seaboards? This will be a fourth plateau, an unimaginable urban wilderness, a structural desert, a jungle of traffic, a cacophony of signs and sounds stretching for endless unbroken miles beyond the grasp, comprehension, or imagination of even our architects and planners, let alone the average citizen. In spite of pious platitudes in every Sunday supplement, there are no planning or control efforts in sight which will be able to stem, divert, form, or articulate this cancerous monster of urban fusion, worse than any science fiction, which looms ahead. We can only hope that state and interstate planning bodies, and a possible Federal Department of Urban Affairs, will be able to wake us from our self-congratulatory dream of endless progress before the deluge. In the nineteenth century the restless pioneers moved west in stages, leaving their messy mis-

3

4

takes behind. What price reaching Mars and the Moon, leaving our cities behind?

Science fiction does give us the ultimate projection:

Its urbanization, progressing steadily, had finally reached the ultimate. All the land surface of Trantor, 75,000,000 square miles in extent, was a single city. The population, at its height, was well in excess of forty billions. . . .

He could not see the ground. It was lost in the ever increasing complexities of man-made structures. He could see no horizon other than that of metal against sky. . . .

There was no green to be seen; no green, no soil, no life other than man. Somewhere on the world . . . was the Emperor's palace, set amid one hundred square miles of natural soil, green with trees, rainbowed with flowers. It was a small island, amid an ocean of steel. . . .[47]

Regionalism. Beyond the areas of urban and suburban concentration, even at the metropolitan and megalopolitan levels, lie the rural and primeval hinterlands and the smaller satellite towns and villages, which in reciprocal relations with the urban centers establish recognizable regions. These have an organic integrity which is often in sharp contrast or even conflict with the much more arbitrary political reality of incorporated municipal, county, and state boundaries. There are as many definitions of region as there are persons with specific reasons for making definitions. Without trying for our own hard and fast boundaries we can say that, interested as we are in the physical-social landscape, our regions must be entities of some consistency in both physical and social terms. Physical geography may establish valleys of varying sizes, coastal plains backed by mountains, natural harbor areas, and similar comprehensible units. Drainage patterns are apt to form natural regions and chains of regions. In living, we tend to follow valleys and to be bounded by hills and mountains. Socially, if the community is the area we are apt to cover in normal daily living patterns, perhaps the region is the area we are apt to cover in a year of ordinary weekends. This combination of physical and social controls will not produce precisely defined regions with neat boundaries. Rather, it will produce a system of loosely overlapping micro- and macroregional zones. Each zone will have its own specific geographical landscape character, its own peculiar combination of urban and nonurban elements. It will always have both in some degree. This balance of structural and natural forms will constitute regional landscape character and potential described so well by Brenda Colvin and Brian Hackett.[48] The English still seem to be preserving a tradition of regional-landscape thinking that was developed in this country by Olmsted, Eliot, and Jensen, but has since been submerged in the tides of progress.

Following Colvin and Hackett, we can say that the regional landscape will be one which most of the citizens of the urban center or centers, and their rural and wild hinterlands and satellite towns, can comprehend, experience, and enjoy in the course of the annual cycle of living. We will seek balanced relations between town and country and between agriculture, extraction of raw materials such as lumber, coal, or oil, and untouched, adjusted, or reconstructed nature. Seeking such balance will involve much greater control and direction of the physical form and extent of urban density, suburban sprawl, and exurban scattering than we have today. Likewise, it will involve control of extraction, agriculture, and changes in nature, even beyond those advocated by conservationists and ecologists today. This will be true because the search for the balanced and beautiful regional landscape must go beyond functional and humanitarian planning, as they are at present conceived, beyond the preservation of the balance of nature and the good things that exist (important though all these are), to the potential richness that can emerge from the impact of creative imagination, unfettered by special interests, upon the forms, elements, and resources which exist. Elements of architecture and urbanism, of suburbanism, of rural and primeval living, of topography, of quiet and moving water, of woods and meadows, of brushland and desert sand, of rock and forest, of cropland, orchard, and pasture, of mining and drilling and quarrying and lumbering, of drainage and flood control, of water supply and sewage disposal, of electric distribution and gas and oil storage, of engineering, traffic and transportation, and of active recreation and passive contemplation must be woven together into an integrated landscape which will give pleasure to the senses and sustenance to the questing spirit of mankind day after day through all its parts both great and small.

TYPICAL PATTERNS OF URBANIZATION

1   *Development moving in on agriculture.*
2   *Development begins.*
3   *Flood of suburban sprawl dammed by topography.*

1

2

3

185

4

5

6

7

8

4   *Scatteration.*
5   *Formlessness sets in.*
6   *The flood becomes a sea.*
7   *Urban life.*
8   *Urban life.*

9

9   *Living becomes more congested.*
10   *Slums and public housing.*
11   *Downtown recreation.*
12, 13   *Final urban congestion and squalor—plus beautification.*

10

11

12

13

189

THE MEADS
Morro Bay, Calif.

The Meads is an integrated development on a 100-acre site between highway and beach. Morro Bay is a small community, but it has the potential to be a recreation center for the large area between Santa Barbara and Big Sur. A balanced pattern of facilities includes commercial, transient, and more permanent residential and recreational elements. As an antidote to zoned segregation by use and value, this will be a healthy, stimulating, and exciting place.

190

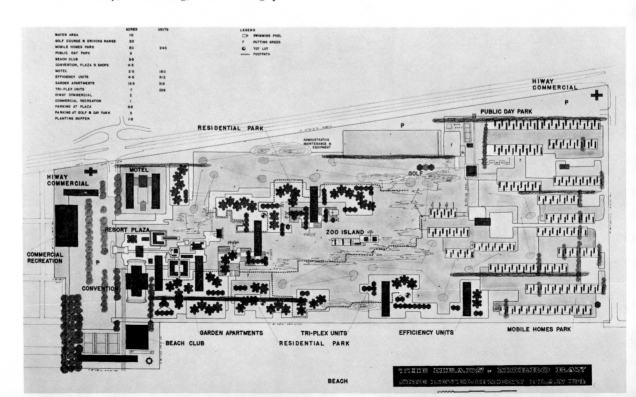

SEA PINES PLANTATION AND FOREST BEACH CORPORATION
Hilton Head, S. C.

Shown here is the complete land planning and detailed design projection for the development of a large island acreage off the coast of the southeastern United States. (Complete story in "Progressive Architecture," July, 1960.)

MASTER PLAN OF SEA PINES PLANTATION AND FOREST BEACH CORPORATION DEVELOPMENT

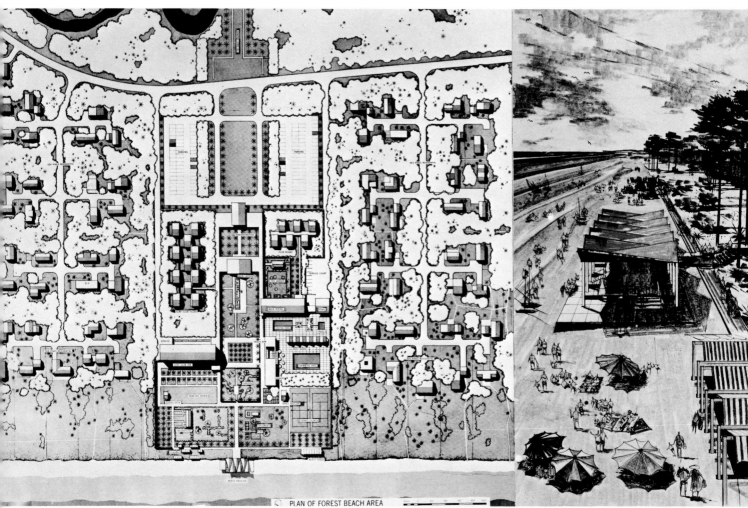

PLAN OF FOREST BEACH AREA

PLAN OF THE SURF AND GOLF CLUB AND SURROUNDING AREA

PLAN OF SEA PINES BEACH RESIDENTIAL AREA

193

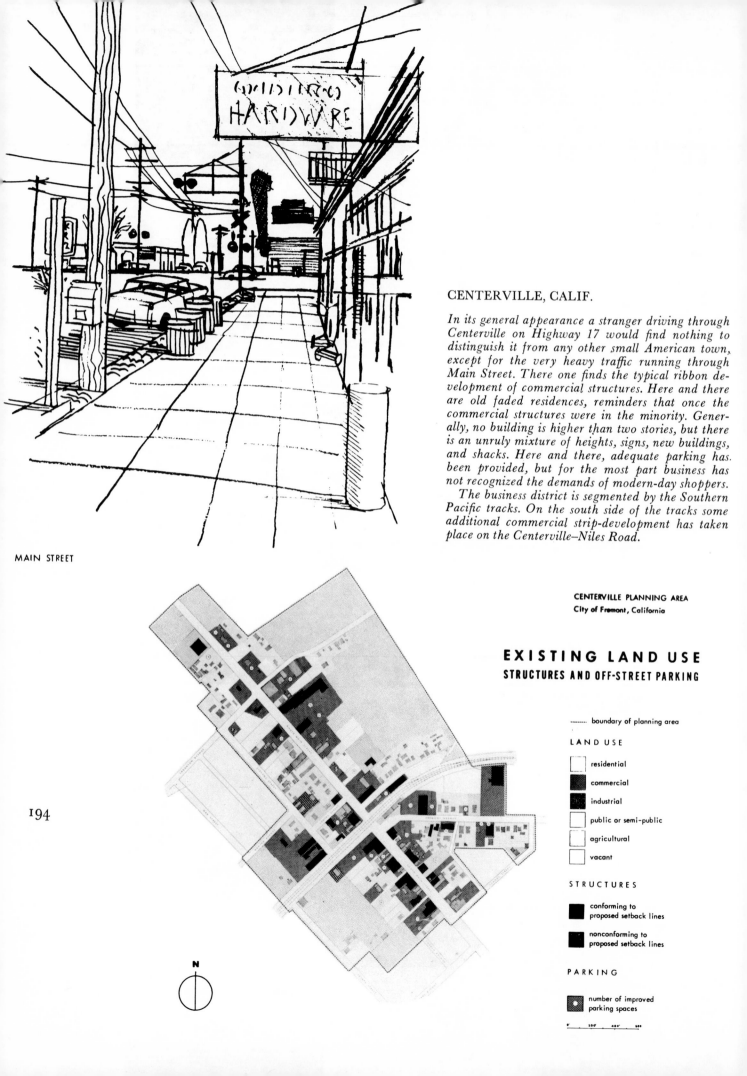

MAIN STREET

CENTERVILLE, CALIF.

In its general appearance a stranger driving through Centerville on Highway 17 would find nothing to distinguish it from any other small American town, except for the very heavy traffic running through Main Street. There one finds the typical ribbon development of commercial structures. Here and there are old faded residences, reminders that once the commercial structures were in the minority. Generally, no building is higher than two stories, but there is an unruly mixture of heights, signs, new buildings, and shacks. Here and there, adequate parking has been provided, but for the most part business has not recognized the demands of modern-day shoppers.

The business district is segmented by the Southern Pacific tracks. On the south side of the tracks some additional commercial strip-development has taken place on the Centerville–Niles Road.

194

CENTERVILLE PLANNING AREA
City of Fremont, California

EXISTING LAND USE
STRUCTURES AND OFF-STREET PARKING

-------- boundary of planning area

LAND USE

residential

commercial

industrial

public or semi-public

agricultural

vacant

STRUCTURES

conforming to
proposed setback lines

nonconforming to
proposed setback lines

PARKING

number of improved
parking spaces

N

Almost hidden in the haphazard mixture of uses is the little Presbyterian church, oldest in the region and designed in classic style. Surrounding it is a cemetery, open but presently in an unkept and uncared-for condition.

THE PROPOSED PLAN. The ultimate success of a shopping district like Centerville depends not only on careful analysis and determination of commercial land needs, the general location of the different commercial zones, and an effective circulation system, but also on general appearance. The size and location of buildings, their interrelationship and the treatment of open areas about them, as well as their design and the design of other structures such as outdoor advertisements, street fixtures, etc., establishes the character of the area. It is proposed, therefore, that in addition to the general regulations of the Zoning Ordinance, special regulations will be applied. These will apply to setback lines, building area and height, and landscaping. These proposed regulations are shown graphically on Map 6.

In Centerville, the old architecturally valuable Presbyterian church creates a unique opportunity for environmental design which, if properly utilized, can add considerably to the attractiveness of the area as a whole. It is therefore proposed that the church be retained in its present location and that its surroundings be developed into a park including the cemetery which should be rehabilitated from its present rundown and neglected state. A small public building, e.g., a branch library, could be located in the public part of the park to add to its usefulness.

From an esthetic point of view, consideration should also be given to elimination, step by step, of overhead utility lines. The very presence of numerous utility poles and a mesh of wiring along and across the streets can spoil the efforts made in achieving good design in buildings and other structures.

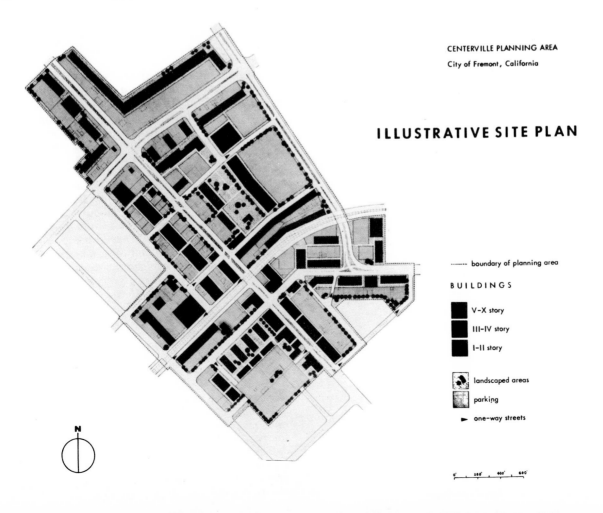

CENTERVILLE PLANNING AREA

City of Fremont, California

ILLUSTRATIVE SITE PLAN

-------- boundary of planning area

BUILDINGS

■ V–X story

■ III–IV story

■ I–II story

landscaped areas

parking

► one-way streets

N

195

1 *Site as is.*

PORT HOLIDAY
near Las Vegas, Nev.

Client owns the only private land of any size abutting Lake Mead. It is surrounded by the federally owned Lake Mead National Recreational Area.

This land will be developed into a recreation city which will be able to offer recreation facilities for all age groups and all economic levels, unlike the nearby Las Vegas, where recreation facilities for teenagers and younger members of the family are virtually nonexistent.

Because of the great seasonal fluctuation of the level of Lake Mead, it has been decided to dam the Las Vegas Wash which meanders through the site. Thus a separate water-recreation area has been created on which, unlike the huge Lake Mead, safe water activities can be enjoyed by all age groups.

The very rugged terrain of the surrounding washes, mountains, and desert areas determined to a large extent the locations of some of the other recreation facilities.

Motel, hotel, and residential areas, as well as mobile estate provisions, were carefully predicated upon economic feasibility studies.

By creating a Port Holiday "Authority" under the State Act of the Government of the State of Nevada, the owners were able not only to fully control architectural design, but also to create their own zoning ordinances, and police powers, as well as set up their own utility companies.

The great advantage of developing a "new town" instead of working with an established community is, of course, that there are no arbitrary property lines, or worse, a gridiron of streets, which had been established many years ago. Port Holiday, due to the lack of such arbitrary boundaries, could thus establish "building envelopes," which would meet all required densities as established by lessees' requirements or as required by the economic feasibility studies, without forgoing vistas or relationships to their immediate environment, by simply juxtaposing building units with each other. To avoid the scattered appearance which most developments have, the grouping of units on the site was studied for a long time. Out of these design sessions evolved a grouping of a large central unit, dominated by a geodesic dome of some 600-ft diameter, which will encompass the central plaza, casinos, and motor hotels. These groupings not only lend a feeling of unity to the project, but also allow the creation of a desired density without losing the needed openness to maintain a resort quality.

After the large geodesic dome over the plaza, the next most important elements are the apartment units which grow out from under the shelter of the dome and, closely following the contours of the terrain, make maximum use of the dramatic views of the rugged desert land of Nevada. Some small geodesic domes located at the mobile estates park lend a focal point to the south shore of Lake Adair and provide shelter to some of the community facilities serving the residents of this facility.

2 *General view of proposed development.*

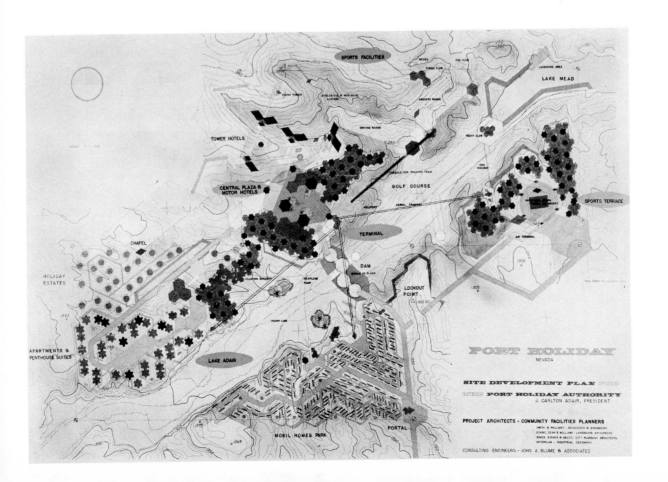

3

3 *View toward Lake Mead from Yacht Club.*
4 *Central plaza.*
5 *Central plaza.*
6 *Typical motor hotel unit.*
7 *Under motor hotel.*
8 *Aerial tramway.*
9 *Floating gardens.*

4

5

198

7

6

8

9

1

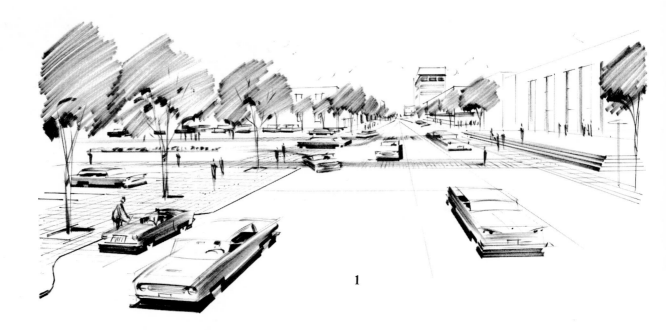

200

3

CASPER, WYO.

2 *Downtown from the air, showing plaza with city hall to its right.*

3 *Closer air view, showing detail of existing civic center area.*

1, 4, 5, 6 *Studies for development of urban-plaza quality in civic center by the expansion and enrichment of pedestrian areas, the introduction of trees, water, and garden structures, a pedestrian bridge connecting City Hall to the plaza, and a vehicular bridge over the water.*

4

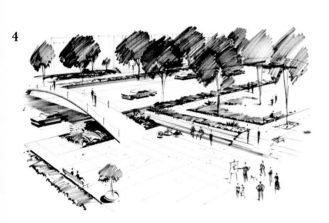

5

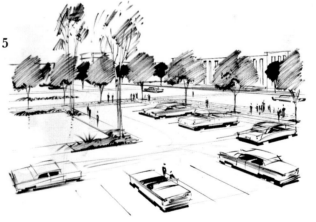

201

6

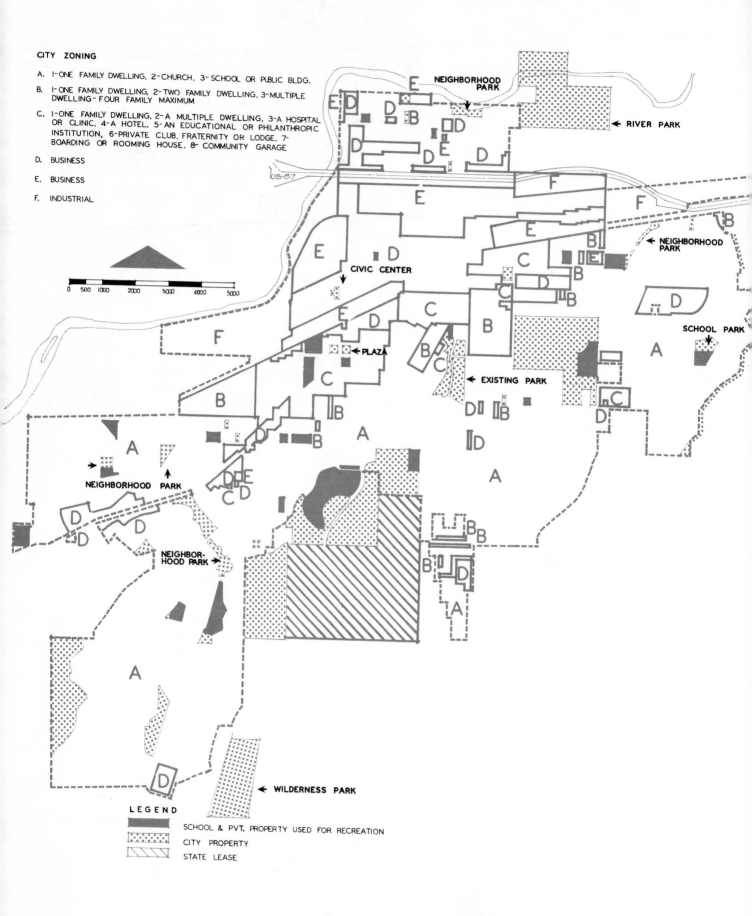

CITY ZONING

A. 1-ONE FAMILY DWELLING, 2-CHURCH, 3-SCHOOL OR PUBLIC BLDG.

B. 1-ONE FAMILY DWELLING, 2-TWO FAMILY DWELLING, 3-MULTIPLE DWELLING-FOUR FAMILY MAXIMUM

C. 1-ONE FAMILY DWELLING, 2-A MULTIPLE DWELLING, 3-A HOSPITAL OR CLINIC, 4-A HOTEL, 5-AN EDUCATIONAL OR PHILANTHROPIC INSTITUTION, 6-PRIVATE CLUB, FRATERNITY OR LODGE, 7-BOARDING OR ROOMING HOUSE, 8- COMMUNITY GARAGE

D. BUSINESS

E. BUSINESS

F. INDUSTRIAL

0 500 1000 2000 3000 4000 5000

NEIGHBORHOOD PARK

← RIVER PARK

CIVIC CENTER

← PLAZA

← NEIGHBORHOOD PARK

SCHOOL PARK

← EXISTING PARK

NEIGHBORHOOD PARK

NEIGHBOR-HOOD PARK →

← WILDERNESS PARK

LEGEND

SCHOOL & PVT. PROPERTY USED FOR RECREATION
CITY PROPERTY
STATE LEASE

7, 8 *Downtown park. Air view and sketch plan for two open square blocks straddling the main street south of downtown. Building in one block has been razed. Both blocks are filled with well-grown trees and both have a considerable cross slope. The design study endeavors to connect the two blocks by realigning the street vertically and horizontally; to integrate the park space with the bordering buildings by closing the peripheral streets and introducing free-flowing paving patterns; and to enrich the resultant spaces further with extensive water patterns and large-scale sculpture.*

9 *Existing city park. Well developed with swimming pool, game courts, baseball field, outdoor theater, and plantings of golden willow and silver poplar.*

8

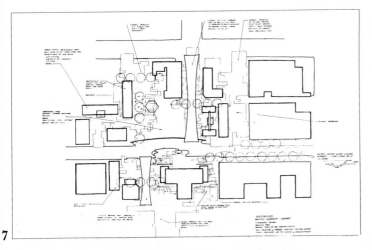

7

9

203

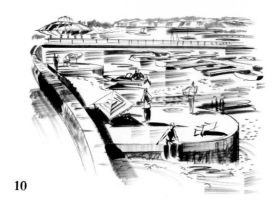

10

11

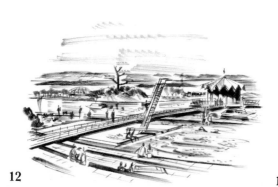

12

10, 11, 12, 13 *River park. The flow of the Platte River has been stabilized by extensive dam construction. It therefore becomes possible to develop it into a predictable recreation resource. Plan and sketches indicate the potential for an aquatic park of multiple richness, including wilderness island, day camp, children's island, controlled boating and swimming, river-going power boats, resorts, launching pad for trailered boats, picnic areas, gun club, three-par golf, community building, plaza shops, and trailers.*

14, 15, 16 *Wilderness park. A 70-acre site on the mountainside fringe of town, donated by Harry Yessness, leading local merchant. 14 shows part of the site as is, irregular prairie topography with roughly dammed stream. Plan and bird's-eye indicate potential for a woodsy planted development in patterns of blue spruce, dark pines, silver poplar, and golden willow. Trees are in open patterns to permit surrounding prairie to filter in. Eventually the town will grow around park. Most of the area will be for camping, hiking, riding, and nature study. The pond is reshaped and given an island with a snack bar and boat pier. There will also be a substantial community retreat, junior museum, children's zoo, administration, and overlook development.*

14

204

13

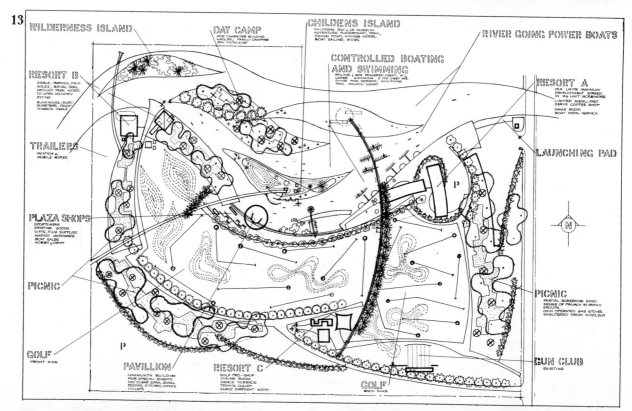

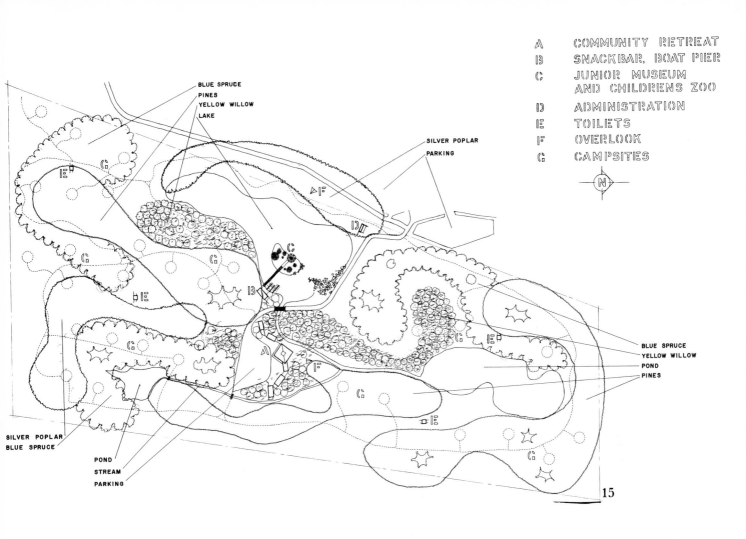

BLUE SPRUCE
PINES
YELLOW WILLOW
LAKE

SILVER POPLAR

PARKING

A   COMMUNITY RETREAT
B   SNACKBAR, BOAT PIER
C   JUNIOR MUSEUM
    AND CHILDRENS ZOO
D   ADMINISTRATION
E   TOILETS
F   OVERLOOK
G   CAMPSITES

N

BLUE SPRUCE
YELLOW WILLOW
POND
PINES

SILVER POPLAR
BLUE SPRUCE

POND
STREAM
PARKING

15

16

17

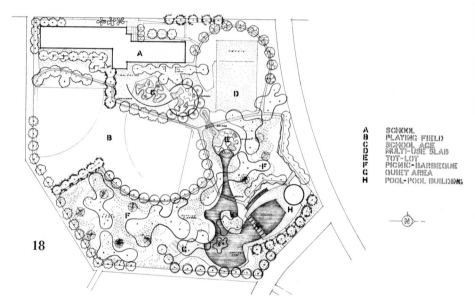

18

A B C D E F G H

SCHOOL
PLAYING FIELD
SCHOOL AGE
MULTI-USE SLAB
TOT-LOT
PICNIC-BARBEQUE
QUIET AREA
POOL-POOL BUILDING

19

206

17, 18 *Neighborhood school park. Plan for development of bare elementary school site into balanced neighborhood facility combining the disciplined facilities required by school programming with the freer and more flexible elements possible in a neighborhood park. Areas include a playing field, school-age play area, multiuse slab (court games), tot-lot, picnic-barbecue area, and combined lagoon and swimming pool with dressing shelter.*

19, 20, 21 *Neighborhood playground parks.* **19** *and* **20** *show the distribution of natural green drainage space through the city. Prototype plan* **21** *was developed to allow repetition in whole or part on several or many sites. It includes complete balance of facilities: entry area with refreshment stand, space for barnyard with animals, picnic facility; preschool area with parents' shelter, pool, maze and play sculpture on contoured ground, other climbing and balancing equipment, riding path; transition to school-age area via stile wall and connecting streetcar (to emphasize interpenetration and joint responsibility); school-age area with pool, shelter, old cars, maze, log pyramids, balancing structure, wrestling bowl, junk building yard, and little theater; and multipurpose slab for games, skating, dancing. Curving pergola connects all elements.*

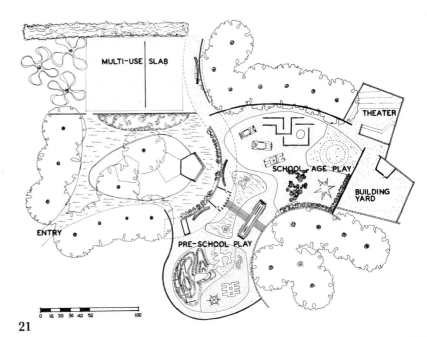

21

20

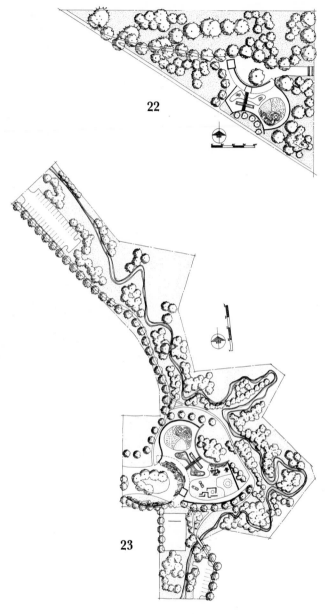

22

22, 23, 24, 25 **22** and **23** are five blocks apart; one concentrates on school-age space, bordering on a school playground; the other on preschool. The former is flat, the latter has considerable cross-slope. **24** is a flat peninsula with a 10-ft deep stream bed winding around three sides. Space requirements meant deletion of building yard and theater. **25** is adjusted to a narrow shelf along the river, with existing trees and a small clubhouse.

23

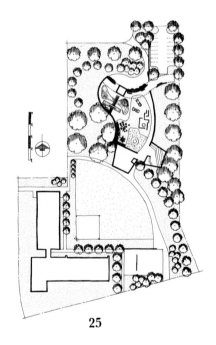

25

24

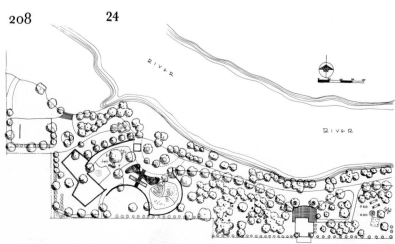

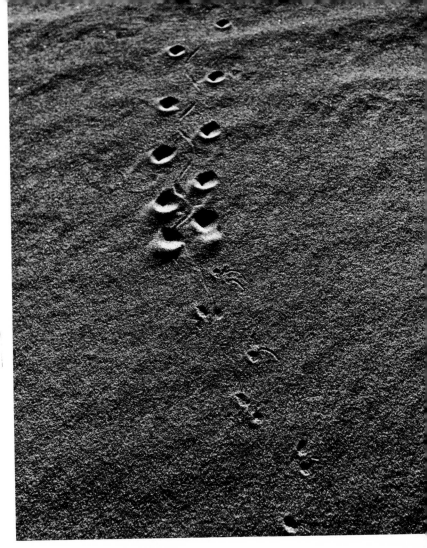

EL CENTRO, CALIF.

El Centro is a compact small city in the center of the richest agricultural valley in the country, Imperial Valley. The valley is bordered east and west by rugged desert mountains. Subject to the most blistering hot summers in the United States, the city has developed a reliance on trees, arcades, and air conditioning. To the last must go the credit for producing a livable year-round climate within buildings, and thus the psychological possibility for stable and continuous community life and spirit. With such choice and control, it becomes possible to enjoy not only the eight months of fine desert weather, but also the magnificent nights of the desert summer. Plans shown here envision the possibility of El Centro becoming one of the great winter-resort areas of the nation.

El Centro is the leading commercial, industrial, and governmental center of the Imperial Valley. People come here to do business, to work, to shop, to vacation, to play, and to learn. The population is now over 18,000.

The planning area covers over 25 square miles of land, of which 3.7 square miles are within the city. Ten square miles are proposed for urban development. The remainder is proposed to remain in agricultural use.

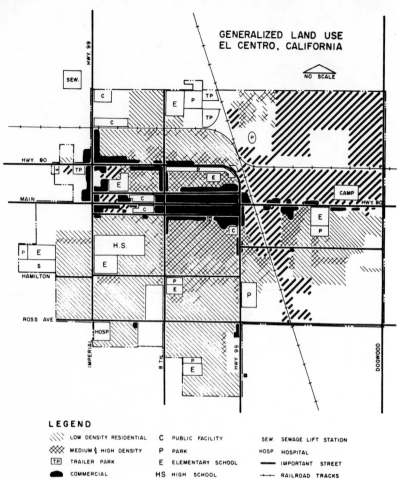

GENERALIZED LAND USE
EL CENTRO, CALIFORNIA

NO SCALE

LEGEND

//// LOW DENSITY RESIDENTIAL	C PUBLIC FACILITY	SEW SEWAGE LIFT STATION	
XXX MEDIUM & HIGH DENSITY	P PARK	HOSP HOSPITAL	
TP TRAILER PARK	E ELEMENTARY SCHOOL	—— IMPORTANT STREET	
● COMMERCIAL	HS HIGH SCHOOL	++++ RAILROAD TRACKS	
/// INDUSTRIAL	S PAROCHIAL SCHOOL	—··— CITY BOUNDARY	

SUMMARY OF GENERAL PLAN OBJECTIVES

The goal of the general plan is the development of a balanced, efficient, and healthy community where the relationship between people, land, and activities and the needs for living, work, and play will satisfy the most desirable standards. The following objectives are the bases which underlie the general plan proposals.

· *The maintenance and protection of the agricultural uses which are the life blood of El Centro and the Imperial Valley.*

· *Sound, healthful, and desirable residential areas, at various densities with properly related amenities and facilities.*

· *Schools, parks, and other public facilities conveniently located to serve the people at the neighborhood level.*

· *A city park integrated with the proposed high school to provide a community recreational, educational, social, and cultural center.*

· *An integrated civic center district combining all levels of governmental agencies.*

· *Commercial facilities to serve the shopping and service needs of the residents of El Centro and its trading area at the neighborhood, community, and regional levels.*

· *A revitalized downtown area and guidance for its expansion and development.*

· *A strong and diversified industrial base. Provision of positive physical separation of uses where industry meets nonindustrial use.*

· *A comprehensive circulation system to serve and integrate the proposed facilities and land uses.*

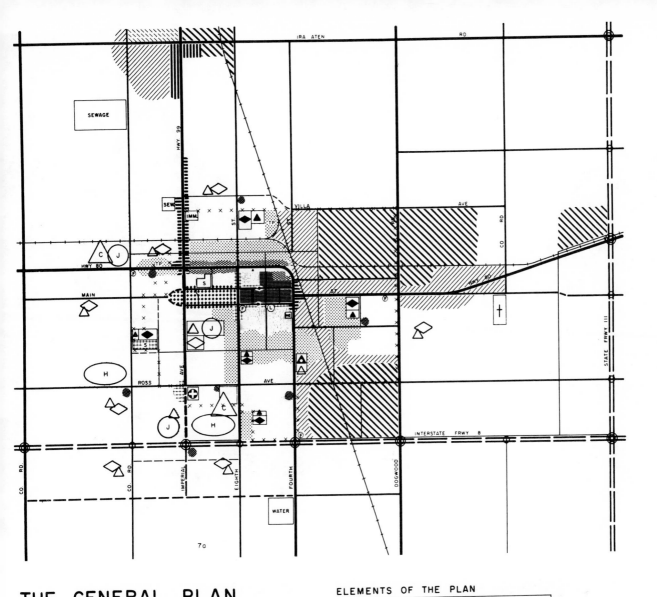

THE GENERAL PLAN
EL CENTRO, CALIFORNIA

ELEMENTS OF THE PLAN

RESIDENTIAL		RECREATION	
	LOW DENSITY 0 - 4 FAM/NET AC.	△	NEIGHBORHOOD PARK ▲
	LOW DENSITY 0 - 6 FAM/NET AC.	△C	COMMUNITY PARK
	MEDIUM DENSITY 7 - 15 FAM/NET AC.	▲	SPECIAL USE PARK
	HIGH DENSITY 16 - 29 FAM/NET AC.		ADAMS PARK
T.P.	TRAILER PARK 10 - 13 FAM/NET AC.		

COMMERCIAL		PUBLIC FACILITIES	
	CENTRAL BUSINESS DIST		CIVIC CENTER DISTRICT
	NEIGHBORHOOD CENTER	F	FIRE STATION
	OFFICE - INSTITUTIONAL	L	LIBRARY
	MOTEL ROW	NG	NATIONAL GUARD
	HIGHWAY COMMERCIAL	IMM	IMMIGRATION OFFICE
	COMMERCIAL - RECREATION	◇	ELEMENTARY SCH ◆
		J	JUNIOR HIGH SCHOOL

INDUSTRIAL		H	HIGH SCHOOL
	LIGHT INDUSTRY	S	SPECIAL SCHOOL
	GENERAL INDUSTRY	× ×	CITY BOUNDARY

STREETS & HWYS.	
	FREEWAY

QUASI PUBLIC			MAJOR HIGHWAY
	OFFICE - INSTITUTIONAL		SECONDARY HIGHWAY
✚	HOSPITAL		TRAFFIC COLLECTOR
S	PAROCHIAL SCHOOL	◎	INTERCHANGE
✝	CEMETERY	○	GRADE SEPARATION
		←	ONE WAY STREET

CONSERVATION		TRANSPORTATION	
	AGRICULTURE		AIRPORT
		←→	RAILROAD R-O-W

0   1/2 MILE   1 MILE   2 MILES

LAND–USE: AGRICULTURAL

OBJECTIVES

· *Maintain the agriculture which is the basis of the El Centro and the Imperial Valley economy*

· *Protect agriculture against piecemeal, hop-scotching, and uncontrolled encroachment by urban uses*

LAND–USE: RESIDENTIAL

OBJECTIVES

· *A sound, healthful, and desirable living environment based on space and occupancy standards that will promote stable residential areas*

· *Designation of appropriate areas to meet the demand for various types of housing with properly related amenities and facilities*

· *Conservation and/or rehabilitation of stable residential areas; no mixing of residential and incompatible nonresidential uses*

To fulfill the objectives listed above, the general plan proposes future neighborhood guides and standards to take advantage of the excellent living conditions in El Centro by:

1. Providing several different densities of residential development

2. Proposing public facilities for good neighborhood living—including schools and parks close enough to walk to without traffic hazards

3. Proposing planned, integrated shopping facilities to serve the residential areas—convenient, pleasant, adequate parking

4. Proposing a comprehensive street system, routing nonresidential traffic around neighborhood areas and not through them

5. Protecting.the home environment; no intrusion of incompatible nonresidential uses

6. Improving the appearance of the neighborhoods by improved street designs, higher development standards, street improvements, street trees, and better maintenance of front yards

214

LAND–USE: COMMERCIAL

OBJECTIVES

· *To revitalize the downtown area and guide its expansion and development and to maintain its position as the dominant shopping district in the Imperial Valley*

· *To serve the shopping service needs of residents efficiently and conveniently by providing neighborhood shopping facilities*

· *To encourage planned, integrated commercial development which will look well, function well, and not create traffic conflicts*

· *To provide for groups of commercial uses related to or dependent upon highway traffic*

CENTRAL BUSINESS DISTRICT

The central business district of El Centro represents the strongest and most vital shopping area in the Imperial Valley. In the construction of the buildings in the area, some efforts were made to meet the problem of extreme summer temperature by the development of arcaded walks. In order to meet the challenge of the completely designed, one-stop shopping center with totally air-conditioned enclosed space and extensive and well-planned parking areas, the present business district will have to adopt some of the features of the new shopping centers. If this challenge is not faced, there is likely to be a decline in the service that the central area will provide. This would be extremely dangerous to the economy of the community and to the individuals who work in, have their places of business in, or own property in the central business district

215

El Centro, at present, has a substantial central business district with a dollar volume of retail sales equivalent to cities twice its size.

Its per capita sales figure of $2,640 is much higher than the $1,673 for the county and the $1,447 for the state.

El Centro has a higher percentage than the county or the state in all major categories of retail sales. It is over double per capita in general merchandise and automotive sales and is high in apparel, though far below Calexico in this category.

These figures reveal that El Centro has a considerable outside-trading area. This was substantiated by the Trading Area Survey which revealed that over half of the shoppers were from out of town on the day of the survey.

The present central business district core extends from Eighth Street to Fourth Street between Broadway and State Street. The high value commercial frontage is on both sides of Main Street. Sears, J. C. Penney, and MacDonalds are the anchor stores. Most of the existing off-street parking lots are located in back of these frontages and have access off Broadway and State Streets.

For the central business district the general plan proposes:

A. FOR IMMEDIATE ACTION

1. A cleanup campaign to tidy alleys, parking lots, and all spaces around buildings. Some of the alleys are unsightly and are sometimes used for storage of trash and other items. Some parking areas are in need of paving or improvement.

2. An improvement or remodeling of fronts, sides, and backs of buildings is needed. Coordinated design, color schemes, and harmonious signs will greatly improve the downtown appearance. Double-fronted stores with inviting, well-designed parking lot entrances as well as street entrances are also essential. Existing parking lot entrances are far from inviting even though a high percentage of people enter from the rear because of the location of parking there.

3. The retention of commercial frontage on both sides of Main Street. Retail sales businesses which require a central business district location should be concentrated in the core area. Offices and other uses which do not require a central business district location or do not depend on walk-in business should be located on the periphery where office and institutional areas have been designated on the plan.

4. The expansion and improvement of parking facilities to meet the present and future needs and demands of the shopper. The minimum standard for downtown parking should be at least 1:1—one square foot of parking for each square foot of commercial floor space, plus employee parking at one space for each three employees. These standards are now considered inadequate by the Urban Land Institute, which recommends parking ratios of 3:1 or 4:1. The plan proposes that the portions of the blocks behind the Main Street frontages and facing on Broadway and State Street be converted to off-street parking. This process is already under way.

5. The development of better merchandising policies. Attention should be called to the many possibilities that exist for complete shopping in one center with all of the pleasant features suggested above. Advertising should emphasize the "center."

6. A Central Area Committee should be developed to carry out the proposals and to work closely with the city so that it may do its part.

B. LONG-TERM OBJECTIVES

1. The conversion of Broadway and State Street to one-way streets from 700 ft west of Imperial Avenue to Fourth Street, with State Street traffic heading east and Broadway traffic heading west. This will bring more efficient movement of traffic, less congestion, and better access to off-street parking areas. Much of the congestion on Main Street will also be relieved.

2. The provision of areas for future expansion of the central business district by extending the central business district northward on Sixth Street. Expansion in this direction is feasible and desirable as Sixth and Main Streets are the center of the central business district. Access from Adams Avenue would be facilitated with Sixth Street as the primary accessway to downtown El Centro. The revitalization and renewal of the fringe areas of the existing district should provide for additional expansion of retail uses.

3. The closing of Main Street from Fourth Street to 700 ft west of Imperial Avenue. Between Fourth and Eighth Streets, a pedestrian shopping mall to eliminate automotive traffic congestion and create a pedestrian shoppers' paradise is proposed. Pleasant landscaping, benches, paving, pools, fountains, and shade could make this an attractive place to shop even in the heat of summer. An overhead screen or shade element is the key. The arcades are only a partial solution to the problem. The proposed screen or shade element should span the mall, thereby creating a total and unified shopping environment.

LAND–USE: INDUSTRIAL

OBJECTIVES

· To strengthen the City's industrial base
· To secure sound industrial development, well

located in relation to transportation routes, utilities, and other compatible land uses

To provide buffering where industry meets non-industrial use

INDUSTRY

Industry is essential to the economy of a city for it provides work opportunities, shares the tax load for city services and facilities, and provides personal incomes which are spent at local stores.

The general plan proposes a sound industrial base by:

1. Setting aside adequate land suitable for industry
2. Establishing standards for industrial development
3. Recommending adequate off-street parking
4. Integrating industrial land-use and circulation
5. Recommending the prohibition of future mixing of industrial and nonindustrial land-uses

PUBLIC FACILITIES

In order to accommodate and serve properly tomorrow's population, the city must plan now to acquire and reserve sites for public facilities where they will be needed before good sites are no longer available. Examples of missed opportunities and improperly located public facilities with their undesirable consequences are found in all cities. The price of land tomorrow will not be as low as it is today. Therefore, the agencies responsible must act to ensure that necessary sites and facilities will be available in proper locations.

SCHOOLS

Schools in the general plan have been located to serve the population expected from the land-uses proposed. The direct responsibility for providing schools rests, of course, with the school districts, but the general plan assists by:

1. Indicating a long-range plan of land-use to guide future development and establish proper land-use relationships
2. Relating schools to ultimate population, based on proposed residential densities and anticipated population characteristics, other land-uses, and traffic ways
3. Proposing integrated school-park facilities wherever possible

School population at ultimate land development is the basic element in long-range school facility planning.

From the projected ultimate population of 52,000 people, 7,650 kindergarten through sixth grade students have been estimated for the planning area. To serve them the general plan proposes 13 ele-

mentary schools with an average enrollment of 590 students.

Five elementary schools are existing.
Eight elementary schools have been proposed.
Three junior high schools have been proposed.
Two new high school sites have been proposed.

A site 500 ft north of the proposed Interstate Freeway 8 between Eighth Street and Imperial Avenue will replace the existing inadequate high school site. The new site is now under consideration by the School Board and has been strongly recommended by the City Planning Commission. The advantages of locating the high school here are great. It is the closest available large site centrally located to serve the entire city; it is the area of greatest future growth; it has good access. For the school districts its principal advantage is that students will be able to utilize the auditorium and swimming pool which will be located in the city park. To the city, the principal advantage is not only the utilization of the high school's facilities for recreational purposes but the creation of a combined center for community activities.

RECREATION

The general plan seeks to establish a foundation upon which to build a system of facilities which will bring recreation into the daily life of each citizen, making leisure time productive for the family, the neighborhood, and the community.

In the community survey the people revealed that they were acutely aware of the shortage of park and recreation facilities in El Centro. The recreation facilities they most expressed a need for were: a swimming pool, parks, playgrounds, a recreation center, dancing facilities, teenage facilities, an auditorium, and a skating rink.

To meet these present needs and to meet future needs (ultimate population of 52,000), the general plan proposes a comprehensive system of recreation facilities for all ages and all new neighborhoods.

NEIGHBORHOOD RECREATION CENTERS, the anchor of the recreation system, should be within walking distance of homes. They are planned primarily for young children and family groups.

A total of 17 neighborhood parks are proposed in the planning area, a standard of one park for each 3,000 population (3 existing and developed, 4 existing but undeveloped, and 10 proposed). The parks should be located adjacent to elementary schools and where possible should be 7 to 10 acres in size. Many of the existing sites are too small for proper development and use.

COMMUNITY RECREATION CENTERS should serve several neighborhoods with a wide range of indoor and outdoor recreation opportunities. Although planned primarily for young people and adults, community parks also include facilities for younger children and serve as neighborhood recreation centers for families in the vicinity.

Two community parks are proposed in the planning area, a standard of one park for each 25,000 population. These parks are best located adjacent to a senior or junior high school where play facilities can be shared. The city park plans are discussed and presented in detail in a separate portion of this study.

SPECIAL-USE PARKS include a separate area providing space for a single activity or facility or for several closely related activities or facilities.

Two existing special-use parks are proposed to remain—Adams Park which is a visual asset to the city and Stark Field which is a baseball park. It is also proposed that they include facilities for younger children and serve as neighborhood parks.

CIVIC CENTER

The general plan proposes that all city, county, state, federal, and irrigation district buildings be combined and integrated in one civic center district. Such a functionally integrated, architecturally unified civic center will facilitate governmental operation and will promote a civic identity and pride.

The area should be given first consideration by all public agencies as the preferred location for all public buildings and activities. However, the civic center district is not exclusively reserved for public buildings but includes related quasi-public and private uses.

CIRCULATION ELEMENT

OBJECTIVE

A comprehensive transportation system for the movement of persons and goods with maximum efficiency and convenience and minimum danger and delay.

The circulation element of the general plan is a comprehensive transportation system for the movement of people and goods within and through the city with maximum efficiency and safety. It deals with various modes of vehicular transportation including: freeways, major and secondary highways, traffic collectors, a possible one-way street system, a truck route system, railroad lines, grade separations, airport, heliport, bus transit service.

Traffic planning must be approached on a regional as well as a local level. It must take into consideration both the overall land-use patterns and the major traffic generators in the region and the city —interstate traffic destinations, regional recreation areas, downtown business areas, industrial areas, military bases, and intensively developed residential areas; and the patterns of traffic flow between them

The circulation system proposed in the general plan is based on and coordinated with county, state, and city established and proposed routes.

CIVIC CENTER

PRINCIPLES

This study of a proposed civic center for El Centro is based on the following principles:

1. That a civic center or town center of some size will provide a needed focal point for El Centro, now absent

2. That because of the relatively small size of the city's and state's requirements, it will be mutually beneficial to group city and state facilities with county and irrigation district facilities

3. That agriculture, because of its importance to this area, deserves a building, or group of buildings, related to the civic center

4. That to emphasize the importance of the center, further areas should be designated for—
   A. Quasi-public uses
   B. Private-civic uses

5. That the civic center, by its design and location, should reinforce the existing commercial and government centers, rather than disperse and separate them

6. That a civic center boundary be established as soon as possible, to control use, density, landscaping, and other qualities

ARCHITECTURAL CHARACTER. We believe that the El Centro civic center complex can and should be a unique architectural expression, particularly suited to this environment and climate. We believe this can be achieved by adhering to three principles (in addition to retaining a sensitive architect):

1. Space the buildings so there are generous land areas between. Space is a characteristic of Imperial Valley and should be exploited. This principle was well understood by the architects of the courthouse, and not as well understood by the architects of the veterans' building.

2. Use water as a feature in fountains and pools throughout the civic center.

3. Use shade devices both man-made (trellises, canopies) and natural (groves of trees) to provide a special regional architectural quality.

This civic center, as proposed, cannot grow in a haphazard hit-and-miss fashion. To some, the scale of the center may appear sparse. This was done deliberately. We believe the space is elegant and that the open green vistas combined with water features will prove to be of both esthetic and financial advantage to the city and county. Space, once lost, can never be brought back, except at great cost. Space is the greatest assurance against obsolescence, as future needs (which we cannot possibly predict) have a better chance of being met where there is plenty of elbow room for creative thinking.

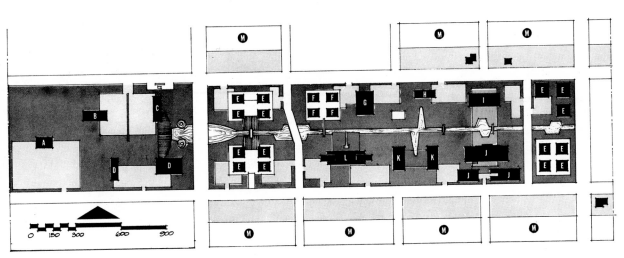

LEGEND

- [ ] PARKING AREAS
- [■] BUILDINGS
- [ ] WATER
- [ ] LANDSCAPED AREAS

BUILDING KEY

A·D IMPERIAL IRRIGATION DISTRICT
B COUNTY OF IMPERIAL ROAD DEPT.
C COUNTY OF IMP., STATE OF CALIF.,
   FEDERAL AGRICULTURAL CENTER

E QUASI PUBLIC
F CITY OF EL CENTRO
G EX. COMMERCIAL, FUTURE CIVIC
H EX. CITY OF EL CENTRO POLICE

I EXISTING COUNTY HEALTH
J EXISTING COURT HOUSE
K COUNTY OF IMPERIAL
L STATE OF CALIFORNIA
M PRIVATE CIVIC

Suggested expansion, Imperial County Office Building.

View of Imperial County Building through palm- shaded plaza.

219

Toward quiet area.

CITY PARK

The new city park for the city of El Centro will serve as a focus for social and recreational life for the entire community. It will develop a physical framework of unprecedented quality and visual interest for desert recreation. The special character of the park will also give El Centro a memorable symbol of nationwide interest in attracting tourists. The basic concept of the plan is to produce a green and hilly oasis, well equipped with diversified recreation facilities, surrounding a lake of 5.7 acres, in the center of which will sit the new community auditorium. The park site is now 36 acres of which 20 are already owned by the City. Extending from this, parallel to the future freeway, is a pitch and putt golf course site of 20.63 acres. West of these, the proposed high school site of 47.39 acres includes a suggested parking area of 6.7 acres which would serve all three facilities. This parking area should perhaps be shared by the park and the high school, or even belong entirely to the city.

The park area, exclusive of lake, auditorium, and swimming pool area which are covered elsewhere in this study, is planned in general on the basis of the Guide for Planning Recreation Parks in California published in 1956 by the State of California. Included in the park area are:

1. Preschool age play lot and mothers' area of 1/3 acre

2. Play area for elementary school age children of 2/5 acres

3. Parklike meadow area for free play of about 6 acres

4. Multipurpose slab for court games

5. Picnic and barbecue area of 4 acres

6. One acre of free space for special events (community festivals, trade fairs, agricultural meetings, etc.)

7. Nature area of 3 1/2 acres

8. Older people's quiet-game center of 2 1/2 acres

9. Off-street parking of about 2 acres

However, the park is viewed as more than a cafeteria of facilities. It is viewed as a comprehensive and harmonious landscape unit in which the special facilities, the general landscape development, the lake and the buildings are integrated elements. From the lake area and the facilities in and around it, one will look into an open meadow surrounded by contoured hillocks and ridges, 10 to 20 ft high, developed from the surplus soil now existing on the site, and the material excavated for the lake. The special facilities and the pedestrian circulation paths will be tucked in among the folds of these hillocks, leaving the main central meadow as free green space. The entire contoured area, surrounding that meadow on three sides, will be planted with trees in a woodsy grove. Tree patterns of the many kinds which do well in El Centro will be used in structural groups, patterns, and masses, to give three-dimensional form and continuity to the entire park space, linking together lake, buildings, and contoured ground areas into one comprehensive whole.

The park facilities are distributed and arranged in patterns based on functional relationships and neighborhood relationships.

1. The auditorium, community center, and swimming pool area are grouped in and around the lake at the south end of the park site where they center in the entire complex of facilities projected for this area, forming a hub.

2. The golf course, extending the green space of the park, provides a 500-ft buffer strip between the freeway and the suggested site for the high school.

3. The children's play areas and multipurpose slab are placed on the west side of the park, closest

EL CENTRO CITY PARK

THE PREPARATION OF THIS PLAN WAS FINANCED IN PART THROUGH AN URBAN PLANNING GRANT FROM THE HOUSING AND HOME FINANCE AGENCY, UNDER THE PROVISIONS OF SECTION 701 OF THE HOUSING ACT OF 1954, AS AMENDED STATE OF CALIFORNIA, DEPARTMENT OF FINANCE.

to the immediate neighborhood which they will serve.

4. *The day-camping, nature, and maintenance areas which are mostly quiet, are distributed along the west side of the park which immediately abuts on this neighborhood.*

5. *The senior citizens' area is located near Ross Avenue for easy access, insulated from the street with contoured ground and tree planting and looking out over the play meadow toward the lake to maintain contact with general park activity.*

7. *The area for special events is immediately adjacent to the community center building.*

8. *Pedestrian circulation is provided completely around and through the park and across the lake, connecting park areas, the golf course, and the high school with the activity center.*

It is implicit in the plan that the detailed design development which will follow it should produce a complete and consistent character in all structural elements from buildings to benches; in all outdoor equipment from play areas to mechanical engineering elements; in all planting from grass to trees; and in the detailed design of the lake itself.

The lake edge treatment should be varied and carefully studied, and it should be stocked with carefully selected fish and water plants. Irrigation and night-lighting systems should be designed in close coordination with all structural and landscape development. The earth work which will begin the development should be carefully planned and specified in order to provide the best possible growing conditions for plants and retention basin for lake water.

This precise plan provides the basic concept and general form for the park, makes it possible to establish a program, functions as a guide to action, but requires implementation with much more detailed

Toward play area.

221

design study in order to be sure that its potentiality is fulfilled. Rough cost estimates, priority schedules, and finance programs can be developed on the basis of this plan.

The park as projected in this study is conceived as both a great and memorable element of physical landscape in the Imperial Valley and a center for great and memorable social and recreational experience for all of the people in its service area. It is felt that these two objectives go hand in hand and that neither one can be attained without the other. This high-quality physical environment can only be developed as the result of spirited and cooperative community action, and this action should be inspired by the promise and later the fulfillment of a park of unprecedented quality.

COMMUNITY DESIGN PLAN

There is growing awareness in community planning and design circles that general planning leads to physical results which must be designed; that the quality of these physical results has a great deal to do with the success of the general planning; and that the gap which commonly exists between general planning and precise design should therefore be narrowed or closed. The presentation of this community design plan is a step in this direction.

The existing elements include important buildings, both public and private, some obvious and some perhaps surprising. The civic center buildings both new and proposed, the arcaded main street, commercial buildings, the hospital, the principal churches and school buildings, and the utility structures such as water plant, sewage plant, generating plant, and water tower are all landmarks identifying the entrance to or the portions of the community.

Park to lake.

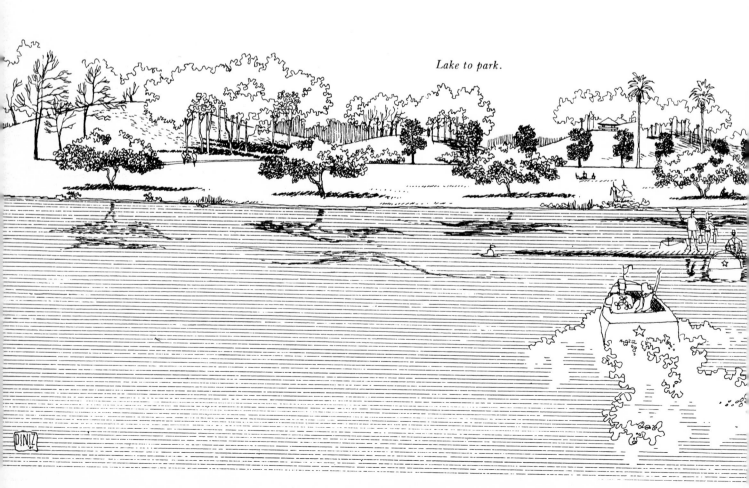

Lake to park.

El Centro is fortunate in having a simple and comprehensible form to begin with, based upon a cross formed by Eighth and Main Streets, with their outer entrances marked by the above-mentioned utility structures, and their center by the Civic Center and the downtown business district. A considerable section of the center of town, south of the business district and a little north, is well planted with mature trees which are a priceless asset in the Imperial Valley. Newer areas south and west are being planted, but it is, of course, too soon for the results to show. Other areas of the town, particularly east of the railroad tracks and immediately around the central business district, are sadly lacking in trees. An energetic, sympathetic, and coordinated program designed to develop tree plantings in these areas would benefit the entire community.

The plan also suggests controlled and consistent tree planting along specific main and secondary streets and special streets around the downtown and civic center areas with the thought that such tree planting, if of the right types of trees, can develop a framework or skyline pattern which will give still more visual unity and continuity to the entire community. These should probably be of the tallest species available. Special consideration should be given to Eighth Street, from Main to the new park site. It is felt that a green belt or greenway can be developed, connecting these two principal elements of the community. Eighth Street is wide enough to have a center dividing strip which would make possible three rows of trees; furthermore, by cooperative programming, tree planting of continuous kinds might be developed throughout the blocks west of Eighth Street, linking the park and the downtown area. A strip of the present northerly acres of the waterworks site which will not be used for park purposes should be preserved along the west side of Eighth Street to continue the greenway concept and link the main park with Harding School and Park.

Thus, the physical structure of the community, based on sound land-use and circulation planning, is seen as a pattern of relations between buildings, streets, trees, and open spaces. These are the primary elements of the community landscape and it is possible, especially in a community of the size and cooperative spirit of El Centro, to project the coordination of these elements in unified and beautiful relationships. Existing important buildings can be emphasized as having community as well as individual importance. New buildings can be so located and designed as to develop the physical community structure (as we suggest in the Civic Center). Likewise, tree plantings based on the careful survey and preservation of existing good specimens and groups, and research into kinds which will do well in El Centro, can develop a sense of the form and structure of the community beyond that provided by buildings and streets alone. An excellent example is the fine row of eucalyptus connecting the south boundary of the developed area with the water plant. These trees are an important landmark and should be preserved.

The water plant, sewage plant, and generating station, viewed as architectural elements at the entrance to the city rather than as mere utilities, should perhaps have more serious thought given to their landscape environment. While it is difficult to give American cities, with their constant tendency to expand, the neat and precise form of medieval and Renaissance cities in Europe, it is nevertheless possible by careful attention to the problem, to develop concepts of form along the lines suggested here that will expand with the growth of the city and control its borders as they push into the countryside. These borders, which are apt to be the more careless and shoddy portions of a city, should receive as careful attention as the Civic Center and downtown business area.

SPECIAL RECREATION FACILITIES

The Citizens Committee on Municipal Improvements strongly recommended the relocation of the public pool near the high school and the construction of a major recreation building. In addition, the city manager and other public officials identified the need for an auditorium-theatre.

Other special facilities that the consultant group feels should be included are:
1. Three- and four-par golf, driving range, and putting green
2. Fishing lagoon
3. Boating marina
4. Prestige restaurant and snack bar
These varied elements suggest the need for establishing a unifying theme for the park and the desirability of treating this great communitywide facility as a resort complex. Too many existing public parks lack any real environmental quality. They manifest only a "cafeteria of activities" approach to park planning.

The successful park, the park that becomes a personal thing to each and every resident, is the one that meets the emotional as well as the physical needs of the people it serves. Here one finds himself in the park, simply because he feels best there. Only after the individual has had time to come out from under the spell of the place does he look around and begin to seek the specific activities available.

This is not only good park planning, it is what the good merchandiser would call the selling difference. We shouldn't be afraid of the commercial connotation—it is founded on some very real and very human basic needs. This quality-that-sets-apart has implications as much for attracting out-of-town visitors as it does for serving the daily needs of permanent residents.

This resort concept, and park-with-a-theme notion serves the public most economically because it has been proven that mood doesn't cost more to attain. It comes about as a result of having a sensitive feeling about the town, the people, and the leisure-time activities, found in the resort park in spirit as well as in the physical form of the park itself. It represents the most inexpensive development policy, because the more compelling the mood, the less critical become detailing and materials—the little things that cost the real money.

From the viewpoint of a city interested in serving its people with the most extensive recreation program and at the same time operating its affairs on a businesslike basis, a nominal fee for area and facility use might be charged. This is an accepted practice today in many communities. The city park can become a place where the family comes to spend the day and with great local pride can invite their out-of-town relatives to come and share this pleasant environment with them.

SWIM PARKS

Swim parks, an idiom long employed in European countries and only recently coming into its own in the United States, are predicated on the notion that facilities as expensive to construct and to maintain as public swimming pools must serve the public; and to the highest extent possible consistent with public use, return revenue for 12 months of the year. At El Centro the ability to achieve all-year usage is further aided by the adoption of the park-school concept, which makes the swim park equally available for the

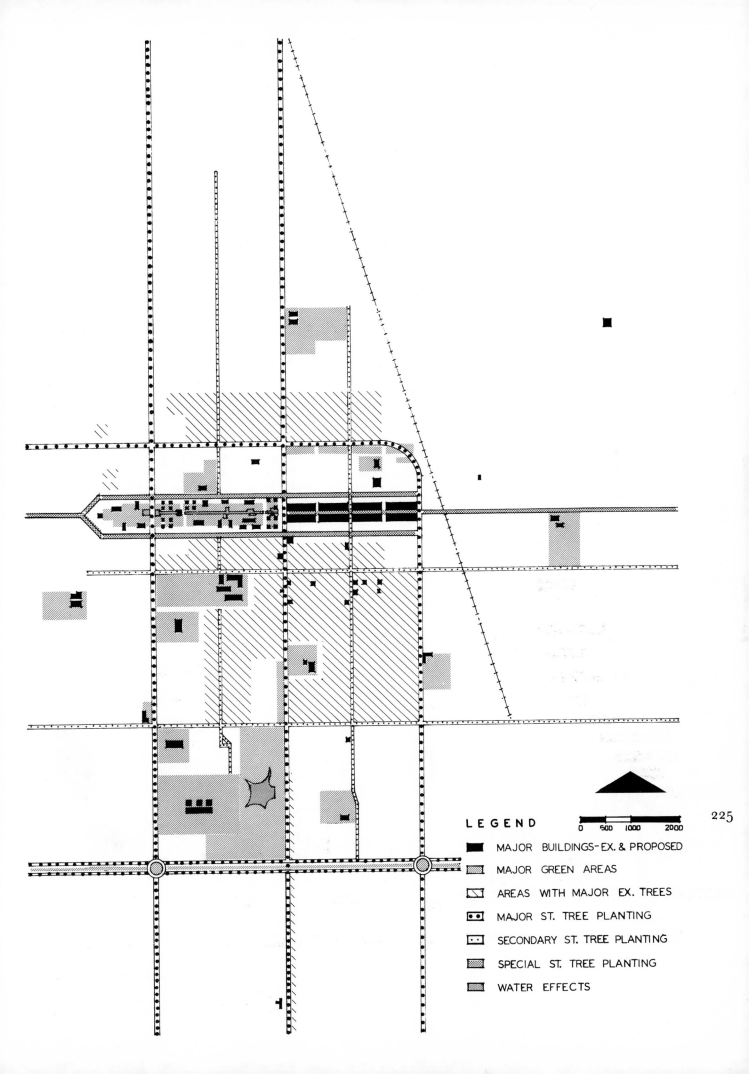

LEGEND

- ■ MAJOR BUILDINGS- EX. & PROPOSED
- ▨ MAJOR GREEN AREAS
- ◩ AREAS WITH MAJOR EX. TREES
- ⚇ MAJOR ST. TREE PLANTING
- ⋯ SECONDARY ST. TREE PLANTING
- ▦ SPECIAL ST. TREE PLANTING
- ▨ WATER EFFECTS

0   500   1000   2000

225

high school physical education programs and for community leisure time.

The swim park recognizes water as much for its environmental potential as for its specific use potential. It is because the water's primary role is that of background mood—background for not one, but twenty or more activities, that the season can be extended so long. For years, recreation planners have sought ways to make the community pool serve more than the few summer months—usually the techniques have fallen into one of two categories. The first has been to try to install a basketball or other game court over the pool, off season, with varying length legs making contact with the pool bottom for stability. The legs sometimes slip however, and players have tripped on the change in level in the floor. The second system has been to construct expensive enclosures over the pool to offer all year cover for the pool. The building, if fixed, has not proved inviting in summer. When a movable roof has been installed, it has proved extremely expensive. Each of these techniques misses on at least two counts.

The plan, as included in the study, exploits flexibility, but not through the method of conversion of use to another activity or enclosure to insulate against the elements. It treats flexibility in another way. The possibility of change in the emphasis placed on the water would not be insulation against, but exploitation of the elements. This can be done by simply setting the pool in a park area that includes:

1. Outdoor gyms (muscle beach)
2. Shady and sunny lawns, for lounging (formerly the exclusive offering of the seashore)
3. Music and rhythm perches on landscaped knolls, for teen guitar and bongo artists

4. Volleyball
5. Shuffleboard
6. Table tennis courts
7. Dance decks

People will pay as individuals during the public sessions or as groups on reserved special sessions after public hours—all through the year. As the weather changes, the emphasis merely shifts. During the hot season most of the interest is centered around swimming, then as the weather becomes less favorable it turns to other activities. Included could be volleyball, weight-lifting and handbalancing, trampoline work, or a good adajio routine. Following, a short refreshing dip in the pool could become that perfect extra sensation before the barbecue picnic. Water casts a spell on the most ordinary activities to the point where users are more than willing to pay an entrance fee 365 days of the year.

The result of establishing a resort of high quality can be the development of a facility which could pay for itself and which also could help to finance programs normally forced out of the public programs because of high production cost versus user frequency ratios.

The measure of success of a swim park, or for that matter any other recreation facility, is the totality of service offered the community. A facility which serves the infant, the young child, the child, the adolescent, and the adult as well as the senior citizen is considerably more successful than the facility which limits itself to only one or a few of the age groups mentioned. Likewise, a facility which is able to serve all sizes of groups from the individual to the family group to large assemblies such as church groups, union groups, or service clubs is apt to be of greater service to the community than the facility too re-

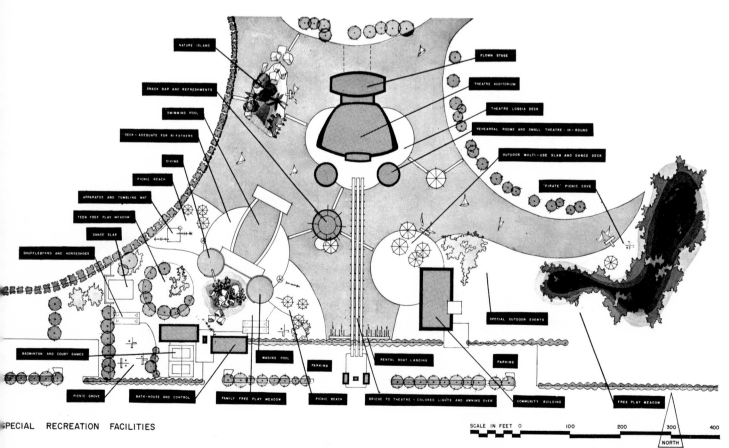

SPECIAL RECREATION FACILITIES

SCALE IN FEET 0   100   200   300   400

NORTH

THE PREPARATION OF THIS MAP WAS FINANCED IN PART THROUGH AN URBAN PLANNING GRANT FROM THE HOUSING AND HOME FINANCE AGENCY, UNDER THE PROVISIONS OF SECTION 701 OF THE HOUSING ACT OF 1954, AS AMENDED
STATE OF CALIFORNIA, DEPARTMENT OF FINANCE.

stricted in size to serve several functions simultaneously. Such dual functions as serving small groups as well as large groups are often accomplished by landscaping, formation of special areas by earth shapes, or obtaining privacy by special screening effects. The location of the swimming pool in the park will enable the new Central Union High School to make full use of it for instructional purposes during certain daytime hours in the school year. The pool's generously sized park setting will permit concurrent use of the wading pool, family area, etc., while the pool itself is being used for instructional purposes by one of the high school classes.

In the special recreation area in El Centro, the swim park serves the young child, older child, teenagers, and young adults. The areas that will be attractive to each of the age groups are carefully insulated from each other. That is to say the teen-age activity areas will appear to have their own identity and will not be mixed with the young child's activity area. This has proved to be important to the acceptance of the area by the various age groups.

AGE GROUPS SERVED

INFANT: *Tot-lot on the Adventure Hill shown on the plan. Fenced, with the supervision coming from paid attendants or mothers' co-op groups.*

YOUNG CHILD: *Adventure playground, not much supervision required. To be most effective for growth and development of the child, however, it should have trained leadership. Wading, model-boat sailing, waterlife study pool.*

CHILD: *Adventure playground—swimming, diving, model-boat sailing, plus participation in the other park facilities.*

ADOLESCENT: *Outdoor gym, dance slab, indoor social space with snack bar serving in- and outdoor, volleyball, shuffleboard courts, turfed open area for informal gatherings centered around conversation and records. All the general activities available in the park. Growing into adulthood, the adolescent seeks experiences that allow him to test strengths and weaknesses, both physical and social. The swim park serves this need well.*

ADULT: *Use community building for receptions, recitals, community club gatherings, fashion shows, lectures, and meetings. Use all park facilities. Main impact will be at the level of the total physical environment, as a place to live and to enjoy life.*

SWIM PARK FACILITIES PROVIDED:

SWIMMING POOL: *Recreational swimming*
Swimming meets
Swimming instruction
Safety classes
Life saving instruction and tests
Water carnivals and ballets
(With temporary dechlorination, fishing for boys' club)

DIVING POOL: *Recreational diving*
Diving meets
Diving instruction
Skin diving instruction
Scuba practice and instruction

WADING POOL: *Recreation for small children*
Model-boat regattas
(With temporary dechlorination, water life study pool)

BEACH AREA: *Big muscle activities*
Parallel bars
Trampolines
Gym equipment
Bar bells
Vaulting bucks
Horizontal bar
Tumbling equipment
Sunbathing
Teen-age area
Tot-lot with spray pool

LAWN AREAS: *Family areas*
Picnic tables
Free-play lawn
Shaded tree grove
Tots' areas with equipment
Sunbathing
Adult quiet area
Croquet

COURT AREAS: *Multipurpose slab:*
Volleyball
Basketball
Dancing
Deck tennis
Pool decking (and pool deck extensions):
Circulation
Shuffleboard
Ping pong
Shaded spectator areas

MAINTENANCE

IX

MAINTENANCE AND DESIGN

How Design Should Recognize and Be Influenced by Maintenance at Public Scale Today

EDWARD A. WILLIAMS

There are many components of gardens that are the result of centuries of counteraction of ideas, people's needs, maintenance and design techniques, with scientific, cultural, and economic forces. These components become matters of tradition and, as such, are taken for granted by gardeners, horticulturists, landscape architects, and the general public.

One of the components pretty well accepted as a part of most landscapes is the lawn. To pursue how the modern lawn developed from the natural meadow through stages of grazed meadow, irrigated meadow, planted meadow, mowed meadow, to what we now accept it as, together with all the history of energies that have gone into its refinement, enjoyment, and exaltation, would be a subject requiring almost as much time, energy, and money as is now being spent upon it by university, state, and Federal government scientists; seed, fertilizer, and equipment company executives; researchers; salesmen; and the public at large. But it takes only a moment to print the four letters L-A-W-N in the space allotted for it on the plan.

Some of the other commonly accepted components of our landscapes are: orchards, rose gardens, cut-flower beds, perennial borders, vegetable gardens, shrub borders, hedges, ground covers, trees of a kind in masses or groups, levels retained by slopes or walls, raised beds, mowing strips, curbs and edgings, and steps and pavings. The reasons, forms, and locations of these are as much derived from a long history of maintenance tradition as they are by the cultural-esthetic requirements of the designer and public. That these are distinctively developed within a tradition is shown by the fact that they are the components that visually differentiate our gardens from those of Japan, for instance, where the maintenance and cultural development are different.

These elements of our public and private gardens are undergoing continual development and change as new ideas and techniques are developed, as old

ideas and techniques are discarded, and as our economic and cultural conditions change. The planted dry-rock wall becomes a concrete wall in scale with the modern building, to better fit our industrialized methods of construction, and to reduce maintenance. The perennial border becomes an area of shrubs. Pavings replace lawns and ground covers. Plants growing naturally replace topiary and clipped trees. The speed of life today suggests larger and bolder scale in our public places. There are opposing tendencies toward massiveness and delicacy, between brutality and humanity. Landscape architects express the current urges and needs of people, and the forms of their landscapes shift and change for reasons of expression; but the basic components continue to remain, though modified, because of the traditional requirements, including those of the maintenance forces.

The landscape architect's awareness of how his project is to be maintained may determine the success or failure of his efforts. Indeed, it is part of his responsibility to determine as nearly as he can what kind of maintenance will be available. In order for him to know what level of maintenance will be available, and in order for him to convey his ideas, there should be direct functioning communication between the designer and the maintenance department.

At the present time there is a fairly sharp division between the design and maintenance fields. The basic reason for the division is that modern society has created the new specialties of landscape architect, landscape contractor, landscape gardener, park executive, nurseryman, horticulturist, specialist in park design, specialist in recreation design, arborist, turf specialist, and many others. At this stage of development, communication between the specialists is relatively poor, because the splintering has happened too fast to permit a continuous, stable liaison. Another reason for the isolation of the fields is overcompetitiveness resulting from the inherent insecurities of a highly competitive society. Over-competitiveness breeds cut-throat competition, arrogance, and frustration which are concealed by secretiveness, diffidence, or more arrogance. These tendencies on the part of many make it difficult for the few who are intent on improving the situation, but it is necessary for them to work consciously to improve communication between the fields.

Public places require different degrees of maintenance consistent with their use and purpose. A design depending upon a highly polished degree of maintenance effort would be inappropriate in a primitive area devoted to hiking, riding, and nature study. On the other hand, a design based upon demonstrating natural forces would be inappropriate where there are to be great concentrations of people, such as in a shopping center. Assuming that the designer is aware of these appropriate degrees of maintenance, and how they affect the character of his design, he must then find out from his client how much and what kinds of maintenance he is capable of providing and wants to provide. Inherent in the resultant design proposals will be certain kinds of required maintenance. These can be outlined in a preliminary maintenance program, discussed with the management and maintenance departments, and the design and maintenance program refined until the final proposal meets with all departments' approval.

Once having determined the levels of maintenance available to the project, the landscape architect then proceeds with the design and supervision of the installation. Most frequently at this point the designer's direct relationship with the job comes to an end. It is ironical that the one who conceived, polished, and refined a design involving living material and saw it through to completion of installation is suddenly isolated from it. Failure at this stage to transfer responsibility from designer to maintenance man is generally the result of lack of adequate communication in the beginning, as well as lack of any arrangement for the designer to make periodic checks on the work as it grows and develops. Such inspections would be helpful to both the maintenance department and the landscape architect and would improve the appearance of the landscape.

One of the distinctive things about parks and gardens that distinguishes them from other things that people design is that their growth and change are inherent and inevitable. Whether the designer likes it or not, changes are going to occur as the plants develop, succeed, or fail, and as all the relationships gradually change. The landscape architect can take part in these changes and exercise some controlling influences that will add to the enhancement of the grounds, or these changes can be left to the chance control of management and maintenance, who at best will have only the haziest idea of the designer's intention. Most grounds develop in one direction or another at this stage, depending upon the intelligence of the management and maintenance forces. This is why many well-designed gardens fall into disrepair while others develop into beautiful places.

The landscape architect is faced with a rapidly changing maintenance situation which, once wholly dependent on manpower, is becoming more and more dependent on machine power and automation. The gardener of old who was designer, engineer, and horticulturist is being replaced by many specialists, while the necessary gardening functions of digging, weeding, pruning, and planting are relegated to low-paid labor, frequently without adequate supervision. Need for solution to this problem has brought about the development of the landscape management field. Training in this field on the college level is now available throughout the country, and graduates are going into federal, state, county, and city park departments, school districts, industries and other areas involved with large landscapes.

Landscape management is a highly specialized field involving administrative, scientific, economic, social, and political functions. Awareness of the responsibilities and problems of this important field can help the landscape architect understand the context within which he works on public scale projects.

A typical large city park department, for instance, will have a director, department heads, landscape architects, draftsmen, engineers, accountants, horticulturists, foresters, superintendents, equipment operators, mechanics, plumbers, carpenters, gardeners, and laborers. All of these specialists are required, in varying degrees, to administer, operate, and keep up a park system. The efforts of these people are directed to one end: to provide and maintain as beau-

tiful and useful a park system as is possible with the resources available.

Among these resources is machine power. Design that permits maximum use of machinery frees manpower to do a better job of maintaining areas that can only be maintained by hand. Machinery has been developed to handle all the operations of planting and maintaining lawn areas. For these machines to operate, lawn areas have to be of sufficient size; and slopes, trees, and shrubs within the lawn areas have to be so located as to permit easy maneuvering. Roads, paths, or open spaces will be designed to allow trucks or maintenance equipment to circulate to all parts of the grounds for pickup, delivery, spraying, cultivating, sweeping, or vacuuming.

Another resource is that of imaginative public relations coupled with imaginative design. The park department that has a high degree of citizen participation and enthusiasm in its program has a powerful ally in its yearly budget struggles. The landscape architect can be helpful in gaining public support by designing the kind of landscapes that the public will be attracted to and appreciate.

Skillful artistic composition of materials and spaces consistent with the purpose, place, and time of the project will produce this desired response. But another important response will be the result of the public's attitude toward project maintenance.

The principal landscape materials are: earth, plants, water, and structural materials, and the maintenance problems involved with them vary according to the appropriateness of their character and use in each particular situation. Following are brief notes and check lists indicating the kinds of investigation and decisions that have to be made in order to design maintenance objectives into a project.

Earth and Maintenance. There are three important ways in which earth is used: first, as a foundation material for structures; second, as a growing medium for plants; and third, as a material for ground forms. The following professions are available and should be consulted for normal and special investigations into earth and soil problems: civil engineers, soil mechanics (foundation) engineers, geologists, and soil management and plant nutrition specialists. Failure to determine the characteristics

of the soils of the site can lead to serious slides, erosion, and failure of structures and plantings, resulting in high replacement and maintenance costs.

1. Earth load bearing qualities range from good to bad, depending on what is to be supported. In extreme cases, pilings or removal and replacement are necessary.

2. Earth structure can range from stable to unstable expansive types requiring special construction methods.

3. The natural structure, fertility, and chemistry of the soil determine the basis for plant selection and soil correction specifications, if required. Initial soil correction may be temporary. What about the long-range maintenance problem?

4. The surface drainage characteristics of earth are a relationship of its absorption qualities, particle sizes, maximum anticipated rainfall, slope, and area of watershed. Methods of avoiding surface erosion, landslides, saturation, and bogging involve both planting and structural control where appropriate.

5. Subsurface investigation, in addition to indicating the load-bearing capacities of the site, will indicate what the subsurface drainage characteristics are. The presence of a hard underlying layer will require strict limitation of the plant list to shallow-rooted plants, unless it is broken through. Other problems accompanying a hard pan are alkalinity and high water table. In low-lying areas, particularly old tidal areas, salinity of the subsurface should be checked as should the presence of underground channels and springs that can create problems with foundations, paving, and plantings.

6. As surface slopes increase in grade, maintenance costs likewise increase because of the difficulty of carrying out maintenance operations on them. If grass is to be planted on slopes, the face slope and vertical curves at top and bottom will be determined for safe and efficient use of mowing machinery. Steeper slopes than those which can be mowed will have to be planted to ground covers or shrubs. Slopes steeper than one foot rise in two feet generally should be avoided, since they cannot be walked upon or worked on safely without special care or equipment.

For walks and roadways, reasonable maximum slopes will be observed to allow for ease in getting

1

2

233

1

2

3

maintenance equipment to all parts of the grounds.

The preceding generalizations about surface slopes are not meant to imply that steeper, sharper, more abrupt ground forms are not to be used, but that where they are considered, their value in the particular landscape will be compared to the cost of maintaining them properly.

Plantings and Maintenance. In considering maintenance, the basic factors in plant selection will be: a) suitability to the weather and soil conditions of the site; b) resistance to insects and disease; c) life expectancy; d) size, shape, and other growth habits. Plants not well suited to the climate of the site will tend to be short-lived and subject to disease or insect attack and eventual replacement. If soil conditions are not right for the particular plant, expensive remaking of the soil will be required. Short-lived plants, unless desired for some special reason, will have to be removed and replaced. Plants that overgrow the space allowed them require continual pruning, shaping, and thinning. Plants with invasive root systems can cause troubles with other plantings, pavement, curbs, and underground utilities.

1. In selecting trees, such matters as proximity to buildings, walls, overhead wires, walks, and curbs, and to each other should be judged on the basis of the growth habits of the trees. When planted in lawns, trees should be spaced for mower clearance and turning. The question of litter of leaves, flowers, and fruit is a relative one, depending upon where the litter falls. Excess litter on heavily-used areas or in pools is an annoyance that should be avoided. The kind of root system, whether spreading or deep, will frequently help determine the suitability of a particular tree variety when judged according to soil conditions, proximity to other plants or structures, or underground utilities. Frequency and duration of irrigation will help to determine how deeply trees will root, and how resistant to drought and wind they will be. Trees, being the largest planting elements, are the most important; so their selection should obviously be made carefully.

2. In selecting and arranging shrubs in rows, groups, or masses, the designer will pay particular attention to the detailed environment. Obviously, shrubs requiring different degrees of sun and shade or water and dryness will not grow well together.

Frequently best design practice will lead to the easiest maintenance. The designer will generally find that economy of variety, resulting in simple arrangements or broad masses, will require less different and exacting kinds of maintenance and will result in a clearer design of greater impact, if well thought out in relation to the total design. In more complicated arrangements, it becomes most important to think in terms of detailed requirements of soil, exposure, size, and shape, so that the plants used together will succeed together. Theories such as natural associations, ecology, and natives versus exotics do not answer all of the questions that have to be answered. Experience will show that the man-made landscape imposes its own conditions affecting the selection and arrangement of plants, and that there are no "natural laws" to free the designer from his responsibility to observe, research, experiment, and use his imagination.

3. Two basic types of ground covers are used in landscapes—shrubby kinds and vining kinds. There are certain maintenance advantages and problems in connection with the use of each of these. Shrubby ground covers, such as prostrate junipers and cotoneasters, are planted with wide spacing between the individual plants. This wide spacing permits spraying or tilling to control weeds until the spaces are covered by the shrubs. The slowness of most of these kinds of shrubs in covering the ground when properly spaced is considered by many to be a disadvantage. In areas where invasive grasses, such as Kikuyu and Bermuda, exist, infiltration of the ground cover by these grasses can become a serious maintenance problem. Vining ground covers such as *Vinca* or *Hedera* require considerable hand weeding during the period that the ground cover is becoming established. Thorough hand weeding is not only expensive but is sometimes met with resistance on the part of gardeners. One advantage of vining types of covers is that they frequently are more rapidly established. The choices of ground covers and maintenance methods should be thoroughly discussed with the maintenance department before final selection.

Ground covers are generally well accepted on banks too steep to mow, in small areas, and under shrubs and trees. Ground covers can also be used as lawn substitutes in areas of no traffic with re-

234

1

2

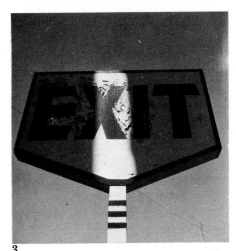

3

sultant savings in watering, mowing, reseeding, fertilization, and top dressing. It is interesting to note, however, that maintenance people frequently prefer the long-term types of maintenance required by lawns to the short-term high maintenance of ground covers, even though the ground covers will require much less maintenance through the years.

4. Great quantities of technical information are available about establishing and maintaining lawns, but there are some points frequently overlooked that it would be well to emphasize here:

a. Aside from the intrinsic beauty of a lawn, its great characteristic of being a planted surface that can be walked and played upon makes it a favorite ground covering. Location is, however, a factor to be considered, and maintenance-free pavement may be the logical substitute in very highly used areas.

b. The establishment of the best possible soil conditions will result in the lowest possible maintenance. Particular attention should be paid to the mechanical properties of the soil, since these cannot be changed once the lawn is installed.

c. Surface and underground drainage conditions can be analyzed and corrections favorable to lawn growth determined in the design stage.

d. The lawn shape, edges, slopes, and spacing of interruptions such as plant beds and trees should be considered in relation to the use of modern construction and mowing equipment.

e. In regions where there is a choice available between grass varieties or strains, the seed selection can be made on the basis of the kind of traffic or use the lawn or turf will receive and the level of maintenance available.

5. Herbaceous material (including perennials, annuals, short-lived shrubs, and biennials), bulbs, and roses are the highest maintenance plants used in landscape. They are desirable in certain plantings because of the color and fragrance which are otherwise unavailable. They include some of the most universally loved plants.

4

5

235

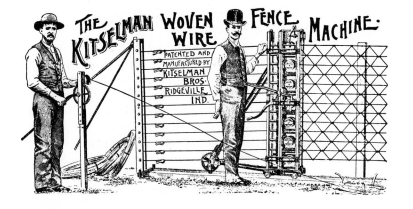

Using them requires judgment and predecision. If they are to be used, spaces must be provided that fit into the overall design, and schedules of colors, types, and planting seasons must be furnished.

In the cases of annuals, roses, perennials, and bulbs, it has become common practice to put them in separate areas or beds because of the similar maintenance requirements, rather than to mix them into areas of shrubbery. This is not to say that there are not other possibilities, such as perennials and bulbs spicing up a ground cover or shrubbery area, but only to point out that there are choices to be made and that where extremely low maintenance is required, these plants will not be used or depended on or will be used sparingly in special areas. A result of this in design is the use of raised beds (so-called planters) or the hedged rose or cut-flower bed, so that the overall design does not suffer too much when the "color" planting is dormant or being changed. Maintenance is simplified by the setting off of the special area requiring special feeding, soil, spraying, staking, disbudding, cutting, and changing.

Structural Materials and Maintenance. Generally the strongest, most durable material or equipment will last the longest and be the cheapest to maintain during its life if it has been well installed. If material selection were based upon this kind of criteria alone, there would not be very many choices to make. When esthetic considerations are balanced with maintenance, initial cost considerations, and needs, the decisions can become quite complicated and difficult. The answers arrived at sometimes have little relation to apparent logic. Most people like to see things well-built and hate to see obvious waste, but in between these two alternatives is a whole range of possible choices. Most public projects are begun because of the existence of a critical need for a school, park, playground, highway, or other public facility. The budget is generally set up by a pulling and hauling of political forces and preliminary estimates and, more than likely, is then fixed and unchangeable. The designer's role is to fulfill the need in the best possible way within the budget, and he cannot do this in a professionally responsible way without considering the maintenance of the project. The designer cannot, however, sacrifice fulfillment of need to maintenance considerations or vice-versa.

Structural materials are used in landscape projects in pavings, drainage structures, curbs, walls, fences, arbors, small buildings, pools, benches, tables, and other miscellaneous furnishings. Related to these are mechanical and electrical systems and equipment of many diverse uses and purposes. The professions of engineering and architecture are frequently more widely familiar with the properties of structural materials and new inventions and processes in this category of material. Collaborative relationships with these professions, travel, observation, and wide communication are the best possible sources for information about structural materials, old and new. From the widest knowledge about material can emerge the best inventory on which selections can be made with some confidence. Lack of knowledge and lack of experience with materials and techniques can be a limitation affecting both design and maintenance.

If a formula for selection of structural material and equipment is required, perhaps this is a good one: fulfill prior social needs first and then, if sufficient money is available, do it with the most permanent and appropriate material. The danger of ready acceptance of this theory is that "willingness to make-do" can be an avoidance of responsibility for pressing for a reasonable budget. The danger of the reverse of this theory is the slick permanent monument that no one is interested in but is so easy to maintain.

How Does Design Affect Management and Maintenance: A Survey of Park and College Experience

GARRETT ECKBO

A questionnaire asking for information on several aspects of landscape management, maintenance, design, and their interrelationships was sent out to park departments and college grounds superintendents in 1961. The charts and notes on the following pages summarize the usable answers received. Answers to other questions were too fragmentary, ambiguous, or noncomparable for effective tabulation and analysis. The questionnaire used is included at the end of this section.

The Respondents. Respondent park departments represent 34 cities in 17 states, ranging in population from about 13,000 (Redding, California) to nearly a million (Houston, Texas). These park departments are responsible for acreages varying from only 2 in Bellevue, Washington, to 5,533 acres in Minneapolis.

It was not the intent of this survey to evaluate the quality of park facilities, hence we calculated only one such indicator: population per acre of park (with due recognition of the limitations of this rough measurement). Respondent cities varied tremendously—from a high ratio of 1 acre per 23 persons to a low of 1 acre per 6,405 persons. This satisfied us that we had a broadly representative sample not only of sizes, types, and locations of cities, but also of adequacy of recreation space.

Schools responding to the survey include 23 colleges, universities, and vocational schools in 16 states, with campuses ranging in size from 18½ to 1,164 acres.

Total land coverage by buildings and vehicular paving reached a median of 4 per cent for parks, 18 per cent for schools. Pedestrian paving coverage was 1 per cent for parks, 5 per cent for schools. Parks had 12 to 19 per cent raw land, schools none.

Item	Parks		Schools	
	Range	Median	Range	Median
Population (1960 census)	12,773–938,219	43,456		
Area of grounds maintenance	2–5,533 acres	633 acres	18½–1,164 acres	90 acres
Persons per acre (a rough indicator of adequacy of recreational area) ...	23–6,405	177		
Maximum maintenance area as per cent of total	0–100%	69%	22–100%	75%
Minimum maintenance area as per cent of total	0–100%	31%	0–78%	25%
Annual maintenance budget	$8,000–$2,969,400	$137,000	$5,000–$329,000	$60,000
Maintenance cost per acre	$78–$5,118	$332	$93–$8,571	$444

Notes

Most cities with very high maintenance-cost-per-acre figures have relatively small total acreage and a high proportion of maximum maintenance area. The same is true for schools.

There is unfortunately no clear straight-line decrease in acre-maintenance cost with increase in total acreage; the figures seem to show some economy in acre costs with larger areas, but there are many exceptions and contradictions.

The proportion of maximum maintenance area does not necessarily decrease as acreage increases. Seattle, Houston, and Fort Worth, with 3,150, 4,454, and 5,096 acres respectively, had between 75 and 80% maximum maintenance. Their maintenance-cost-per-acre figures vary widely, with Fort Worth quite low at $131, Houston on middle ground at $461, and Seattle very high at $936.

Park figures showed maintenance-cost-per-acre increasing as the proportion of maximum maintenance area increases. For 16 cities with 50% or more maximum maintenance area, the median acre-maintenance cost was $372, for 10 cities with 75% or more maximum maintenance area, $411, as compared to the overall median of $332. School figures were too fragmentary to reveal a clear pattern.

Nearly half the schools which answered the maximum-minimum question reported 100% maximum maintenance. It is interesting that one of these 100-percenters had the lowest maintenance-cost-per-acre and another had the highest. Nearly two-thirds of the schools had an acre-maintenance cost under $650; those above this figure rose sharply and may not be valid.

Division of Annual Maintenance Budget

Item in budget	Parks		Schools	
	Range, %	Median, %	Range, %	Median, %
Labor	45–85	65	43–95	78
New equipment	1–35 (⅔ under 10%)	10	1–17 (⅔ under 10%)	5
Supplies and services ..	4–41	20	2–46	19

Notes

When park figures were arranged in order of size of budget, it became apparent that the percentage spent on labor generally increases as the budget increases. For cities with budgets under $100,000, the median percentage expended for labor was 59%; for cities with budgets between $100,000 and $500,000 it was 68%. Data was inadequate for cities with budgets over $500,000, but the direction seemed to continue upward.

School data are insufficient to derive either a similar or different pattern. The higher proportion for labor may indicate the generally smaller areas and budgets for schools, below the point where labor-saving equipment is economic.

The per cent of budget for new equipment was more substantial for parks than for schools, probably reflecting the larger areas cared for.

The large proportion of the total budget spent on labor is characteristic of nearly all parks and schools and seems to bear little relationship to the proportion of total area in maximum maintenance.

Labor	Parks		Schools	
	Range, %	Median, %	Range, %	Median, %
Mowing	7–45	19	2–50	15
Watering	0.5–30	3	1–15	4
Weeding and trimming	0.5–21	7	2–25	10
Clean up	1–23	10	3–25	10
Fertilizing	0.1–23	10	1–10	5
Lawn repair	0.5–5	2	1–10	3
Seeding, planting, digging	1–6	2	1–17	7.5
Tree work	1–25	7.5	0.5–17	4
Sick and vacation	1–12	4	0.5–10	5
Snow removal	1–10	4.5	1–10	5
Supervision and foremen	1–30	9	0.5–15	6
Rubbish collection	1–12	5	2–15	5.5
Equipment repair	0.5–20	4	1–9	5
Nursery	0.5–10	2.5	1–9.5	2
Police services	0.1–15	1	0.5–9	4
Walks, roads, etc.	1–7	3	1–5.5	5
Miscellaneous or other	3–45	10.5	2–56	8.5

Notes

Mowing is clearly the largest single labor item, followed by weeding, trimming, and clean up. For parks, fertilizing, supervision, and tree work were also important items. For schools, seeding-planting-digging was an important item.

The above chart summarizes rather limited data. Jurisdictions have widely varying accounting methods and we have presented only those answers adding to 100%, and including most of the categories given. Zero answers were not calculated, since it was not known whether a zero meant that no expenditure was made on that item or that it was included in another category.

Division of Supplies-and-Services Costs

Supplies-and-Services Expenditure	Parks		Schools	
	Range, %	Median, %	Range, %	Median, %
Service garage charges	2–62	17.5	0.5–30	7.5
Equipment repair	1.2–50	20	1–40	15
Fertilizers and chemicals	2–60	10	1–60	20
Plant materials	1–35	6	1–50	12.5
Miscellaneous or others	3–82.5	25	10–94	30

Notes

The parks' larger expenditures on service garage charges and equipment repair reflects the larger areas maintained. For schools, where areas are smaller, equipment items are less important and plant and fertilizer items account for a larger proportion of the supplies-and-services budget.

Item	Parks		Schools	
	Range	Median	Range	Median
Gap between real and optimum budget —*today*	0–100%	20%	0–50%	20%
Gap between real and optimum budget —*10 years ago*	0–450%	50%	0–60%	15%
Number with *larger* gap today	5		6	
Number with *smaller* gap today	9		7	
Number with *same* gap today	2		0	

Notes

For parks, the trend seems favorable, the gap is narrowing. It is encouraging to note that when park answers were arranged in order of increasing budgets, those with higher budgets cited smaller gaps than those with low budgets.

For schools the trend seems less favorable, but there were fewer answers.

Present and Optimum Budgets. The questionnaire asked, "How much higher is your optimum or desirable budget today than what you have?" and "What was the gap ten years ago?" Most respondents did acknowledge a gap, but some did not. In this question, "OK" and "no difference" answers were counted as zero in calculating medians.

Most respondents answered the question on today's budget gap; there were fewer answers to the second since many parks and schools did not exist ten years ago or had inadequate records.

How Much Does a Long Plant List Increase Maintenance over a Short List?

This is one of the classical questions in planting design circles. The answers are interesting if inconclusive.

Six park departments estimated the increase at 0 to 50 per cent, and two estimated 150 to 200 per cent. The median, questionable as it is with this limited number of responses, was about 21 per cent. Comments ranged from "very little" increase to "considerable, depending on length of list."

Seven schools estimated the increase between 0 and 50 per cent; none estimated higher. The median, again questionable, was 10 per cent. Five respondents commented, ranging from "very little, if any" cost increase to "appreciably."

HOW DOES DESIGN AFFECT MANAGEMENT AND MAINTENANCE?

1. What type development are you responsible for? (school, park, or _____) _____

   Where is it located? _____

   What total *area* of grounds maintenance are you responsible for? _____

   In one or _____ sites?

   If more than one, what range of sizes?   Smallest_____
   Largest_____
   Typical_____

   How much of this is maximum maintenance? _____
   minimum maintenance? _____

   What percentage of the area is covered by:
   buildings _____
   vehicular paving _____
   pedestrian paving _____
   water _____
   raw land (no maintenance) _____

2. What is your current annual maintenance budget? _____

   How is this divided between:
   labor _____%
   new equipment _____%
   supplies and services _____%

   How does labor divide among:
   mowing _____%
   watering _____%
   weeding and trimming _____%
   clean up _____%
   fertilizing _____%
   lawn repair _____%
   seeding, planting and digging _____%
   tree work _____%
   sick and vacation _____%
   snow removal _____%
   supervision and foremen _____%
   rubbish collection _____%
   equipment repair _____%
   nursery _____%
   police services _____%
   walks, roads, etc. _____%
   miscellaneous or other _____%

   How do supplies and services divide among:
   service garage charges _____%
   equipment repair _____%
   fertilizers and chemicals _____%
   plant materials _____%
   miscellaneous or others _____%

What has been the average annual maintenance cost rise in the past ten years in:
labor _____%
new equipment _____%
supplies and services _____%

How much higher is your optimum or desirable budget today than what you have? _____%

What was the gap 10 years ago? _____%

What are your annual maintenance costs per acre for:
lawn with few or no trees _____
rough grass with same _____
lawn with many trees _____
rough grass with same _____
ground cover planted less than 3' o.c.
first 3 years _____
thereafter _____
herbaceous or special planting beds _____
shrub beds _____
aquatic areas _____
vehicular paving _____
pedestrian paving _____

How much does a complex layout increase maintenance over a simple layout? _____

How much does a long plant list increase maintenance over a short list? _____

3. Does design and/or development (construction, installation) come within your jurisdiction? Or, are they within your organization under separate jurisdiction? _____

   Can you send an organization chart? _____

   What are the percentage relations?

	Super-vision	Person-nel	Budget
design	___	___	___
development	___	___	___
maintenance	___	___	___

   Is there an annual relation between development cost and maintenance increase? _____

   What percentage of total construction budget does site work usually represent? _____%

   What percentage of site work is of an engineering nature (rough grading, drainage, main utilities, vehicular paving, heavy construction)? _____%

   and of a landscape nature (finish grading, sprinklers, rock arrangement, pedestrian paving and furnishing, lawns and planting, light construction)? _____%

   What has been the average annual development cost rise in the past ten years? _____%

   Engineering work _____% Landscape work _____%

BIBLIOGRAPHY

Bacon, Edmund N., "Urban Design as a Force in Comprehensive Planning," *A.I.P. Journal*, February, 1963, Baltimore Md.

Conover, H. S., *Grounds Maintenance Handbook*, McGraw-Hill Book Company, New York, 1958.

> Although it has been subject to considerable criticism, this book remains the only one in its field, and is very useful.

Cullen, Gordon, *Townscape*, The Architectural Press, London, 1961.

> This approach, now well known in professional circles, treats the urban scene as a continuous landscape rather than a collection of architectural *objets d'art*. It is an important and basic book.

Halprin, Lawrence, *Cities*, Reinhold Publishing Corporation, New York, 1963.

Dakin, John, "An Evaluation of the 'Choice' Theory of Planning," *A.I.P. Journal*, February, 1963, Baltimore, Md.

Feiss, Carl, Guest Editor, Urban Design issue, *A.I.A. Journal*, March, 1961, Washington, D.C.

Hoppenfeld, Morton, "Towards a Consensus of Approach to Urban Design," *A.I.A. Journal*, September, 1962, Washington, D.C.

Jacobs, Jane, *The Death and Life of Great American Cities*, Random House, New York, 1961.

> This is a healthy book, in the classical tradition of debunking ideas and theories grown perhaps a little pompous. This debunking may include some ideas presented herein. Jacobs, an architectural journalist married to an architect, has been a source of considerable annoyance to the architectural-planning professions. She may well have provided some ammunition for those opportunist and reactionary forces who oppose any reform of the established process of exploiting the landscape for all it is worth. But this is one of the very few serious attempts to analyze the reciprocal relations between form and content in cities, and hence should be required reading for everyone concerned with either. What we do with it is up to us. Certainly it opens more doors than it closes.

REFERENCES AND ACKNOWLEDGMENTS

1. See *Man's Role in Changing the Face of the Earth*, University of Chicago Press, Chicago, 1956.

2. Alfred North Whitehead, *The Aims of Education*, copyright 1929, reprinted by permission of The Macmillan Company, New York.

3. Robert B. Downs, *Books That Changed the World*, Mentor Books, The New American Library of World Literature, Inc., New York, 1956.

4. See Whitehead, *op. cit.*, ref. 2.

5. Helmut Paul Schaber, "The Five-Dimensional Space of Man," *Synthesis*, Graduate School of Design, Harvard University, Cambridge, Mass., 1958.

6. See Harland Bartholomew and Jack Wood, *Land Uses in American Cities*, Harvard University Press, Cambridge, Mass., 1955.

7. The American Institute of Architects, *Southern California Chapter Bulletin*, Autumn, 1960.

8. Robin Boyd, "The New Vision in Architecture," *Harper's Magazine*, July, 1961.

9. Paul Rudolph, "The Determinance of Architectural Form," *Architectural Record*, October, 1956.

10. Reprinted by permission of *Punch* (c) 1960.

11. See Kevin Lynch, *The Image of the City*, M.I.T. Press and Harvard University Press, Cambridge, Mass., 1960.

12. See Aldous Huxley, *Brave New World Revisited*, Harper, New York, 1958.

13. See Lynch, *op. cit.*, ref. 11.

14. See George Wald, *Eye and Camera*, Scientific American Reader, Simon and Schuster, Inc., New York, 1953.

15. Camillo Sitte, *The Art of Building Cities*, Reinhold Publishing Corporation, New York, 1945.

15a. *Ibid.*

16. See Eliel Saarinen, *The City, Its Growth, Its Decay, Its Future. . . .*, Reinhold Publishing Corporation, New York, 1943.

17. See Paul Zucker, *Town and Square*, Columbia University Press, New York, 1959.

18. See G. E. Kidder Smith, *Italy Builds*, Reinhold Publishing Corporation, New York, 1959.

19. Reprinted by permission of *Punch* (c) 1960.

20. Sydney Williams, "Urban Aesthetics," *The Town Planning Review*, Liverpool, England, July, 1954.

21. New York Chapters American Institute of Architects and American Institute of Planners, *Planning and Community Appearance*, Regional Plan Association, New York, 1958.

22. Lynch, *op. cit.*, ref. 11.

23. Harrison Brown and James Real, *Community of Fear*, Center for the Study of Democratic Institutions, Santa Barbara, California, 1960.

24. See Sitte, *op. cit.*, ref. 11.

25. See California Committee on Planning for Recreation, Park Areas and Facilities, *Guide for Planning Recreation Parks in California*, Documents Section, Printing Division, Sacramento 14, California, 1956.

26. From the American Institute of Park Executives, "The Crisis in Open Land," *Park Education Program*, Wheeling, West Virginia, 1959.

27. Prof. Joseph Brown, "Play Communities," *Princeton Alumni Weekly*, Oct. 1, 1954.

28. Hank Ketcham, "A Playground Really Built for Kids," reprinted from *This Week Magazine*, Copyright 1957 by the United Newspapers Magazine Corporation, issue of January 20, 1957.

29. See Sitte, *op. cit.*, ref. 11.

30. *Ibid.*

31. See Boris Pushkarev, "The Esthetics of Freeway Design," *Landscape*, Winter, 1960–61, Santa Fe, New Mexico. See also Christopher Tunnard and Boris Pushkarev, *Man-made America: Chaos or Control?* Yale University Press, New Haven, Conn., 1963.

32. See *Architectural Forum*, September, 1956.

33. Albert Wohlstetter, "No Highway to High Purpose," *Life*, June 20, 1960.

34. G. E. Kidder Smith, *Italy Builds*, Reinhold Publishing Corporation, New York, 1954.

35. See Sitte, *op. cit.*, ref. 11.

36. Lucio Costa, "In Search of a New Monumentality" (symposium), *Architectural Review*, London, England, September, 1948.

37. Zucker, *op. cit.*, ref. 17.

38. Paul Rudolph, "Changing the Face of New York," *The Saturday Review,* October 18, 1958.

39. Edmund Bacon, Executive Director, Philadelphia City Planning Commission, statement before Harvard Conference on Urban Design, April 12, 1957.

40. From Catherine Bauer Wurster, "Architecture and the Cityscape," *Journal of the American Institute of Architects,* Washington, D.C., March, 1961.

41. See Williams, *op. cit.,* ref. 20.

42. See New York Chapters AIA-AIP, ref. 21.

43. Lynch, *op. cit.,* ref. 11.

44. From Paul and Percival Goodman, *Communitas,* Vintage Books, a division of Random House, Inc., New York, copyright by the authors 1947, 1960.

45. From Christopher Tunnard, *The City of Man,* Charles Scribner's Sons, New York, 1953.

46. From Lewis Mumford, "The Social Function of Open Spaces," *Landscapes,* Santa Fe, New Mexico, Winter, 1960–61.

47. From Isaac Asimov, *Foundation,* copyright, 1951 by Isaac Asimov. Reprinted by permission of Doubleday & Company, Inc., Garden City, N.Y.

48. See Brenda Colvin, *Land and Landscape,* John Murray, London, England, 1948; Brian Hackett, *Man, Society and Environment,* Percival Marshall, London, 1950; Sylvia Crowe, *Tomorrow's Landscapes,* Architectural Press, London, 1956.

DESIGN AND ILLUSTRATION CREDITS

Frontispiece *Photograph by Dick Petrie.*

Page 2 *Photograph by Dick Petrie.*

Page 4 Los Angeles Civic Center with parking from City Hall. *Photograph by Harry Drinkwater.*

Page 5 *Photograph by Gordon Sommers.*

Page 6 *Photograph by Dick Petrie.*

Page 8 1. Photograph by Al Greene and Associates.
2. Kaibab Forest. *Photograph courtesy Union Pacific Railroad.*
3. Mole tunnels.
4. Zion Canyon. *Photograph courtesy Union Pacific Railroad.*

Page 9 1. *Photograph by Gordon Sommers.*
2. *Photograph courtesy Mt. Holyoke College.*

Page 10 1, 2. *Photographs by Harry Drinkwater.*
3. St. Andrew's Village plan. *Drawing by Carlos Diniz.*

Page 11 1. Gas tanks and City Hall, Los Angeles. *Photograph by Harry Drinkwater.*
2. MacArthur Park, Los Angeles. *Photograph by Harry Drinkwater.*
3, 4. *Photographs by Max Yavno.*
5. *Photograph by Dick Petrie.*

Page 12 1. Candela shell forms. *Drawing by Frederick Usher, Jr.*
2. New and old buildings, New York. *Photograph by author.*
3. Grauman's Chinese Theatre, Hollywood. *Photograph by Harry Drinkwater.*

Page 13 1, 2, 4, 5, 7. *Photographs by Dick Petrie.*
3. Watts Towers wall. *Photograph by Harry Drinkwater.*
6. Allen Art Building. *Photograph courtesy Oberlin College.*
8. Bunker Hill, Los Angeles. *Photograph by Harry Drinkwater.*

Page 14 1. *Photograph by Dick Petrie.*
2. *Photograph by Maynard Omerberg.*
3. *Photograph by author.*

Page 15 1. Shopping center. *Drawing by Carlos Diniz.*

Page 16 1. San Francisco street. *Photograph by Ben Wildman.*
2. *Photograph by Harry Drinkwater.*
3. Aspen tent. *Photograph by Berko Studio.*

Page 17 1. American Cement Building detail, Los Angeles. ARCHITECTS: Daniel, Mann, Johnson and Mendenhall; SCULPTURAL DESIGN: Malcolm Leland.
2. Connecticut General Life Insurance Company. ARCHITECTS: Skidmore, Owings and Merrill; SCULPTOR: Isamu Noguchi. *Photograph by Ezra Stoller Associates.*
3. Euclid Avenue, Ontario, Calif. *Photograph courtesy Los Angeles Chamber of Commerce.*

Page 19 1. Drawing by Mies van der Rohe.
2. Central quadrangle. *Photograph courtesy Occidental College.*
3. Air view, Scripps College. *Photograph by Robert C. Frampton.*

Page 20 1. *Photograph by Dick Petrie.*
2. Villa Adriana. *Photograph by Carlos Diniz.*
3. Death Valley. *Photograph courtesy Union Pacific Railroad.*

Page 22 1. Campidoglio, Rome. *Photograph by Carlos Diniz.*
2. Elysian Park, Los Angeles. *Photograph by Ralph Cornell.*
3. Medical Plaza. ARCHITECTS: Wurster, Bernardi and Emmons; LANDSCAPE ARCHITECTS: Lawrence Halprin and Associates.

Page 23 1. Los Angeles panorama. *Photograph by Harry Drinkwater.*
2. Sun Valley mountains. *Photograph courtesy Union Pacific Railroad.*

Page 24 1, 2. Alcoa garden. LANDSCAPE ARCHITECTS: Eckbo, Dean, Austin and Williams. *Photographs by Julius Shulman.*

Page 25 1. Choate estate, Berkshires, Mass. LANDSCAPE ARCHITECT: Fletcher Steele. *Photograph by Paul J. Weber.*
2. Shopping center. *Drawing by Carlos Diniz.*

Page 26 1. *Photograph by Dick Petrie.*
2. San Francisco freeways. *Photograph by State of California, Division of Highways.*
3. *Photograph courtesy Wellesley College.*

Page 28 1. Downtown San Francisco. *Photograph courtesy Union Pacific Railroad.*
2. *Photograph courtesy U.S. Soil Conservation Service.*

Page 29 1. *Giant tule tree, Mexico.*
2. *Photograph by Carlos Diniz.*
3. *Photograph by Harry Drinkwater.*

Page 30 1. *Photograph by Gordon Sommers.*
3. Shelter Manor. Cartoon by Robert Day, courtesy *The New Yorker Magazine, Inc.*

241

Page 31　4. Monaco. *Drawing by Carlos Diniz.*
　　　　2. *Photograph by Dick Petrie.*

Page 32　1. *Photograph courtesy U.S. Soil Conservation Service.*
　　　　2. *Photograph courtesy San Diego Department of City Planning.*

Page 33　1. Cincinnati. *Photograph by U.S. Army Air Corps, courtesy of U.S. Housing Authority.*
　　　　2. California City plan. COMMUNITY FACILITIES PLANNERS: Smith and Williams, architects; Eisner and Stewart, city planners; Eckbo, Dean, Austin and Williams, landscape architects.

Pages 34–35　Text for "Example" part title pages from Prof. Thomas E. Hill, *Hill's Manual of Social and Business Forms, A Guide to Correct Writing,* Hill Standard Book Company, Chicago, 1882.

Page 36　*Photograph courtesy U.S. Housing Authority.*

Page 38　Alcoa garden. *Photograph by Julius Shulman.*

Page 39　Patio for Turner and Stevens, funeral directors. LANDSCAPE ARCHITECTS: Eckbo, Dean, Austin and Williams. *Photographs by Harry Drinkwater.*

Pages 40,41　Restaurant garden. ARCHITECT: Leif Valand; LANDSCAPE ARCHITECT: Lewis Clarke. *Photographs by Watson.*

Pages 42,43　28th Church of Christ, Scientist. ARCHITECT: Maynard Lyndon; LANDSCAPE ARCHITECTS: Eckbo, Dean, Austin and Williams.
　　　　1, 3, 4. *Photographs by Harry Drinkwater.*
　　　　2, 5, 6, 7,8. *Photographs by author.*

Page 44　Chateau de Vianden. *Photograph courtesy Office Luxembourgeois de Tourisme.*

Page 46　Stanford Medical Center. ARCHITECT: Edward D. Stone; LANDSCAPE ARCHITECTS: Thomas D. Church and Associates. *Photographs by Stanford University Photographic Department.*

Pages 47–49　Fireman's Fund Insurance Company. ARCHITECT: Edward B. Page; LANDSCAPE ARCHITECTS: Eckbo, Dean, Austin and Williams. *Photographs by Phil Palmer.*

Pages 50,51　Washington Water Power Company. ARCHITECTS: Brooks and Walker; LANDSCAPE ARCHITECTS: Lawrence Halprin and Associates.
　　　　1, 2, 4. *Photographs by Morley Baer.*
　　　　3. *Photograph by Donald Ray Carter.*

Page 52　Industrial Indemnity Company. ARCHITECTS: White, Hermann and Steinau; LANDSCAPE ARCHITECTS: Thomas D. Church and Associates. *Photographs by Phil Fein.*

Pages 53–55　Faculty Club. ARCHITECTS: Paul Hayden Kirk and Associates; Victor Steinbrueck; LANDSCAPE ARCHITECTS: Eckbo, Dean, Austin and Williams. *Photographs by Robert Eyre.*

Pages 56–57　Temple, Brandeis Camp Institute. ARCHITECT: J. R. Davidson; LANDSCAPE ARCHITECTS: Eckbo, Dean, Austin and Williams; DIRECTOR, Shlomo Bardin.
　　　　1, 5, 7, 8. *Sketches by Tito Patri.*
　　　　6. *Sketch by E. Jay Christopherson.*
　　　　2, 3, 4. Site *photographs by author.*

Page 58　*Photograph by Cascade Cameras, Ltd., Banff, Alberta, Canada.*

Pages 60,61　Cherry Hill Shopping Center. ARCHITECTURE, PLANNING, AND ENGINEERING: Victor Gruen Associates; LANDSCAPE ARCHITECT: Lewis Clarke.

Pages 62,63　Old Orchard. ARCHITECTS: Loebl,

Schlossman and Bennett; LANDSCAPE ARCHITECTS: Lawrence Halprin and Associates.

Pages 64–67　Polytechnic High School. ARCHITECT: High Gibbs; *landscape architects:* Eckbo, Dean, Austin and Williams.
　　　　1, 5, 8–13. *Photographs by Harry Drinkwater.*
　　　　2, 3, 4, 6, 7. *Photographs by author.*

Pages 68–77　Ambassador College. ARCHITECTS, remodeling: Norman Entwistle; new work: Daniel, Mann, Johnson and Mendenhall; LANDSCAPE ARCHITECTS: Eckbo, Dean, Austin and Williams.
　　　　1. Old photograph, circa 1900–1910.
　　　　2, 3, 4, 14, 20, 21, 23, 24, 28, 29, 30, 31, 32, 33. *Photographs by Harry Drinkwater.*
　　　　5, 6, 7, 8, 9, 10, 11, 12, 13, 15, 16, 17, 18, 19, 22, 25, 26, 27. *Photographs by author.*

Pages 78–81　University of New Mexico. ARCHITECTS: John Gaw Meem, Santa Fe; Edward Holien and William Buckley, Santa Fe; Flatow, Moore, Bryan and Fairborn, Albuquerque; William Ellison and Associates, Albuquerque; Ferguson, Stevens, Mallory and Pearl, Albuquerque; MASTER PLANNER: John Carl Warnecke, architect, San Francisco; LANDSCAPE ARCHITECTS AND CAMPUS PLANNERS: Eckbo, Dean, Austin and Williams; ASSOCIATE LANDSCAPE ARCHITECT: Kenneth Larsen, Alburquerque; DIRECTOR OF UNM PHYSICAL PLANT DEPARTMENT: M. F. Fifield. *Sketches by Ted Keoseyan.*

Pages 82–87　Scripps College. ARCHITECTS: Gordon Kaufman, 1926; Sumner Hunt, 1930; Whitney Smith, 1959–1960; Theodore Criley 1960–1961; LANDSCAPE ARCHITECT: Edward Huntsman-Trout. *Photographs by Edward Huntsman-Trout.*

Pages 88–95　Longwood Redevelopment. ARCHITECT: Richard A. Keller; CONSULTING ARCHITECTS: Mayer, Whittlesey and Glass; TIME-SPACE UNIT DESIGN: Leo Lionni; LANDSCAPE ARCHITECTS: Eckbo, Dean, Austin and Williams; ASSOCIATE LANDSCAPE ARCHITECT: Grier Riemer.
　　　　1, 6, 15, 20, 26. *Photographs by Balthazar Korab. Other photographs by author.*

Pages 96–97　Harper Humanities Garden, University of Denver. LANDSCAPE ARCHITECTS: Eckbo, Dean, Austin and Williams; CAMPUS PLANNING COORDINATOR: Harold Baird; *Sketch by Ted Keoseyan.*

Page 98　*Photograph by Dick Petrie.*

Page 100　1. Camden outdoor theater. LANDSCAPE ARCHITECT: Fletcher Steele. *Photograph by Paul Weber.*
　　　　2. Bird sanctuary, Santa Barbara. *Photograph courtesy Union Pacific Railroad.*

Page 101　1. La Jolla. *Photograph courtesy San Diego Department of City Planning.*
　　　　2. Balboa Park. *Photograph courtesy San Diego Department of City Planning.*
　　　　3. Mission Bay Park. *Photograph courtesy San Diego Department of City Planning.*

Page 102　1. Kate Greenaway children. *Drawing from American type printer craft.*
　　　　2. *Photograph by Dick Petrie.*

Page 103　*Photographs by Dick Petrie.*

Page 104　1. *Photograph by Claire Kofsky, courtesy Philadelphia City Planning Commission.*
　　　　2. Fern Dell. *Photograph courtesy Los Angeles Board of Education.*

242

Child Study Center. ARCHITECT: Welton Becket and Associates; LANDSCAPE ARCHITECTS: Eckbo, Dean, Austin and Williams. *Photographs by author.*

Page 105 Playground studies. DESIGNER: Saul Bass.

Pages 106,107 Playground details. LANDSCAPE ARCHITECTS: Royston, Hanamoto, Mayes, and Beck.
2, 4, 6, 7. Photographs by Lonnie Wilson.

Page 108 Duarte Playground. LANDSCAPE ARCHITECTS: Eckbo, Dean, Austin and Williams. *Bird's-eye view by Tito Patri; photographs by author.*

Page 109 Chopin Park. LANDSCAPE ARCHITECT: F. K. Polkowski.

Pages 110,111 La Loma Park. LANDSCAPE ARCHITECTS: Eckbo, Dean, Austin and Williams.

Pages 112–114 Municipal Park. LANDSCAPE ARCHITECTS: Eckbo, Dean, Austin and Williams. *Sketches by Tito Patri.*

Pages 115–117 Eagle Rock Park. LANDSCAPE ARCHITECTS: Eckbo, Dean, Austin and Williams. *Sketches by Tito Patri.*

Pages 118–126 Del Valle, Bolivar, San Martin, and Biscailuz Parks. COMMUNITY FACILITIES PLANNERS: Eckbo, Dean, Austin and Williams, landscape architects; Smith and Williams, architects; Eisner and Stewart, city planners; SHELTER DESIGN: Jeffrey Lindsay. *Photographs by Harry Drinkwater; sketches by Frank Sato; play-area plans drawn by Tito Patri; bird's-eye view by Al Spencer.*

Page 127 Sunset Demonstration Gardens. LANDSCAPE ARCHITECTS: Baldwin and Peters. *Photographs by William Aplin.*

Page 128 Marina. COMMUNITY FACILITIES PLANNERS: Smith and Williams, architects; Eckbo, Dean, Austin and Williams, landscape architects; Eisner and Stewart, city planners; CONSULTING ENGINEERS: John Blume and Associates.

Page 129 Newport Dunes. COMMUNITY FACILITIES PLANNERS: Smith and Williams, architects; Eckbo, Dean, Austin and Williams, landscape architects; Eisner and Stewart, city planners. *Sketches by Al Spencer.*

Pages 130,131 Fairfield Park. ARCHITECTS: John Lyon Reid and Partners; LANDSCAPE ARCHITECTS: Eckbo, Dean, Austin and Williams. *Sketches by Tito Patri.*

Pages 132–149 Mission Bay Park. COMMUNITY FACILITIES PLANNERS: Eckbo, Dean, Austin and Williams, landscape architects; Smith and Williams, architects; Eisner, Stewart and Associates, city planners. *Report edited by Royce Neuschatz.*

Pages 132,133 *Air views courtesy City of San Diego.* Mission Beach (page 133). *Photograph by Lyle Stewart.*

Pages 134–143 *1. Middle Rouge Parkway, Northville area, Wayne County, Mich. Photograph courtesy Huron-Clinton Metropolitan Authority.*
2–10, 17–20. Sketches by Al Spencer.
11–16. Furniture models. DESIGNERS: Selje' and Bond.

Page 144 Horseback riders in Michigan. *Photograph by William E. Bradley.*
Busch Gardens, Van Nuys, Calif. ARCHITECTS: Ladd and Kelsey; LANDSCAPE CONSULTANT: Morgan "Bill" Evans. *Sketch by Carlos Diniz.*

Pages 146,147 Quivira Basin. *Elevation sketch by Smith and Williams.*

Pages 148,149 Cabrillo Island. *Elevation sketch by E. Jay Christopherson.*

Page 152 *Photograph by Dick Petrie.*

Pages 154,155 *1. Photograph by Harry Drinkwater.*
2, 3. Before and after, Welwyn Garden City, England. LANDSCAPE ARCHITECT: Mr. Sefton. *Photographs courtesy Welwyn Garden City Development Corporation.*
4. Cincinnati, 1934. Photograph by U.S. Army Air Corps.
5. Miscellaneous fences. Photograph by Dick Petrie.
6, 7, 8. Sketches by Carlos Diniz.

Pages 156, 157 *1. Los Angeles. Photograph by Harry Drinkwater.*
2, 3. Golden Gateway. ARCHITECTS: Welton Becket and Associates. *Sketches by Carlos Diniz.*
4. Square detail, Los Angeles International Exposition of 1966. ARCHITECTS: Ladd and Kelsey; DESIGNER: Herb Rosenthal. *Sketch by Carlos Diniz.*

Page 159 Kersey Kinsey Office Buildings. ARCHITECTS: Farrell, Larsen and Kahn; LANDSCAPE ARCHITECTS: Eckbo, Dean, Austin and Williams.
1, 2. Photographs by Harry Drinkwater.
3, 4. Photographs by author.

Pages 160,161 Fresno Downtown Mall. PLANNING, ARCHITECTURE, ENGINEERING, GRAPHIC DESIGN: Victor Gruen Associates; LANDSCAPE ARCHITECTS AND SITE PLANNERS: Eckbo, Dean, Austin and Williams; IRRIGATION CONSULTANT: Robert Cloud; SCULPTORS: Jan de Swart, Claire Falkenstein, Jacques Overhoff, Stan Bitters. *Model photographs by Gordon Sommers.*

Page 162 Street studies. LANDSCAPE ARCHITECTS: Eckbo, Dean, Austin and Williams; DESIGNER: Eric Hoyte.

Pages 163,164 Texas Sculpture Entrance Plaza. ARCHITECTS: Skidmore, Owings, and Merrill; SCULPTOR: Isamu Noguchi. *Photographs by Lee Angle.*

Pages 165–167 Rich's Department Store. ARCHITECTS: Stevens and Wilkinson; LANDSCAPE ARCHITECTS: Eckbo, Dean, Austin and Williams. *Photographs by Gottscho-Schleisner, Inc.*

Page 168 Business and Technical Division. LANDSCAPE ARCHITECTS: Eckbo, Dean, Austin and Williams. *Photographs by Harry Drinkwater.*

Page 169 Waterside Promenade. LANDSCAPE ARCHITECTS: Eckbo, Dean, Austin and Williams.
1. Photograph by author.
2, 3. Photographs by Julius Shulman.

Page 170 Sather Gate Entrance Complex. STUDENT UNION ARCHITECTS: Vernon De Mars, Don Reay, Don Hardison; STUDENT UNION LANDSCAPE ARCHITECTS: Lawrence Halprin and Associates; DWINNELLE HALL AREA LANDSCAPE ARCHITECTS: Eckbo, Royston and Williams; SUPERVISING LANDSCAPE ARCHITECTS: Thomas D. Church and Associates.
1, 2. Photographs by Morley Baer.
3. Photograph by Robert Royston.
Plan courtesy Thomas D. Church and Associates.

Page 171 Omega, Vällingby. ARCHITECT: Ragnar Uppman, SAR; LANDSCAPE ARCHITECT: Sylvia Gibson. *Photographs by Gibson.*

Pages 172–175 Long Beach City College Quadrangle. LANDSCAPE ARCHITECTS: Eckbo, Dean, Austin and Williams. *Photographs by Harry Drinkwater; sketches by Tito Patri.*

243

Page 176   *Photograph by Dick Petrie.*

Page 179   *Photographs courtesy New York Convention and Visitors Bureau.*

Page 180   1. Copenhagen. *Photograph courtesy SAS News.*
            2. Stockholm. *Photograph courtesy SAS News.*

Page 181   1. *Photograph by Pacific Air Industries.*
            2. *Photograph courtesy San Diego Department of City Planning.*

Page 182   1. Bryant Park, New York. *Photograph by author.*
            2. City Hall, Penn Center, Hospitality Center Court. *Photograph by Claire Kofsky, courtesy Philadelphia City Planning Commission.*

Page 183   1. New York housing. *Photograph by author.*
            2. Des Moines, Iowa, covered by trees. *Photograph by author.*
            3. Cleveland. *Photograph courtesy U.S. Housing Authority.*
            4. San Francisco freeways. *Photograph courtesy Division of Highways, State of California.*

Pages 185–189 1–8. *Photographs courtesy San Diego Department of City Planning.*
            9. South Boston. *Photograph courtesy U.S. Housing Authority.*
            10. Chicago. *Photograph courtesy U.S. Housing Authority.*
            11. Downtown recreation. *Photograph courtesy San Francisco Chamber of Commerce.*
            12, 13. Cincinnati, 1934. *Photographs by U.S. Army Air Corps.*

Page 190   The Meads. COMMUNITY FACILITIES PLANNERS: Smith and Williams, architects; Eckbo, Dean, Austin and Williams, landscape architects; Eisner and Stewart, city planners.

Pages 191–193 Sea Pines Plantation and Forest Beach Corporation. LANDSCAPE ARCHITECTS AND PLANNING CONSULTANTS: Sasaki, Walker and Associates.

Pages, 194,195 Centerville, Calif. CITY PLANNERS: Sydney Williams and Leo Jacobson. *Sketch by Chad Michael.*

Pages 196–199 Port Holiday. COMMUNITY FACILITIES PLANNERS: Smith and Williams, architects; Eckbo, Dean, Austin and Williams, landscape architects; Eisner and Stewart, city planners; CONSULTING ENGINEERS: John A. Blume and Associates. *Site photograph by author; sketches by Al Spencer.*

Pages 200–208 Casper, Wyo. COMMUNITY FACILITIES PLANNERS: Smith and Williams, architects; Eckbo, Dean, Austin and Williams, landscape architects; Eisner and Stewart, city planners. *Photographs courtesy City of Casper; sketches by Al Spencer.*

Page 205   Wilderness Park. *Bird's-eye view by Stan Repp.*

Pages 209–227 El Centro, California. COMMUNITY FACILITIES PLANNERS: Eisner, Stewart and Associates, city planners; Eckbo, Dean, Austin and Williams, landscape architects; Smith and Williams, architects and recreational consultants. *Photographs courtesy El Centro Chamber of Commerce.*

Page 213   *Air view courtesy San Diego Union.*

Page 219   *Sketches by Al Spencer.*

Pages 220–223 *Sketches by Carlos Diniz.*

Page 230   *Photograph by Harry Drinkwater.*

Page 232   Castle Weldan in Goor. *Photograph courtesy Netherlands National Tourist Office.*

Page 233   1. Mulholland Drive, cracked. *Photograph courtesy Grading Section, Los Angeles Department of Building and Safety.*
            2. Drawing of ant nest from an old book.

Page 234   1. Acacia verticillata blossoms. *Photograph by Childress-Halberstadt.*
            2. Liquidambar leaves. *Photograph by author.*
            3. Terrace, Connecticut General Life Insurance Company. ARCHITECTS: Skidmore, Owings, and Merrill; SCULPTOR: Isamu Noguchi. *Photograph by Ezra Stoller.*

Page 235   1. Drawing of flowers and bees from an old book.
            2. Shack. *Photograph by Greg La Chapelle.*
            3, 4, 5. *Photographs by Dick Petrie.*

Pages 236–239 Maintenance survey. *Edited and compiled by Royce Neuschatz.*

Pages 245–248 Index. *Coordinated by Margaret Omerberg.*

INDEX

Accent, continuity related to, 27, 181
  as landmark, 27
Access and utilities, problems of, 15
Access roads, 9
Acreage, 100
AIA–AIP, 31, 180
AIPE, 100
Air conditioner, 14
Ambassador College, Pasadena, California, 68–77
Analysis as beginning of design, 4
Angle, Lee, photographs by, 163–164
Aplin, William, photographs by, 127
Architecture, and cityscape, 180
  colonial, 45
  contemporary, 11–12, 16, 27
  in design of landscape, 5
  expression necessary to urban design, 179
  literature of, 16
  modern, 178
  pure, 158
  in relation to trees and space, 14–15
  rural and park, 11
Arid regions, 9
Art, compared with design, 4
  search for quality, 19
Asphalt, percentage in total landscape, 11
Asphalt deserts of twentieth century, 10
Atmosphere, variations in, 8
Autos, domination of circulation routes by, 178
  parking requirements, 45
  and pedestrians, 153–154
  as service to community, 10, 156

Bacon, Edmund, 154, 179
Bacon, Francis, 12
Baer, Morley, photographs by, 50–51, Nos. 1, 2, 4; 170, Nos. 1, 2
Baldwin and Peters, 127
Bass, Saul, playground studies, 105
Beauty, interpretation of, 30
  in landscape, 5
Becket, Welton and Associates, 104, 156–157
Berko Studio, photograph by, 16, No. 3
Biscailuz, Eugene, Park, Lakewood, California, 126
Blume, John A., and Associates, 128, 196–199
Body, human, 21
Bolivar, Simon, Park, Lakewood, California, 121–124
Boyd, Robin, 12
Bradley, William, photograph by, 144
Brandeis Camp Institute, Temple, Santa Susana, California, 56–57
Brooks and Walker, 50–51

Brown, Harrison, 31
Brown, Joseph, 102
Budget, 33
Buildings, definition, 10
  grouping of, 56, 59
  problems, 16
  prominent siting, 178
  relation to each other, 179
  relation to street landscaping, 153
  role in subdivision, 32
  types, hierarchy of, 178

California, State of, Division of Highways, photograph by, 26, No. 2
California, University of, Sather Gate Entrance Complex, Berkeley, 170
Camera, 21
Car (see Auto)
Carter, Donald Ray, photograph by, 51, No. 3
Cascade Cameras, Ltd., photograph by, 58
Casper, Wyoming, 200–208
Ceilings in landscape, 25–26
Centerville, California, 194–195
Change in structure of landscape, 29
Cherry Hill Shopping Center, Haddonfield, New Jersey, 60–61
Child Study Center, Los Angeles, California, 104
Children, 101
Chopin Memorial Park, Zelazowa Wola, Poland, 109
Christopherson, E. Jay, sketch by, 56, No. 6, 148–149
Church, Thomas D., and Associates, 46, 52
Circulation, 27
Clarke, Lewis, 40–41, 60–61
Climate, control, 45
  as determinant of form, 16
  difficult, 37
  and trees, 14
Collaboration, 5, 179
Colonial architecture, 45
Color, effect on space enclosure, 25
Colvin, Brenda, 184
Commercial landscape, 30
Communitas, discussion of, 181–182
Community, 27
  impact of right-of-way on, 156
  landmarks, 29
  landscape, 153, 158, 177
  needs, 45
  planning, 100–101
Community Facilities Planners, 33, No. 2; 118–126, 128–129, 132–149, 190, 196–227
Community of Fear, 31
Congestion, 10

Connections, between building and landscape, 4
  emotional, with moon, 22
Conservation, 3
Continuity, accent related to, 27
  of experience, 25
  of reciprocal relations, 158
  spatial and sensory, 178
  of time, 7
  within urban site forms, 181
Contour, 7
Contrast in urban scene, 178
Control, arbitrary, in zoning and subdivision, 32
  centralization of, 5
  of land use, 10
  loss of, over vistas and panoramas, 24
  and perception, 20
Copenhagen, 180
Le Corbusier, 28
Cornell, Ralph, photograph by, 22, No. 2
Costa, Lucio, 158
Court, 23
Coverage, land, 10

Daniel, Mann, Johnson and Mendenhall, 17, No. 1; 68–77
Davidson, J. R., 56–57
Day, Robert, cartoon by, 30, No. 3
Decisions, on development of land, 18
  on materials within designated area, 4–5
Del Valle, Jose, Park, Lakewood, California, 118–120
De Mars, Reay and Hardison, 170
Democratic processes, 5
Dennis the Menace, 103
Design, conscious processes, 3–4
  detail by, 19
  finding a way, 158
  influenced by maintenance, 231
  landscape, two kinds, 5
  multidirectional, 24
  of physical elements in land use, 32
  as problem-solving activity, 15
  processes and patterns, 33
  regional, 29
  spatial, 7, 9
Detail, of space organization, 24, 37
  of street design, 154–155
Development, 3, 9
Dimension in space organization, 7
Diniz, Carlos, drawings, photographs, and sketches by, 10, No. 3; 15, No. 1; 20, No. 4; 22, No. 1; 25, No. 2; 29, No. 2; 30, No. 4; 144, 154, Nos. 6–8; 156–157, Nos. 2–4; 220–223
Districts, analysis of, 180
Downtown centers, 27–28

Drainage, 9, 15
Drinkwater, Harry, photographs by, 4, 10, Nos. 1, 2; 11, Nos. 1, 2, 5; 12, No. 3; 13, No. 3; 8, 16, No. 2; 23, No. 1; 29, No. 3; 39, 42–43, Nos. 1, 3, 4; 64–67, Nos. 1, 5, 8–13; 68–77, Nos. 2–4, 14, 20, 21, 23, 24, 28–33; 118–126, 154–155, No. 1; 156–157, No. 1; 159, Nos. 1, 2; 168, 172–175, 230
Duarte Playground, Duarte, California, 108

Eagle Rock Park, Los Angeles, California, 115–117
Earth, movement of, and seasonal change, 8
Eckbo, Dean, Austin & Williams, 24, Nos. 1, 2; 33, No. 2; 39, 42–43, 47–49, 53–57, 64–81, 88–97, 104, 108, 110–126, 128–149, 159–162, 165–169, 172–175, 190, 196–227
Edges, definition of, 180
Education as conditioner, 17–18
Einstein, Albert, 7
Eisner & Stewart, 33, No. 2; 118–126, 128–129, 132–149, 190, 196–227
El Centro, California, 209–227
Emphasis, development of, 27
Enclosure, environmental effects of, 23
    as garden space, 25
    visual, on streets, 156
Energy, individual, personal, and physical, 7
Entry, 38
Entwistle, Norman, 68–77
Experience, close-up, 15
    conditioned by time, 7
    garden-house relations, 24–25
    historically memorable, 18
    landscape as one continuous, 17
    sequential, 20, 27
Eyes, perception and control, 21
Eyre, Robert, photographs by, 53–55

Fairfield Park, Fairfield, California, 130–131
Farrell, Larsen and Kahn, 159
Fein, Phil, photographs by, 52
Finance, conservation of, 27
Fireman's Fund Insurance Company, San Francisco, California, 47–49
Floors, materials, 25
    structure, 19
Form, architectural, 16
    in garden design, 24
    search for, 5
    three-dimensional, 180
    variety of land, 9
Frampton, Robert C., photograph by, 19, No. 3
Freeways, 9
    large scale of, 27
    major, 155
    scale of planned, 156
Fresno Downtown Mall, Fresno, California, 160–161
Future, 7

Galbraith, J. K., 15
Gardens, landmarks in, 29
    space organization of, 24
Gestalt psychology, 18
Gibbs, Hugh, 64–67
Gibson, Sylvia, 171

Goodman, Paul, 182
Goodman, Percival, 182
Gottscho-Schleisner, Inc., photographs by, 165–167
Greene, Al, & Associates, photograph by, 8, No. 1
Greenway system, 179
Gridiron, as feature of American landscape, 27
    in older sections of town, 177
    patterns, 59, 154
    plan, 153
    rationalization of, 29
    street block system, 178
Groups, buildings in, 56, 59
Gruen, Victor, Associates, 60–61, 160–161

Hacket, Brian, 184
Halprin, Lawrence, and Associates, 22, No. 3; 50–51, 62–63, 170
Handicraft, 3
Harmony, 18
Harper Humanities Garden, University of Denver, Denver, Colorado, 96–97
Hayward, California, 107
Hedrick-Blessing, photographs by, 62–63
Hierarchy of building types, 178
Highways, 9
History as teacher, 5
Hjelte, George, 99
Holien & Buckley, 78–81
Housing, three main levels of, 177
Human body, 21
Human energy, 7
Human perception of landscape, 17–18
Huntsman-Trout, Edward, 82–87
Huxley, Aldous, 19

Image, shifting of type, 181
Individual, experiences of, 18
Industrial Indemnity Company, Fresno, California, 52
Industrial society, 3, 5
Integration, 99–100
International style, 12, 16

Johnson, Philip, 12
Jungle as boundary of building, 18

Keller, Richard A., 88–95
Keoseyan, Ted, sketches by, 78–81, 96–97
Kersey Kinsey Office Buildings, Studio City, California, 159
Ketcham, Hank, 103
Kidder-Smith, G. E., 157
Kirk, Paul Hayden, and Associates, 53–55
Kofsky, Claire, photographs by, 104, No. 1; 182, No. 2
Korab, Balthazar, photographs by, 88–95, Nos. 1, 6, 15, 20, 26
Krusi Park, Alameda, California, 106–107

Labor in maintenance, 17
La Chapelle, Greg, photograph by, 235, No. 2
Ladd & Kelsey, 144, 157
Lakewood Parks, Lakewood, California, 118–126
La Loma Park, Monterey Park, California, 110–111
Land, as fundamental element, 9
    natural structure, 15
    as open space, 100
    as parks and playgrounds, 99
    use of, 10

Landmark, as accent, 27
    definition, 29
    as point-reference, 180
Landscape, change in structure of, 29
    commercial, 30
    community, 153
    and continuity of all elements, 15, 158
    development, 33
    human experience and, 18
    and mass-produced housing, 26
    quality of, 10, 18
        physical, 3
    regional character, 184
    remodeling of, 5
    result of existing, 5
    spaces, 23–24
    subdivision, 32–33
    suburban, 28
    world around us, 17
Landscape architect, 12
Landscape design, objective of, 21
Landscape elements, 12, 16, 32
Latin patio house, 45
Le Corbusier, 28
Light, as affected by earth's movement, 8
    as element, 8
Linear surfacing patterns, 25
Living rooms, 37
Loebl, Schlossman and Bennett, 62–63
Long Beach City College, Long Beach, California, Business and Technical Division, 168
    Quadrangle, 172–175
Longwood Redevelopment, Cleveland, Ohio, 88–95
Love in maintenance, 17
Lynch, Kevin, 18, 19, 31, 180
Lyndon, Maynard, 42–43

Maintenance, 17, 231
Man (see under Human)
Manhattan, continuity and accent in, 27–28
    skyline, 27–28
    space in, 178
Manipulation of space, 16
Marina, South San Francisco, California, 128
Mathematics and space organization, 7
Mayer, Whittlesey & Glass, 88–95
Meadows, 23, 100
Meads, The, Morro Bay, California, 190
Meem, John Gaw, 78–81
Megalopolis, 182–183
Merchandising, 27
Metropolis, 182
Michael, Chad, sketch by, 194
Mies Van der Rohe, Ludwig, drawing by, 19, No. 1
Mission Bay Park, San Diego, California, 132–149
Mitchell Park, Palo Alto, California, 106–107
Mobility, human, 21
Monotony, continuity in suburbscape, 28
    creating confusion, 30
    in landscape, 11
    and variety of construction, 178
    visual, 18
Moon, emotional connections with, 22
Mumford, Lewis, 182, 183
Municipal Park, Buena Park, California, 112–114

Nairn, Ian, 18, 27
National Park Service, 11

Nature, 3
  important in design of landscape, 5
  as naturalizer, 18–19
  preserves, 99
  rhythm of, 21
  stylistic monumentalization and, 157
  trees in, 14
Neighborhood, 177
Neighborliness, 45
New Mexico, University of, Albuquerque, New Mexico, 78–81
Newport Beach, Waterside Promenade, California, 169
Newport Dunes, Newport Beach, California, 129
New York City (see Manhattan)
Nodes, definition of, 180–181
Noguchi, Isamu, sculpture by, 7, 17, No. 2; 163–174

Objective, 3
  of landscape design, 21
Olmsted, F. L., 23, 99, 100, 184
Old Orchard, Skokie, Illinois, 62–63
Omega, Vällingby, Stockholm, Sweden, 171
Omerberg, Maynard, photograph by, 14, No. 2
Open space, 3
  adequate, in recreation programming, 100
  as basic complementary element, 14–15
  historical discussion of, 182
  landscaped pedestrian, 12
  in parks, 27
  passive, 100
  public, 29
  relation between buildings and, 59
  system, 179
  uncontrolled, 23
  urban, 10
Order, 18
Ordinary landscapes, 5
Organic impact on gridiron, 27
Organic residues, 9
Organization, campus-type space, 27
  detailed space, 24
  elements of space, 7
  of habitual living patterns, 10
Orientation, physical, 29, 102
Owner and land development, 33

Pacific Air Industries, photograph by, 181, No. 1
Page, Edward B., 47–49
Palmer, Phil, photographs by, 47–49
Panorama, 23
Paris, 153
Parking, 10, 45
Parks, 99, 182
Passing through, 38
Passive space in parks, 100
Past, 7
Paths, 180
Patio, 37, 45
Pattern of surface materials, 25
Patri, Tito, sketches and bird's-eye view by, 56–57, Nos. 1, 5, 7, 8; 108, 112–126, 130–131, 172–175
Pedestrian, experience, loss of, 178
  incompatibility with autos, 153–154
  separation from autos, 157
  spaces for, 156
People, 5, 29, 181
Perception and control of space, 20
Perspective, 21

Petrie, Dick, photographs by, frontispiece, 2, 6, 11, No. 5; 13, Nos. 1, 2, 4, 5, 7; 14, No. 1; 20, No. 3; 26, No. 1; 31, No. 2; 98, 102, No. 2; 103, 152, 155, No. 5; 176, 235, Nos. 3, 4, 5
Philadelphia, 29–30
Photographer, 9, 27
Planning, 5
  in building developments, 99
  controls, 45
  and human relations, 19
  master, 32
  and trees, 14
Play area, 102
Play equipment, 102–103
Playground studies, models by Saul Bass, 105
Polkowski, F. K., 109
Polytechnic High School, Long Beach, California, 64–67
Port Holiday, Lake Mead, near Las Vegas, Nevada, 196–199
Practical subdividers, 32
Present time, 7
Primeval time, 28–29
Privacy, 45
Problems, 3–5
  of building and site, 45
  in landscaping street, 153
  of regional design, 29
  of transition and sequence in design, 15
  with utilities and trees, 154
  visual, 21
Professional design, 5
Professional space planning, 30–31
Programs, 5
Prototype, 27
  for given problem, 21
  for outdoor space organization, 24
Pushkarev, Boris, 156

Quality, 3, 5
  definition, 18
  of experience, 7
  of garden space, 25
  in landscape, 3, 18
    as land-use control, 10

Real, James, 31
Real estate, 9
Reality, 4
Recreation, area design, 99
  programming, balanced, 100
Regimentation, 5, 30
Region, definition of, 184
  as determinant of architectural forms, 16
  landmarks in, 29
  for weekend recreation, 182
Regional planning, traffic control in, 9–10
Reid, John Lyon, 130–131
Relations, of balance, between buildings, 178
  between town and country, 184
  between building, site, and landscape, 4
  between building size and auto parking, 45
  of building to its environment, 16
  faulty, in building design, 33
  lack of, in U.S. building, 18
  of neighborhoods to community, 177
  between privacy and neighborliness, 45
  reciprocal, between individual and community scale, 158

Relations, technical, functional, and esthetic in buildings, 59
Repp, Stan, bird's-eye view by, 200–208
Responsibility, in development of landscape, 29
  implied in street planning, 153
  for planning contact lines, 157
Restaurant Garden, Raleigh, North Carolina, 40–41
Rich's Department Store, Knoxville, Tennessee, 165–167
Roads, alignment of, for access, 15–16
  related to subdivision, 32
  and utilities, 9
  (See also Freeways)
Rock, 9
Room, spaces, 23–25, 37
Royston, Hanamoto, Mays & Beck, 106–107
Royston, Robert, photograph by, 170, No. 3
Rudolph, Paul, 16, 178
Rural landscapes, 24
Rural regional context, 28–29
Rural regionalism, 184
Rusticism, 11

Saarinen, Eliel, 23
San Martin, Jose, Park, Lakewood, California, 125
Sasaki-Walker, 191–193
Sato, Frank, sketches by, 118–126
Scale, community, 27–28
  of continuity in landmarks, 29
  expansion of, in space organization, 15
  role in landscape, 17
Science, 4
Scripps College, Claremont, California, 82–87
Sculpture, 5
Sea Pines Plantation and Forest Beach Corp., Hilton Head, South Carolina, 191–193
Seasonal earth movement, 8
Seattle, Washington, street studies, 162
Sequence, in architecture and landscape design, 178
  of continuity and accent in single spaces, 27
  of landscape experience, 20
  problems of, in scale expansion, 15
  of space in buildings, 16, 179
  in terms of experience, 4
Service radius, 100
Setback, 156
Shade, 8
Shelter, 25, 31
Shulman, Julius, photographs by, 24, Nos. 1, 2; 38, 169, Nos. 2, 3
Site, 45
Sitté, Camillo, 21, 23, 24, 59, 154, 157
Skidmore, Owings & Merrill, 17, No. 2; 162–164
Smith and Williams, 33, No. 2; 118–126, 128–129, 132–149, 190, 196–227
Society, 5
  democratic, use of space, 15
  industrialized, 31–32
  lack of interest in environment, 32
  and landscape, 17–18
Soil, 9
Sommers, Gordon, photographs by, 5, 9, No. 1; 30, No. 1; 160–161 model
Space, 7
  as determinant of form, 16

247

Space, open (*see* Open space)
  organization outdoors, 24
  passive, 100
  unique, in New York, 178
Space planning, 30–31
Speed, 156
Spencer, Al, sketches by, 129, 134–143,
  Nos. 5–13, Nos. 20–23; 196–199,
  200–208, 219
Square, definition, 157
  multidirectional qualities in, 23
  public, 24, 26
Stanford University, Palo Alto, Califor-
  nia, Medical Center, 46
  Photographic Department, photo-
   graphs by, 46
Steele, Fletcher, 25, No. 1; 100, No. 1
Steinbrueck, Victor, 53–55
Stevens & Wilkinson, 165–167
Stewart, Lyle, photograph by, 133
Stockholm, 180
Stoller, Ezra, Associates, photographs by,
  17, No. 2; 234, No. 3
Stone, Edward D., 46
Streets, 9–10, 153
Structure, 3, 19
Subdivision, discussion of, 31
  new, mass, 11
  patterns, 45
  political boundaries and property lines,
   18
  process, vagaries of, 9
  similar to important institutions,
   59
  and street patterns, 157
Suburban areas, building in, 11
  continuity of, 28
  development, 29
  landscape, street vistas, 24
  requirements for open, 182
  typical street, 153
Sunset Demonstration Gardens, Los Angeles County Arboretum, Arcadia,
  California, 127
Survey, 161
Symmetry, human, 21
Synthesis, 4
System, Greenway, 179

Taste, 18
Technocrats, 3

Technology, 4
  pressures of, 45
Texas Sculpture Entrance Plaza, First National Bank, Fort Worth, Texas,
  '163–164
Texture, 25
Time, 7
Topography, 9
Tradition, 18
Traffic, organized by planning proce-
  dures, 10
  planning, 155
  preindustrial concept of, 157
Transition, problem of expanding scale,
  15
Trees, in cities, 182
  lack of planning for, 157
  lining streets, 153
  as measure of civilized landscape, 12
  as shelter pattern, 25
Tunnard, Christopher, 182
Turner and Stevens Funeral Directors,
  patio for, Pasadena, California, 39
Twenty-eighth Church of Christ Scientist,
  Westwood Village, Los Angeles, Cali-
  fornia, 42–43
Types and variables, 27
Tyrranopolis, 183

Unity, 18, 21
Uppman, Ragnar, 171
Urban design, 14–15, 19, 99, 179, 182
Urban redevelopment, 5, 18, 33
Urbanization, 3
  as complex jumble, 28
  concern for quality in, 180
  and landscape spaces, 23–24
  and metropolitan areas, 182–183
  pattern of modern, 45
  redevelopment pressure, 33
  in roads and utilities, 10
Usher, Frederick, Jr., drawing by, 12,
  No. 1
Utah, University of, married students'
  housing, 107
Utilities, and access, 15–16
  conflict with trees, 154
  coordinated with subdivision design,
   32
  matters of practical engineering, 10
  and roads, 9

Valand, Leif, 40–41
Van der Rohe, Ludwig Mies, drawing by,
  19, No. 1
Variables, 27
Variation in atmospheric seeing condi-
  tion, 8
Variety, among similar elements, 18–19
  monotony of, 18
  in older suburban areas, 11
  within symmetry, 21
View, 25
Vista, 22
Visual demands created by buildings, 45
Visual needs of streets, 155–156
Visual problem, of modern street, 154
  in perception and control, 21

Walls, 19, 25
Warnecke, John Carl, 78–81
Washington, University of, Faculty Club,
  Seattle, Washington, 53–55
Washington Water and Power Company,
  Spokane, Washington, 50–51
Waste of living space, 10
Waste space in building design, 33
Water, 9
Watson, photograph by, 40–41
Weather, 9
Weber, Paul J., photograph by, 25, No. 1;
  100, No. 1
Wells, H. G., 31
White, Hermann and Steinau, 52
Whitehead, Alfred North, 7
Wild landscapes, 24
Wildman, Ben, photograph by, 16, No. 1
Williams, E. A., 231
Williams, Sidney, 31, 180, 194–195
Williams, Wayne, 100
Wilson, Lonnie, photographs by, 106–107
Wohlstetter, Albert, 157
Work spaces, 37
Wright, Frank Lloyd, 11, 28
Wurster, C. B., 180
Wurster, Bernardi and Emmons, 22,
  No. 3

Yavno, Max, photographs by, 11, Nos.
  3, 4

Zoning, subdivision and, 32
Zucker, Paul, 158